ISBN 978-0-259-50938-7
PIBN 10820839

1 MONTH OF
FREE
READING

at

www.ForgottenBooks.com

By purchasing this book you are eligible for one month membership to ForgottenBooks.com, giving you unlimited access to our entire collection of over 1,000,000 titles via our web site and mobile apps.

To claim your free month visit:

www.forgottenbooks.com/free820839

English
Français
Deutsche
Italiano
Español
Português

www.forgottenbooks.com

Mythology Photography **Fiction**
Fishing Christianity **Art** Cooking
Essays Buddhism Freemasonry
Medicine **Biology** Music **Ancient
Egypt** Evolution Carpentry Physics
Dance Geology **Mathematics** Fitness
Shakespeare **Folklore** Yoga Marketing
Confidence Immortality Biographies
Poetry **Psychology** Witchcraft
Electronics Chemistry History **Law**
Accounting **Philosophy** Anthropology
Alchemy Drama Quantum Mechanics
Atheism Sexual Health **Ancient History**
Entrepreneurship Languages Sport
Paleontology Needlework Islam
Metaphysics Investment Archaeology
Parenting Statistics Criminology
Motivational

HANDBOOK OF THE
EARLY CHRISTIAN FATHERS

Handbook of the Early Christian Fathers

BY

ERNEST LEIGH-BENNETT

" That Christianity should become the religion of the Roman Empire is the miracle of history; but that it did so become is the leading fact of all history from that day onwards."—FREEMAN.

LONDON

WILLIAMS & NORGATE

14 HENRIETTA STREET, COVENT GARDEN, W.C.

1920

DEDICATED

TO

"THE BLESSED COMPANY OF ALL
FAITHFUL PEOPLE"

INTRODUCTION

The importance to history of those brilliant thinkers, writers, organizers, and in many cases statesmen, whom we know as the Early Church Fathers, was thus well described on their intellectual side by Charles Kingsley in his Preface to *Hypatia*—

"To exhibit the Catholic Church as possessing, in the great facts which she proclaimed, full satisfaction even for the most subtle metaphysical cravings of a diseased age—that was the work of the time; and men were sent to do it, and aided in their labour by the very causes which had produced the intellectual revolution. The general intermixture of ideas, creeds and races, even the mere physical facilities for intercourse between different parts of the Empire, helped to give the great Christian Fathers of the fourth and fifth centuries [1] a breadth of observation, a depth of thought, a large-hearted and large-minded patience and tolerance, such as, we may say boldly, the Church has since beheld but rarely and the world never: at least, if we are to judge those great men by what they had, and not by what they had not, and to believe, as we are bound, that had they lived now and not then, they would have towered as far above the heads of this generation, as they did above the heads of their own. And thus an age, which to the shallow insight of a sneerer like Gibbon, seems only a rotting and aimless chaos of sensuality and anarchy, fanaticism and hypocrisy, produced a Clement and an Athanase, a

[1] Why not also the third ?

v

Chrysostom and an Augustine: absorbed into the sphere of Christianity all that was most valuable in the philosophies of Greece and Egypt, and in the social organization of Rome, as an heirloom for nations yet unborn; and laid in foreign lands, by unconscious agents, the foundations of all European thought and Ethics."

So much for the intellectual work of the Fathers, and the victory which they achieved for Christianity over the philosophical systems of their age. But besides all that, it was these men who conquered the Roman Empire, and subjected it to the Christian Church; and in that work many of them proved themselves diplomats and statesmen of the highest order, notably St. Athanasius, St. Basil and St. Ambrose.

The object then of this book is to give as briefly as possible, and in a condensed form, rough notes which will enable a beginner to get a general view of the progress of Christianity during the first four centuries, of the scientific development of its philosophy and theology, of its struggle with the world power, of its internal organization as a community. And this is shown by a series of chapters, each of which is devoted to one of these great men, who passed on from hand to hand the work that had to be done.

It is often less necessary to go minutely into the details of their lives than to point out their environment, and the opposing forces with which they had to contend: and an attempt has been made to show them in correct perspective in their relation to one another.

It is possible that an undue proportion of space will seem to have been given to two subjects, the Apostolic Tradition, and the Invocation of Saints. The intention in the first of these two cases is not to uphold any special view of tradition, but to show that the importance assigned to the oral tradition is one of the strongest historical evidences of the truth of Christianity. And the interest of the second lies in this: that the Church of England claims to see eye to eye with the Primitive Church, and this period she seems to consider as ending with the Fourth General Council, viz. A.D. 450. It seems to the writer that her general attitude on the Communion of Saints differs widely from that of the fourth, or even the third century.

In view of the prominence given to Eucharistic controversy in later times, the leading quotations from the various Fathers have generally been cited, but so far as possible without comment, except where it has been necessary to explain words; but once or twice, especially in the chapter on St. Cyril, it has been thought desirable to point out what was evidently, whether rightly or wrongly, the view of the Father in question.

With St. Augustine the work is brought, somewhat reluctantly, to a close. It might have seemed good to add a chapter on St. Cyril of Alexandria and a few others, and to complete the history up to the time of the Fourth General Council, when the development of Christian Theology was complete. But St. Cyril's conflict with Nestorius opens up in many respects a new phase of history, while the acts and the character of Cyril differed widely from those of his predecessors.

Arguments which can be drawn from these early days in the controversy about the infallibility or supreme authority of Rome have generally been given, but only from the purely historical standpoint. It is not desired, on this subject or any other, to grind the axe of any particular section of Christianity.

The author's grateful thanks are due to Rev. G. E. Catlin, who read most of the MS. and gave him much valuable advice.

CONTENTS

CHAPTER I

CHAPTER II

CHAPTER III

CHAPTER IV

CHAPTER V

ix

CHAPTER VI

CHAPTER VII

CHAPTER VIII

CHAPTER IX

CHAPTER X

CHAPTER XI

CHAPTER XII

CHAPTER XIII

CHAPTER XIV

CHAPTER XV

CONTENTS

HANDBOOK OF THE
EARLY CHRISTIAN FATHERS

CHAPTER I

ST. CLEMENT OF ROME

(Bishop of Rome from about A.D. *92 to* 99)

ALL that we know of this first of the Apostolic Fathers may be summed up in the account of St. Irenæus given about 100 years later. " The blessed Apostles, Peter and Paul, having built up the Church of Rome, entrusted the bishopric to Linus, who was followed by Anacletus, and third in succession to the Apostles Clement obtained the bishopric; who had also himself seen the blessed Apostles, and had conferred with them, and had still their preaching sounding in his ears, and their traditions before his eyes; not alone, for there were still many left of those who had been taught by the Apostles. In the time of this Clement, no small dissension arising among the brethren at Corinth, the Church at Rome sent a very weighty epistle to the Corinthians reconciling them to peace, and restoring their faith, and declaring to them the traditions they had recently received from the Apostles." [1]

From this statement we gather, (1) that there is no proof that the Church of the first century regarded St. Peter as bishop of Rome in any special sense apart from St. Paul; for after stating that that Church was founded jointly by the two Apostles (which the Roman Church has always admitted), it proceeds to say that

[1] *Hær.*, III. 3. 3.

B

they both jointly appointed Linus as bishop. (2) It helps materially to fix the date of St. Clement's bishopric, which is generally given as from 92 to 99 : because it makes him third after the Apostles (the tradition still preserved in the Roman Mass); whereas at a later date it was held that Clement came next to Linus, and was consecrated by St. Peter. (3) It attributed to St. Clement, or rather to the Roman Church, the Epistle known as the First to the Corinthians, ignoring other writings now known to be spurious, but for a long time attributed to him. (4) Although St. Clement was doubtless mainly responsible for that Epistle, and may have entirely composed it, the personal element of the mediæval and modern Papacy is not found in it. It was sent from the Church of Rome by the hand of Clement. On the other hand the Roman Church as such took rather an authoritative line in the Epistle.

There has been some controversy about the origin of St. Clement. He was at one time supposed to have been the Titus Flavius Clemens, cousin of the Emperor Domitian, who was executed and possibly martyred; but Lightfoot thinks it more probable that he was a Jewish freedman of Flavius, or the son of one, and brought up in the Imperial household. He also finds tradition " early constant and definite " that he was a disciple of either St. Paul or St. Peter. Beyond this little is known of him, except what can be gathered from his Epistle. But before passing to this it is necessary to allude to *The Clementine Recognitions.*

This religious romance, at one time attributed to St. Clement, was probably written between 180 and 220, the author being quite unknown. The plot is as follows : Clement's father is given as Faustus, a connection of Vespasian and Domitian, who were of the Flavian family. His mother, Fausta, having rejected the improper overtures of her brother-in-law, was denounced by him to her husband, and in consequence fled from home with her two elder children; who afterwards were separated from her in consequence of shipwreck, and became disciples of St. Peter. After an interval of ten years, the father left Clement, who was then twelve years old, to search for his wife. Fausta, after long wanderings, fell in also with St. Peter, and was healed of some paralytic trouble. St. Peter then effected the recognition of the two sons by their mother; and a little later the father was recognized in a similar manner. In due course, St. Clement himself, having studied all the philosophies of the time without getting satisfaction, hears of Christ, and travels to Judæa to make enquiry. He also is introduced to St. Peter, and baptized by him; and then at last the recognitions of the whole family are completed.

The story has no literary or artistic interest, but a controversial one. St. Peter is the hero, and it seems to have been written by Judaizing Christians, in order to emphasize the position of St. Peter at the expense of St. Paul. To the romance was attached a spurious letter from St. Clement to St. James at Jerusalem, announcing that St. Peter had consecrated him Bishop of Rome and entrusted to him his " Chair of discourse,"; and that in consequence, though reluctantly, he occupied the chair of Peter. Anglican writers, notably Father Puller,[1] claim that this romance, though condemned at Rome, encouraged by reason of its wide circulation the general tradition that St. Peter was Bishop of Rome. The same story appears in the Clementine Homilies: and both the Recognitions and the Homilies are founded on a still earlier romance, called The Circuit of Peter. So far from St. Clement having travelled through the East with St. Peter, it is most probable that his life was spent in Rome : for that reason it is unlikely that he was the Clement referred to in St. Paul's Epistle to the Philippians, as is sometimes supposed.

[1] *Primitive Saints and the See of Rome.*

The Church of Corinth, which had given so much
trouble to St. Paul, was again, after a meritorious interval,
torn by dissensions. Not apparently by any specific
heresy, unless perhaps some scepticism about the resurrection of the body, but by jealousy of the laity towards
the clergy. Discipline was slack and some presbyters
had even been driven from their cures by the insub-
ordinate laity. The first section of Clement's *Epistle
to the Corinthians* (according to a general division of
subjects made by Lightfoot), after praising the former
virtues of the Corinthian Church, rebukes them for
their quarrels, the result of envy or a grudging spirit,
and illustrates the bad effects of envy by several quotations from the Old Testament. " Repent, therefore,"
says Clement; " imitate the lowliness and long-suffering
of Christ and you will be at peace." That peace and
harmony are according to God's will is shown by everything in nature. The second section expounds the
doctrine of the Resurrection of the Body, illustrated
again by nature (night and day, winter and summer),
and especially by the grotesque myth of the phœnix.
The third section exhorts to purity of life, with a view
to that resurrection, and especially counsels faith, but
not without works. In the fourth section, he returns
again to the question of their divisions, but more especially to the importance of the laity recognizing the claims
of the clergy. It is no longer a question of peace, but
of obedience; subordination of rank and division of
office being of divine appointment both under the Mosaic
law and also by the apostolic arrangement. In the
fifth section he suddenly breaks into a long prayer;
and in the sixth he gives certain personal directions,
ending with the customary benediction.

The main interest of this Epistle lies in the fact that
not only was it the first work that emanated from the
" apostolic men," that is, men who were not themselves
apostles, but on whom the apostolic cloak had fallen;

but also it combined in a remarkable way the teaching of the various apostles. For instance, it gives to Faith and Works an equal importance, discussing the two virtues side by side at some length. There is evidence throughout that the writer was influenced alike by St. Paul, St. Peter and St. James; also that he was perfectly acquainted with the first three gospels; St. John's had probably not reached him. Our Lord's words are quoted, and there is in the fifth section a curious paraphrase of part of the Magnificat, which, unless the Magnificat was a well-known Jewish hymn, seems to imply a knowledge of St. Luke. There is also in this epistle an evident love of nature as displaying the order and uniformity of God's works; the sense of order being carried also into the moral world, and enforced at great length from the Old Testament. The whole epistle is worded in a calm spirit of moderation. It is, as Lightfoot says, a serene meditation on the Christian scheme; though it neither has the depth and clearness of conception of the apostolic literature, nor displays the logical and scientific spirit of later writers, who were forced by intellectual opponents to meet them on their own ground. It was fortunate for the Christian Church that the first writer, who, after the Apostles' death, took up the threads of their teaching, was, as Bishop of Rome, brought under the influence of both St. Peter and St. Paul.

A striking sentence appears in the third section bearing on the apostolic succession. " The Apostles knew through our Lord Jesus Christ that there would be strife over the name of the bishop's office. For this cause therefore, having complete foreknowledge, they appointed the aforesaid persons and afterwards they provided a continuance, that if these should fall asleep, other approved men should succeed to their ministrations."

The prayer which occupies the fifth section is regarded

as being the earliest Christian liturgical form extant.
Lightfoot's view is that, though prayers were for the
most part at that date extempore, some of them
were beginning to assume a stereotyped form; and
that this one may have been commonly used in the
service of the Roman church. It is at any rate
the earliest Christian prayer recorded after the Lord's
Prayer.

The theology of St. Clement is of a very simple character, but his idea of the atonement is given along the
lines of the epistle to the Hebrews, which he quotes
copiously. Indeed, the authorship of that epistle has
sometimes been attributed to him. Eusebius went
so far as to say that St. Paul wrote it, and St. Clement
translated it into Greek: but it is not likely that St.
Clement was the author. The doctrine of the Trinity
was of course not formulated at this time as a theological
dogma; but Clement expresses it in these words: " As
God liveth and Jesus Christ liveth, and the Holy Spirit,
who are the faith and hope of the elect:" this assevera-
tion taking the place of the Jewish, " As the Lord
Jehovah liveth."

The Epistle was written in Greek, for the earliest
Roman church was a sort of religious Greek colony.[1]
Christianity first spread among the lower orders, and
the poorer classes in Rome were at that period mostly
of Greek descent and speech. Already no doubt many
patricians had accepted the Faith, for even St. Paul
was able to say, " They of the household of Cæsar salute
you "; but they would equally understand Greek; for
it was generally known to the educated classes, and was
the channel of communication with distant parts of
the Empire. As the Roman Church became Latinized,
during the following two centuries, St. Clement's epistle
passed out of the ken of the Western Church, having

---

[1] A trace of the earliest Roman Liturgy still lingers in the
Greek words Kyrie eleison.

little bearing on the dogmatic controversies of the later Fathers. At the Reformation, however, when questions of·Church order became of interest, it was hunted up, and first printed in 1633; but from a MS. from which Lightfoot's fifth section was lost. The complete epistle went through the Press for the first time in 1875. The edition of 1633 was translated from a copy presented to Charles I by the Patriarch of Constantinople, bound up with a complete MS. of the New Testament.

The fact that St. Clement's epistle, and also a spurious second epistle, which was attributed to him, were so bound up in early times with the New Testament, gave rise to the idea that it was at one time regarded as canonical; but this is very unlikely. Were it so, it would have appeared in its place among the epistles, whereas it comes after the apocalypse. It was, however, publicly read at Corinth, Alexandria, and in many Eastern Churches, and was probably bound up for convenience.

The so-called Second Epistle to the Corinthians, which is really rather a homily than an epistle, and may therefore be treated as the earliest specimen of a published sermon, was probably written about A.D. 200, or at the earliest 150. Eusebius, the historian (about A.D. 300), doubts the authorship of St. Clement on the ground that no ancient authorities recognized it. It was probably a sermon first delivered at Corinth; and so became part of the literature of that church. The other spurious works are two epistles on Virginity in Syriac; a letter to St. James, already alluded to in connection with the Recognitions; and another to the same saint. The authenticity of these works was repudiated by Eusebius.

Little as we know of St. Clement's life, the memory of him long lingered as of an important personality. Of his two predecessors we hear practically nothing. It is the figure of St. Clement that always stands as the living embodiment of the sub-apostolic Roman Church; which even at that early date, St. John being still alive, was already becoming the central force of Christianity.

[This and the next two chapters are almost entirely based on Lightfoot's *Apostolic Fathers*.]

CHAPTER II

(Bishop of Antioch from about A.D. 69 *to* 107)

✓ FROM Rome we pass to another " see of Peter," Antioch; at that time a city of great splendour, which, though repeatedly injured and sometimes destroyed by earthquakes, was continually restored with increased magnificence; a haunt of Roman Emperors, who visited it for the games and the theatre; notorious also for the licentious worship of Apollo at Daphne, which was a suburb of the city; and yet one of the earliest centres of Christian life, and the place in which the very name of Christian had its origin. To-day literally no trace remains of this ancient city, which at its zenith contained a population of half a million and at one time a hundred thousand Christians. On the site is the wretched modern town of Antak, where less than a century ago the Christian population lacked even a church.

Antioch was situated in the north-west of Syria, about twenty miles up the Orontes from the port Seleucia; which derived its name from Seleucus, the general, who, on Alexander the Great's death, took Syria as his share of the Macedonian empire. According to the account in the Acts of the Apostles, St. Paul and St. Barnabas were more concerned than St. Peter in first preaching the gospel at Antioch : but tradition has always attributed the foundation of the church to St. Peter, and declared that he lived there as bishop for seven or eight years before visiting Rome. On this account, it was an apostolic church; and later a patriarchate with jurisdiction extending far away into the East. The successors of St. Peter at Antioch, however,

9

never made the claims to universal rule, which were made by Roman bishops.

St. Clement and St. Ignatius stand in marked contrast to each other, and seem typical of the Western and Eastern Churches that were to be. In Clement we see the calm, practical, judicious spirit, which characterized the West; in Ignatius the fervid spirit of the East. But the spirit of Ignatius expended itself not, as in the subsequent history of the East, in championing scientific definitions of dogma, but in upholding Church order; although Church order was rather a means to an end, than an end in itself, the end being the avoidance of heresies and divisions. But the fervid spirit of Ignatius was especially seen in his thirst for martyrdom; and connected with his death and his letters is everything that we know of him.

Of his life, as of St. Clement's, we know practically nothing. Legends grew up round his second name, Theophorus (God-borne or God-bearer); as for instance that he was the little child whom Jesus took up and showed to his disciples. He was generally believed to have had intercourse with apostles, and to have been a pupil of St. John. The last is quite likely, although there is no clear evidence of it. He never mentions him in his own writings, though he seems to have been influenced by St. John's. About the year 69, according to Eusebius, he succeeded Evodius as third bishop of Antioch. St. Chrysostom and Theodoret, however, say that he immediately followed St. Peter, and was consecrated by him. There is no record of any of his episcopal acts, unless we except the institution of antiphonal singing at Antioch. This may perhaps be rightly attributed to him, as there are in his epistles several analogies from music. It had, however, long been the custom in Jewish worship, and is mentioned by Pliny as characteristic of Christian in Bithynia in A.D. 112. There are also eleven analogies from medicine, from which it is suggested that in early life he may have been a physician.

It seems probable, from the great humility that he displays in his epistles, his description of himself as the last [1] of the Antiochenes, and his fear that he will not be counted worthy of martyrdom, that only late in life, after a career that he looked back on with remorse, did he become a Christian. But of all this we really know nothing. All the picture we have of him is in the last few months of his life, when he is on his way to Rome to receive the crown of martyrdom. The date of this is generally given as 107, but Lightfoot gives any year up to 118, and Harnack fixes it at 125. Trajan was emperor at the earlier date : and though he was a humane man, it is probable that in his reign the first definite laws were enacted against Christianity. Some suppose that Nero made the profession of our religion a capital offence; indeed Tertullian said this was the only act of Nero that was never repealed. Probably till Trajan's time, Christianity was hardly distinguished from Judaism in the judicial mind. Trajan, however, had always a dread of secret societies, guilds, or combinations of any kind, and allowed none except burial clubs. The Church in Rome existed in the eyes of the state at first as a burial club ; when it was clearly recognized as something more than this, it became a *religio illicita*. But Trajan forbade hunting out Christians : only where obvious cases came before the tribunals, were they to be punished. Some sort of disturbance had arisen in Antioch, which seemed graver than it might otherwise have been, owing to rumours of a pending insurrection of Jews : so Ignatius gave himself up for the peace of his Church, and was despatched to Rome as food for the beasts in the Coliseum, the manner of his death showing that he was not a Roman citizen.

[1] Eph. 21.

The route of this journey to Rome is interesting, from the glimpse we get of the Churches on the way. He may possibly have gone by land to the west coast of Asia Minor; but it is more probable that he went by sea from the port of Seleucia to Attalia in Pamphylia on the south coast. Thence he would cross by land to Smyrna, a port on the west coast. On the way he stayed at Laodicea, Hierapolis, Philadelphia, and Sardis, composing certain difficulties that had arisen at Philadelphia. At Smyrna he was comforted by Polycarp, then a young bishop, but forty years later to become a famous martyr. He also received deputations from Ephesus, Tralles and Magnesia, which lay out of his route, though not far away. By them he despatched epistles to their respective Churches; at the same time he wrote to the Romans in advance, begging them not to use their influence to prevent his martyrdom; for the persecution being only local, the Roman church was just then at rest. We next hear of him at Alexandria Troas, a port north-west of Asia Minor, to which he was probably conveyed by sea. There he learnt with joy that peace was restored to his own church, and thence he sent three more Epistles—to the Church of Smyrna, to Polycarp personally, and to the Philadelphians. He then crossed via Neapolis to Philippi in Macedonia, and after that we hear no more. Although he complained of his treatment on the way from the " ten leopards," [1] as he called his soldier guards, he seems to have been granted leisure and even freedom at the halting places; but this was easily granted, for escape within the Roman Empire was impossible.

The seven Epistles already mentioned are now fully ascertained to be the only genuine ones of Ignatius; but eight other spurious letters were at one time associated with his name—viz. one to St. John, one to our Lady (with her reply), and letters to Mary of Cassabela,

[1] Rom. 5.

the Tarsians, Philippians, Antiochenes, and Hero his successor as bishop of Antioch. All these are now finally put out of court. The authenticity of the correspondence with the B.V.M. and St. John was disproved at a comparatively early date. There then remained twelve in an edition, which was known as the longer Recension, and was first published in Latin in 1495, in Greek in 1557. In 1664 Archbishop Ussher discovered at Oxford an edition containing only the real seven letters, and in a much shorter form. Six, according to this reading, were published by Voss in 1644 in Greek, and so are sometimes spoken of as the Vossian epistles : the seventh was published by Ruinart in 1689. It was soon shown from the anachronisms and historical errors in the longer Recension, that the new discovery was the real work of Ignatius : although French and English non-Episcopal Protestants tried, but without success, to impugn the authenticity of these letters altogether. This edition used to be known as the shorter Recension, but Lightfoot calls it the Middle Recension, because in 1845 Canon Cureton found a still shorter edition of three Epistles only in Syriac, which Lightfoot has now called the short Recension. It has been, however, conclusively shown that the Middle Recension can be relied on, and that the short Syriac one was only an abridgement of those particular epistles for edification. The following list shows the various Recensions :—

Polycarp	Short	Middle	Longer Recension,
Romans	in	Recension	supported for a
Ephesians	Syriac	correct;	long time by
Smyrnæans		acknowledged	Roman Catholics,
Magnesians		by	but now entirely
Philadelphians		Eusebius	abandoned.
Trallians			
Correspondence with			
Mary of Casiobela			
Tarsians			
Antiochenes			
Bishop Hero			
Philippians			

Judaizing and Docetism are the heresies denounced in these epistles; but, according to Lightfoot, these were really one; or rather the same set of teachers in each case were at work, Jews by birth, who were teaching a form of Docetism. This word will be more fully explained later in connection with Gnosticism. It is enough for the present to say that the Docetic view was that Christ never really suffered in the flesh, but only seemed to do so. Either the whole life of Christ was phantasmal; or else they distinguished between the Divine Being and the human Jesus, affirming that the Christ, or Logos, descended on Jesus at His Baptism, and deserted Him before the crucifixion. Thus Ignatius continually speaks of the *real* Passion, and says that Christ was truly born, died, and rose again, and that the Christ, who reappeared, ate and drank, and was no incorporeal phantom.

The best way to guard against such errors was to cling to the bishop, to remain united, and to follow his teaching. "Where the bishop is, there is the Church." This idea runs through nearly all the Epistles, and Ignatius is therefore quoted by all Episcopalians as a witness to the truth of Episcopacy from the earliest times. And so he is. He clearly shows that bishops existed throughout Asia Minor, for he alludes to those of Ephesus, Magnesia, Tralles, Philadelphia, and Smyrna; he also speaks of them as established in the farthest parts of the earth.[1] Nor were they itinerant, like Timothy and Titus, but localized; and they ruled, though they were constitutional monarchs. In Rome also there was a bishop, though apparently with even less autocratic power than in Asia; perhaps because there was less heresy. The point that Ignatius leaves undecided is whether at that time Episcopacy was considered a divine institution, possessing doctrinal significance, and therefore a necessity to a true Church;

[1] Eph. 3.

or whether it was to be supported because it happened to be the order of the Churches he was addressing, and therefore the only existing bond of discipline. There is no proof that he looked on it as more than the latter. On the other hand there is no proof that he did not. In face of the very strong words he used, it is dangerous to argue from silence.

Unlike the other Epistles, that to the Romans makes no allusion to heresy, the Roman Church being " filtered clear from every alien colouring; " [1] nor to the bishop. It is full of his approaching martyrdom; the object being to implore them not to beg him off. Elsewhere he alludes to what was coming gravely and quietly : all his passionate aspirations for the crown are here. " I am God's wheat, and I am ground by the teeth of wild beasts, that I may be found Christ's pure bread." " Provoke the beasts, that they may become my sepulchre, and leave no part of my body behind." [2] " Permit me to be the imitator of the passion of my God." [3] " Come fire and cross and grappling with wild beasts, wrenching of bones and hacking of limbs and crushings of my whole body : come, cruel tortures of the devil and assail me; only be it mine to attain unto Christ." [4]

The other Epistles deal mainly with heresy and unity. Public worship and the Eucharist are incidentally recommended as a means of making religion not only a profession but a power. The following are some of the chief episcopal quotations. " Wherever the bishop is there let the people be, as where Jesus is, there is the Catholic Church." [5] This, by the way, is the first known instance of the term " Catholic Church," and " Catholic " is here synonymous with " Universal," not " Orthodox." The quotation is referred to equally by Catholics and Protestants. To the former it implies that the bishop is indispensable : to the latter that

---

[1] Rom. 1. [2] *Ibid.*, 4. [3] *Ibid.*, 6.
[4] *Ibid.*, 5. [5] Smyr. 8.

wherever Christ is, there is the Church. " Respect the
bishop as a type of God, and the presbyters as the
council of God and the college of the Apostles. Apart
from these there is not even the name of a Church." [1]
It will be seen that to the presbyters also is attributed
a great sanctity, as the successors of the Apostles.
Elsewhere he says, " The presbyters are to the bishop
as the strings to the lyre " [2] (one of his musical metaphors). Again, " Let no man do aught of the things
pertaining to the Church apart from the bishop. Let
that be held a valid Eucharist, which is under the
bishop, or one to whom he shall have committed it. . . .
It is not lawful, apart from the bishop, to baptize or
hold the Love feast." [3]   And again, " If any one follow
one who maketh a schism, he doth not inherit the
kingdom. If any man walk in strange doctrines, he
has no fellowship with the Passion." [4]

As regards Docetism, the following is the strongest
quotation, and a splendid defence of Christ's bodily
Resurrection : " For I know and believe that He was
in the flesh after the Resurrection : and when He came
to Peter and his company, He said ' Lay hold and
handle me, and see that I am not a bodiless spirit, and
straightway they touched Him and believed, being joined
to His flesh and blood. Wherefore also they despised
death, nay, were found superior to it; and after His
resurrection He ate and drank with them, as one in the
flesh, though spiritually He was united with the Father."[5]

Following this argument he gives an example of high
sacramental doctrine. " They abstain from the Eucharist, because they allow not that It is the flesh of our
Saviour, which flesh suffered for our sins, and which
the Father of His goodness raised up." [6]   The following sentence seems to mark the influence of St. John :
" The Spirit knoweth whence it cometh and whither

[1] Tral. 3.   [2] Eph. 4.   [3] Smyr. 8.
[4] Philad. 3.   [5] Smyr. 3.   [6] *Ibid.*, 6.

it goeth." [1] The following shows that he was an intense admirer of St. Paul, whom the Judaizers depreciated : " Sharers in the mysteries with Paul, the holy, the martyred, the ever-blessed Paul, in whose footsteps may I be treading when I come to meet God." [2] Here and there in his writings are little flashes of epigram; such as, " He that truly possesses the words of Jesus is able also to listen to His silence; " [3] " Form yourselves into an harmonious chorus, of which the key-note is God; " [4] " The one Bread, which is the medicine of life, the antidote of death; " [5] " Faith is the beginning of life, Love is the end." [6] Here is a very elaborate metaphor : " Ye are stones of a temple, which were prepared beforehand for a building of God the Father, hoisted up to the heights through the engine of Christ, which is the Cross, and using for a rope the Holy Spirit, while your faith is your windlass, and love is the way that leads up to God." [7]

One other subject deserves a passing notice. He once says that he could reveal to them the mysteries of the angelic host.[8] This seems to refer to the angelology of that time, the insight which some Christians in the early church believed they possessed into the disposition of the angels. It appears later in the Alexandrian school, and was presumably hinted at by St. Paul in the Epistle to the Colossians; " things visible and invisible, whether thrones or dominions or principalities or powers," and again when he warns the faithful against " a voluntary humility and the worshipping of angels."

Two Acts are extant of the martyrdom of St. Ignatius, one Roman and one Antiochene; but it is not likely that either dates from earlier than the sixth century, and they are therefore quite legendary.

---

[1] Philad. 7.   [2] Eph. 12.   [3] Ibid., 15.   [4] Ibid., 4.
[5] Ibid., 20.   [6] Ibid., 14.   [7] Ibid., 9.   [8] Trall. 5.

CHAPTER III

(Bishop of Smyrna. Lived from about A.D. *69 to* 155)

" EIGHTY-SIX years," said Polycarp on his trial before the Proconsul, " have I served the Lord, and He hath done me no wrong. How then can I speak evil of my King who saved me? " In this " eighty-six years " lies the leading thought about Polycarp. His importance in history is not in his relation to any particular events, or heresy, or movement of the time; nor has his one extant Epistle any theological or literary interest; but he is a human link between the apostles and the middle of the second century.

Two statements occur in the works of Irenæus, who was at his zenith in 180, and had been Polycarp's pupil, to the effect that he often spoke of the Apostles, especially St. John, and of his early intercourse with them, and of their teaching. It is not certain who the other Apostles were; but St. Andrew probably died at Ephesus, and St. Philip not far away at Hierapolis. At any rate it is sufficient for us, that he should have been taught by St. John, and that in 155 there should have still survived a prominent bishop, who had been so instructed : and further that he should have exercised personal influence on a man of the intellectual calibre of Irenæus, who would carry on the testimony for forty years more.

The character of Polycarp made him eminently suitable to be such a link. He combined with a charity for non-essentials a sturdy conservatism; a simple faith; great piety; possibly a lack of imagination; a

18

disdain of persecution; and an absolute intolerance of those who attacked the first principles of the faith. We gather all this from the few records we possess of him; from Irenæus' allusions; from his Epistle; from the circular letter of the Church at Smyrna describing his martyrdom; and from Eusebius' account of his visit to Rome shortly before his death. Beyond this all regarding his life is conjecture. At the end of the fourth century a life of Polycarp by Pionius was current, who had been alive in 250; but it is full of legendary lore to which no credence can be attached.

St. Polycarp was probably born of Christian parents in 69, just before the fall of Jerusalem; and as we find him not long after at the feet of St. John at Ephesus, his family may have been one of the many who migrated at that time to Asia Minor. If, as Tertullian says, he was consecrated Bishop of Smyrna by St. John, he then could hardly have been thirty : but there is nothing in this contrary to the custom of the time. Less than ten years after, he is comforting Ignatius on his march; and a little later Ignatius writes him with sound advice, the old man to the young; making us feel, from the way he singles him out, that he was the most important personality of the many bishops he had met *en route*. Then we have his letter to Philippi. Ignatius had asked him to communicate with the church at Antioch on the occasion of their restored tranquillity, and had asked the Philippian church to do the same. The latter sent their letter to Smyrna, and asked Polycarp to forward it with his own.

He sends them in reply his Epistle, which contains nothing novel; except that for the first time the word " Catholic " appears, not in the sense of " Universal," but " Orthodox." There is copious quotation from the New Testament; but nothing bearing on either the Church institutions of the day or modern controversy. Quotations from the Old, of which Clement's Epistle had been so full, are scarce : making us feel how completely the Old and New were changing places. His anger against heretics is shown by his alluding to those who denied the Resurrection as " the first born of Satan," [1] a term of reproach which he addressed to the Gnostic, Marcion, in the streets of Rome : also in a letter of Irenæus to Florinus, who had been his fellow-pupil, in which he describes the horror with which Polycarp would have heard of Florinus' heretical opinions.

In the last year of his life he made a journey to Rome to convey to the bishop, Anicetus, the views of the Asia Minor Churches on the proper day for the observance of Easter, which differed from the Roman custom. The Asiatics, taught, as they claimed, by St. John, always observed the day of the Crucifixion on the fourteenth day of the month Nizam, regardless of the day of the week; the Romans kept it on the nearest Friday, and the Resurrection on the Lord's Day. From the date, 14th, arose the term " Quarto-deciman Controversy." More will be heard of this later. What is noteworthy at present is that Polycarp and Anicetus agreed to differ, and that the former was invited to celebrate the Eucharist in the presence of the latter. The question was not discussed so amicably a little later. Polycarp was evidently treated with great reverence at Rome, where he is reported to have made many converts.

An interesting thought about Polycarp is the extent of his influence in founding the French church. On the south coast of Gaul were a number of Greek colonies from Asia Minor, of which Smyrna was a leading port. Polycarp never visited Gaul; but Irenæus at any rate, who was his pupil, spent most of his life there. Possibly many other missionaries were sent from Smyrna by Polycarp or influenced by him to settle there.

[1] Eph. 7.

The martyrdom of St. Polycarp is fully described in the circular letter of the Church of Smyrna, which has thoroughly established itself as a genuine document, and is of great interest as being the first authentic and contemporary " Act " of a m ᵣyr. It contains portents and miracles; but they ar ᵤch as might be easily founded on facts, though ᵣobably coloured by the heated imagination of the spectators. The persecution at Smyrna in 155, like that of Antioch to which Ignatius had been sacrificed, was a local disturbance. Rénan points out that there was a great revival of Pagan feeling in the middle of the second century; a sort of counter-reformation, after a period of scepticism; which caused keen animosity against those who refused to join in it. This Pagan reaction would no doubt be quite in accordance with the spirit of the Antonine Emperors. The popular indignation against Polycarp broke out on the occasion of the great anniversary of Asia, and was inflamed by the Jews. The proconsul at Smyrna was reluctant to convict him, but was forced by his insistence to carry out the law. Unlike Ignatius, he by no means at first courted persecution, but retired to a farm of his own in the country. But when he learned that the guard was on its way to arrest him, he made no further attempt to escape, but surrendered with the words, " Thanks be to God."

The course of Roman State persecutions of the Christian Church during this century deserves study. Trajan (A.D. 98), Hadrian (117), Antoninus Pius (138), under whom Polycarp suffered, and afterwards Marcus Aurelius (168) were wise and just emperors, and by no means cruel; they did not, like Nero, wreak their spite on unpopular victims. Yet Ignatius died under Trajan, Polycarp under Antoninus Pius, while Marcus Aurelius shed Christian blood freely. Even under Hadrian too the law was enforced, although this dilettante traveller took a friendly interest in all varieties of religion, liked

to be initiated into religious bodies, and seems to have
had a lurking sympathy with Christianity; reserving a
niche among his heathen gods and Jewish patriarchs
for the Sacred Figure; and building, as they say, empty
temples ready for the Christians to take over if they
wished. In sub-apostolic times it is probable that
Christianity was regarded only as a degraded form of
Judaism, a point of view which the Jews themselves
encouraged. It would therefore have some claim to
toleration, along with Judaism, as an ethnic religion.
During the time when Jews were giving trouble, previous
to the fall of Jerusalem, they diverted attention from
themselves to the Christians. By Domitian's time, the
difference between the two religions was beginning to
be understood; and though countless others were
tolerated at Rome, Christianity became *illicita;* yet
probably no definite enactments were made against it
till the time of Trajan.

Christianity came under the ban of the Government,
partly because it tolerated no other faith alongside of
itself; partly because it contained essential elements,
which seemed dangerous to society, to Roman law and
polity, and even to the Roman supremacy. More surely
than any one at that time realized, the new civilization
of Christianity was waging a war of life and death
against the old civilization of Paganism as represented
by Rome; and Paganism, however little individual
Romans may have believed in their deities, was the
established religion of the state. The Antonine Emperors would probably have laughed to scorn the idea
of this danger; but an uneasy feeling arose, when
Christians refused to throw a pinch of incense, like
every one else, on the altars of the state gods; when
they showed also a disinclination for military service;
and especially when they repudiated the divinity of the
Cæsars.

This strange cult of the reigning house sprang out of

something much deeper than bombast. It is difficult
for us to grasp exactly what the Romans understood
by divinity, but we know that their deities were personifications of ideas: was not then the Emperor
the incarnation of the idea of Rome, the Eternal City,
weaving its spell over mankind, as it does even to the
present day? The Christians were indeed unable to
say " We have no king but Cæsar." They had another
king, who was to return and subdue all the Empires
of the world. Indeed, for this reason special search
was sometimes made for relatives of our Lord. It
must also be remembered that the Emperors probably
knew very little about the details of the various persecutions, at any rate at this time, as they were generally
of a local character. The social and popular prejudice
against Christians will be more suitably dealt with in
connection with St. Justin Martyr.

CHAPTER IV

ST. IRENÆUS

(About A.D. *125–200. Bishop of Lyons in* 180)*

ACCORDING to chronological order, St. Justin Martyr should be considered next, as his average date is thirty years earlier than that of St. Irenæus; but he represents altogether a different school, that of the apologists; whereas St. Irenæus is linked through St. Polycarp to the apostolic age.

His life, though he was not an Apostolic Father, is a kind of supplement to theirs; while as the first great constructive theologian, he himself forms a link between the simple sub-apostolic age and that of the great doctors of the Church. His early life was apparently spent in Smyrna. In middle life he was a presbyter at Lyons, and afterwards bishop, the intercourse between Asia Minor and Gaul, especially the port of Lyons, being very close. He was probably often in Rome, where Hegesippus reports having heard him lecture. Once especially he visited Rome, to explain to Eleutherus the position of the Montanists; and while he was there the fearful persecution broke out in Gaul (A.D. 177), when Bishop Pothinus, Blandina the slave-girl, whom the beasts would not attack, and many other Christians were slaughtered, as described in the circular letter of the churches of Lyons and Vienne, which is the second authentic Act of Martyrdom. Then in 180 he became Bishop of Lyons, and was probably consecrated at Rome by Eleutherus, since at that time there seems to have been only one see in Gaul. From 182 to 188 he was engaged on his great work in refutation of Gnostic heresies, originally known as the *Refutation of Knowledge* (*Gnosis*) *falsely so called*, but generally known as *Against Heresies*. Subsequently, or perhaps concurrently, he wrote his letter to Florinus; the *Ogdoad* (a denunciation of the Gnostic Valentinian's system), and a book " on the schism," viz. the dispute about the date of Easter. The letter to Florinus was on the unity of God, and the origin of evil : two fundamental points in all the Gnostic controversies. He died about the close of the century.

As Bishop of Lyons he wrote a celebrated letter to Victor of Rome, protesting against his excommunicating all churches who did not conform to his own rule about observing Easter. St. Irenæus is constantly appealed to in the controversy between Rome and Protestants on two grounds. One is this letter to Victor; and another is a statement in his great work that all Churches must be in agreement with Rome. First, as to the letter. The Quarto-deciman controversy, already alluded to in the last chapter, had by 188 become a burning question; and although it seems to us rather strange that the Church should have been so distracted over a matter of ritual, the proper day for keeping Easter; yet when the Church was struggling under persecution for her very existence, unity in externals in the face of the enemy was of the utmost importance. It was the necessity of a united front that was most prominent in the mind of Ignatius, when he upheld the bishop's office; and later on it was a leading thought with Cyprian. Victor was probably wise in trying to enforce uniformity, though excommunication was a strong measure; especially as the Asiatic churches followed the example of St. John. The fact that he did so is quoted by Roman Catholics as a proof of the position of the Papacy even in the second century, although no Church changed its usage in consequence, and the ban fell quite harmless. It raised a strong protest from Polycrates, bishop of Ephesus, backed by the bishops of his province, and a mild but firm protest from Irenæus, advising Victor that he ought not to cut off whole churches of God for observing an ancient and apostolic custom. Eusebius says only that Victor *tried* to cut off the churches of Asia. These protests are naturally quoted by the other side to prove that Rome was considered to be acting *ultra vires*. One thing is clear, that his idea of keeping Easter on Sunday was the sensible one. The Council of Nicæa 140 years afterwards enforced it, and the Asiatic custom died out; indeed it will generally be found that the decision of Rome in these early days was justified by subsequent events. Irenæus himself, though bred in the East, conformed to Victor's rule, probably in order to maintain uniformity, at any rate in the Western world. It is also doubtful whether Victor himself realized that he was doing more than quarreling with his equals, and refusing to kneel at the same altar with them, if they were unreasonable; or whether he was consciously acting like a mediæval Pope.

The often-quoted saying of Irenæus about the Roman Church is this : " For with this church it is necessary that every church should agree on account of its more potent principality, that is, the faithful everywhere, inasmuch as the apostolic tradition has been preserved in it by those who exist everywhere." [1] This is a very literal translation from the Latin translation, all we possess of the original Greek. On the face of it, it is a strong statement; for if it really means that every one must agree with Rome, it implies that Rome is infallible; the statement coming from the pen of a writer, who had received at only second hand the tradition of the Apostles. A recent Roman Catholic book, however, *The Faith of Catholics* (by Berington & Kirk), translates the passage quite differently. " To this Church it is necessary that all others should resort (convenire *ad* not *cum*)." In other words, all roads lead to Rome.

[1] *Hær.*, III. 3. 2.

To Rome, as the metropolis, representatives of all the Churches come from time to time, and she is a mirror reflecting the views of them all; so in her the tradition has been preserved continuously by those who exist everywhere. But in any case, it is always dangerous to quote isolated passages from the Fathers apart from their context. This will be found specially to be the case in connection with sacramental doctrine. What Irenæus was enforcing here was the apostolic tradition. He showed that all the churches traced their bishops back to the Apostles; and as it would take too long to recount all the successions, he gives Rome as the best example, ending with the above remark.

On the Apostolic Tradition Irenæus is very strong. He is the first of several Fathers who state the creed of the Church, each in their own words, showing that apparently there was as yet no written formula. But their statements all substantially agree, and are in effect the Apostles' creed. This is the form in which Irenæus gives the Tradition: " The Church, though dispersed throughout the whole world even to the ends of the earth, has received from the apostles and their disciples this Faith. In one God the Father Almighty, Maker of Heaven and Earth, the Sea and all things that are in them; and in one Christ Jesus, the Son of God, who became incarnate for our salvation; and in the Holy Spirit, Who proclaimed through the prophets the dispensation of God and the advents and the birth from a virgin, and the passion and the resurrection from the dead, and the ascension into heaven in the flesh of the beloved Christ Jesus our Lord, and His manifestation from heaven in the glory of the Father to gather all things in one, and to raise up anew the flesh of the whole human race, in order that to Christ Jesus, our Lord and Saviour and King, according to the will of the Invisible Father ' every knee should bow,' etc. etc., and that every tongue should confess to Him that

He should execute just judgment upon all, that He may send spiritual wickednesses and the angels who transgressed and became apostate together with the ungodly and unrighteous and wicked and profane among men into eternal fire, but may in the exercise of His grace confer immortality on the righteous and holy and those who have kept His commandments and persevered in His love, some from the beginning and others from repentance, and may surround them with glory. The Church having received this preaching and faith, though scattered throughout the world, yet as if occupying but one house carefully preserves it. . . . For though the languages of the world are dissimilar, yet the import of the tradition is one and the same. For the Churches which have been planted in Germany do not believe or hand down anything different, nor do those in Spain or Gaul, nor those in the East, nor those in Libya, nor those established in the central regions of the world." [1]

The chief reason we have for believing that the Christian Church was essentially the same at the end of the second century as at first, both in faith and practice, is the tenacity with which the tradition of the Apostles was maintained. It could not have been the New Testament on which they relied in the first resort, seeing how few MSS. were obtainable. How many MSS. would be necessary to start with to allow the lessons to be read in every church? Irenæus says, " Polycarp at Rome proclaimed himself to have received from the Apostles the one and only tradition which hath been handed on by the Church." " Yes, and the Church at Ephesus, having had Paul for its founder, and John abiding among them till the time of Trajan, is a true witness of the apostles' tradition." [2] " The Apostles having in the Church as in a rich storehouse most abundantly deposited whatever appertains to the truth. And what if the Apostles themselves had not even left

[1] *Hær.*, I. 10. 1–2.   [2] *Ibid.*, III. 3. 4.

us any Scriptures, ought we not to follow the course of that tradition, which they delivered to those to whom they entrusted the Churches ? " [1] " Many barbarous tribes have salvation written in their hearts without ink and paper." [2]

In fact the Apostles delivered to their successors a certain rule of faith which they were always to remember and which they infallibly remembered. Whether or not there was a definite formula (a "*form* of sound words," as St. Paul wrote to Timothy) we know not; probably not. Gradually the Church collected the sacred writings, and selected from them the Canon. But if the New Testament had at the beginning been the main authority without the tradition behind it, there would have been much more error. Irenæus himself makes a misstatement as to the duration of our Lord's life, and Dean Farrar, in his mistrust of tradition, refers to this as showing how dangerous it was to rely on tradition, unless supported by Scripture. But tradition had nothing to do with a question of that kind. Irenæus explained clearly what the Tradition was; it was in effect, though quite differently worded, the apostles' creed. Tertullian later, and Origen also, explained the Tradition in quite different words, but to exactly the same effect.

Besides the fact that the main articles of the Faith were handed down by tradition, the main institutions, such as the Sacraments, relied on tradition. Origen [3] says, for instance, that Infant Baptism was in accordance with Apostolic tradition; and while there is no *theory* of the Eucharist in the New Testament, a fairly uniform theory runs through the early Fathers. It seems clear that they all believed that the elements were the Body and Blood, and that the Eucharist was an offering or Sacrifice. They do not attempt to explain the Real Presence and probably doubted their ability to do so,

[1] *Hær.*, III. 4. 1.   [2] *Ibid.*, III. 4. 3.   [3] See ch. viii.

but they continually used the analogy of the Eucharist
as an illustration of essential truths, such as the twofold
nature, human and divine, of Christ, or the reality of
His humanity. Sometimes also it was held that even
if the elements of both Sacraments were symbols, they
were at least efficacious symbols. Waterman says
that they understood the union of the bread and the
Body to be something parallel to the union of the Human
and Divine natures.[1] What is important, however,
here is that they had a fairly uniform theory; which
had come down by tradition from the Apostles, transmitted through the Episcopal succession.

Whatever confusion there may have been at first
between the orders of presbyter and bishop, Irenæus,
Tertullian, Clement of Alexandria, Origen, Cyprian
and Eusebius all make a strong point of the successions
of bishops. It is not fair to say that these men invented
the episcopal theory as a bulwark against heresy, or
that it was a new idea; because Irenæus rested his
whole position on the teaching received through Polycarp from the apostles. Gradually of course the New
Testament became, in place of tradition, the foundation
on which the Faith rested.

Here incidentally we may quote two of the leading
statements of Irenæus on the Eucharist :—

" Bread from the earth receiving the summons of
God is no longer common bread, but an Eucharist containing two parts, an earthly and a heavenly." [2]

" The oblation of the Eucharist is not fleshly but
spiritual and therefore clean. For we offer to God
the bread and the cup of blessing, giving thanks to Him
that He bade the earth send forth these fruits for our
nourishment, and afterwards having duly performed
the oblation, we call on the Holy Ghost that He would
make this sacrifice, the bread the Body of Christ, and
the cup the Blood of Christ, that they who receive these

[1] *Post-apostolic Age.*   [2] *Hær.*, IV. 18. 5.

antitypes may receive forgiveness of sins and Eternal Life." [1] Dr. Pusey took this as the general position of the Primitive Church.

Tertullian described Irenæus as a "most curious explorer of all kinds of learning." He often quotes from Greek poets, Homer, Hesiod, Pindar, and also from Plato. Also he had a thorough knowledge of the New Testament, which he approached in scholarly fashion, comparing MSS. and warning people against relying on isolated texts, which he called weaving ropes of sand,[2] instead of taking the Bible as a whole.[3] He took a liberal view of inspiration, deprecating the oratorical flights (hyperbata [4]) of St. Paul being taken quite literally. He always writes in a charitable spirit, never addressing his antagonists in stronger words than " O ye foolish ones," and praying earnestly for their conversion, thus acting up to his name of the Peace-Maker.

The book *Against Heresies* is in five parts. The First describes the Gnostic systems of Valentinian, Basilides and Saturninus, their sources and developments, and also Ebionitism; adding short accounts of the other Gnostics.

The Second points out their absurdities.

The Third, Fourth, and Fifth refute them and incidentally draw up the first philosophical statement of Christianity, the fifth dealing especially with the doctrine of the Incarnation.

It was seen in the chapter on St. Clement that the Roman Church of his time was a Greek community, a great proportion of the Roman population being Greek by descent and speech. Since the time of Alexander the Great the whole of the Eastern world within the Roman Empire, as well as the colonies in Southern Gaul, was Greek; Greek was the chief medium of communication throughout the Empire; Greek was the language

---

[1] Fragment, 36.   [2] *Hær.*, I. 8. 1.   [3] *Ibid.*, III. 7. 1.
[4] Translated " transpositions " in the ante-Nicene library.

of culture and literature. Marcus Aurelius himself wrote in Greek. The Roman philosophical systems, Stoicism and Epicureanism, were chiefly concerned with moral philosophy; it is to the Greek mind and the Greek language that we must look for metaphysics and all the deepest thinking; so that when the Church had to meet the thought of the age, it was Hellenistic theories that she had to conquer.

What then was the general position of that form of Greek thought, which under the name of Gnosticism, tried, as De Pressensé says, to stifle Christianity by embracing it? Based on Plato or on a memory of Plato, it had become debased by dabbling in Orientalism, the mystic systems of Egypt, Syria, Persia and India. Yet from these Eastern influences it had imbibed a desire to convert philosophy into religion. And this is to its credit. The old religion of Polytheism had become unsatisfactory and an object of derision. Some great monotheistic first principle was wanted, and some explanation of the relation of the individual spirit to that first principle. The Roman Empire had a body but no soul; and there was a consciousness that the old order was breaking up and something must fill its place. Scepticism had landed them in despair. The problem before them was how to reconcile the existence of a supreme and perfect God with the existence of evil or matter, for these were one and the same thing; all matter was evil, for it was the thing most removed from spirit. It was said in the last chapter that the second century saw an attempt to revive Paganism; it was only a part of a general yearning for religion of some sort, and the philosophers were not satisfied with Olympus. How far away was God from material things![1] How degraded was the world! How degraded was man by the soiled robe of the flesh! How were they to obtain Redemption from the world, the

[1] Cf. Harnack's *Expansion of Christianity*, ch. iii.

flesh and death! It must come somehow through knowledge; and the way to escape existed somewhere, if they could only find it; either in some ancient religion, or some mystery, or some person; and if the redeeming agency were found, there must be some method by which the redeeming gnosis (knowledge) could be efficaciously applied. In their desire to arrive at this result, they examined all existing religions, and came finally first upon Judaism and afterwards upon Christianity.

It is an open question, how far we are justified in treating the difficulties of belief with which the earliest Christians had to contend as heresies, assuming Canon Bright's definition of heresy as " an erroneous super-structure on a Christian foundation " to be correct. For the most part they were either a conservative cling-ing to early associations, as with the Judaizers; or they were antagonistic religions, as with most of the Gnostics; since the latter, though they claimed to be Christians, cut at the very root of the Faith; their Christianity was in fact only the superstructure. As Bishop Wordsworth pointed out, until the time of Con-stantine, the Church fought the outside world; when the Church became established, the world poured into the Church, and she then had to fight distinct heresies, like Arianism, that sprang up from within. At the same time there was a tendency in quite early days for Christians, especially if of Jewish origin, to get entangled in Oriental speculations; while the current heathen philosophy, Platonic at root, absorbed to some extent Jewish and Christian thought among other Oriental systems, Platonism from the first having been tinged with Orientalism. This is why Ignatius is probably attacking the same error, when in one letter he alludes to Docetics and in another to Judaizers. It was the error of the Jewish mind dabbling in Gnosticism.

What was exactly meant by Gnosticism, it will be always difficult to explain; especially as hardly any

D

Gnostic works remain. We can only reconstruct them
through their Christian antagonists, and by the fifth
century all trace of them had died out, except the
followers of Marcion, who lingered on till the seventh.
All metaphysical schemes of that time were forms of
Gnosticism, that is, Theories of Knowledge; Christianity,
as St. Clement of Alexandria afterwards claimed, being
the highest of all. But through all the other systems
ran one main thought, that Matter was Evil; the
material world having been created by an inferior deity,
or fallen angel, whom they called the demiurge, or
world-maker. There was one Eternal Spirit, from whom
emanated a graduated series of existences, called æons;
each was a personification of some particular attribute
of the Deity; and they all together made up the Pleroma
or Fullness of the Godhead. The eclectic spirit of the
Gnostics tempted them to meddle with Christianity.
They represented Christ (not the Man Jesus, but the
Logos or Word which dwelt in Christ) as an Æon; and
while they adopted the theory of Redemption, they
said the Redeeming work was not life, suffering and
death, but the imparting of a saving knowledge (Gnosis).
The idea that a Divine Being could be tortured was
abhorrent to them, and they invented various ways
of getting over it, such as the Docetic explanations
combated by Ignatius.

Now the Jewish sect, known as Ebionites, only half
accepted Christianity. To them Christ was the Messiah,
but not Divine. Still He was the Messiah; and as
such could not have died on the cross. They therefore
adopted the Docetic views, and it is specially against
them that Ignatius was writing. As time went on,
they drifted more and more into Gnosticism, the
extremist views being held by the Essenes. Ebionitism
probably first appeared at the beginning of the second
century and was rather a Jewish than a Christian sect,
though constantly presenting temptations to Christians.

St. Paul's contention with Judaizers was rather that they should throw off the trammels of the Law and ceremonial, with a view to the conversion of the Gentiles, than with their erroneous doctrines; yet his emphasizing the Resurrection of the body as well as certain phrases like " the fullness (or Pleroma) of the Godhead bodily," seem to point to a nascent Gnosticism. Possibly he did not think it advisable to call too much attention to it, while warning the Church against its development. The expression " Knowledge (Gnosis) falsely so called," also of course occurs to us at once. In the closing years of St. John and of the Century comes the first definite attempt to combine Greek philosophy with Christian teaching. " In the beginning was the Logos and the Logos was made flesh and dwelt among us." Ignatius attempted no philosophical arguments; he merely emphasized the reality of Christ's life, death, and resurrection. Nor did Polycarp. It was reserved for Irenæus to make the first intellectual refutation, and for the doctors of Carthage and Alexandria to follow it up; till at last the Church arrived at the crowning refutation of Docetism, " Not by conversion of the Godhead into flesh, but by the taking of the Manhood into God."

It is startling that even in the reign of Augustus the Jewish population of the Empire was seven per cent. of the whole; it is also strange to think of the Jewish as a missionary church, though our Lord spoke of them as " compassing heaven and earth to make one proselyte." Both these statements, however, are true. Of course the seven per cent. was not made up of Jews by race. There were many grades of Judaism, ranging from other semitic neighbouring tribes to the educated Roman who accepted the doctrines and to some extent adopted the ritual, but remained uncircumcized. But in Judaism the Hellenic mind found much of absorbing interest; a rational system of creation, a just monotheism, and also the oldest and most wonderful book in the world. To a large extent, therefore, it adopted Jewish philosophy; while the Jewish mind, flattered by the social and intellectual importance thus acquired, turned its attention to founding schools of philosophy, of which the most important professor was Philo of Alexandria. But there were two great drawbacks for the Greek in Judaism; one was that the Jewish Jehovah created the material world, and was therefore, as it seemed, responsible for something evil—creation was in fact rather a blunder—and also Judaism was at heart national and not universal; even the circumcized proselyte had not, at any rate in the first generation, full privileges. It was to meet the first difficulty that the Gnostics imagined two Gods; the supreme and perfect God, and the altogether inferior God, or demiurge, who created Matter. The lower God was not a direct emanation from the higher; but came after a long interval, which was bridged over by a succession of Æons, or personifications of abstract ideas, such as Wisdom, Reason (the Logos) and the like. Whether the demiurge was a fallen and malicious angel, or a well-intentioned semi-deity, who was unconscious of any one higher than himself, and did his best, but did it imperfectly, is of no consequence; Matter and Evil remained, and from these Man must be redeemed. But when the Gnostics had in this fashion settled accounts with Judaism, they found themselves confronted by another religion, advancing behind Judaism and often confounded with it, which was a world-wide system and offered the fullest privileges to all; which told them of a Redeemer, and knew of no sacrifices or rites, except the pure and simple mysteries by which the scheme of the Redemption could be applied to their souls. Here then was at last the true Gnosis. Christ was to them the power that was to redeem them from the Demiurge: the New Testament was to redeem them from the old. The

Jews had been called the Second Race; here then was the Third Race (tertium genus), whose nationality was the world.

As a natural consequence of their views, the Greek Gnostics looked on St. Paul as the one great Apostle; because, though himself a Jew of the Jews, he was always fighting against Judaism, on the ground that Judaism had found its completion in Christianity; the New Testament had supplanted the Old, and the Old now existed as a witness to the New. On the other hand the Essenes, the later Ebionites, who became entangled in Gnostic fancies, but still maintained the Law as the basis of all religion, gave great prominence to St. James and St. Peter, in order to throw St. Paul, whom they considered the enemy, into the background. Gnosticism, while it lived, was of great service to the Church; for it taught the Church to think, and to equip herself for an intellectual struggle with the educated classes. It forced the Church to formulate a theological system; it gave her a literature and art. Then it utterly died, except the school of Marcion which lingered on for some centuries. At present hardly any of the Gnostic writings are extant, while the work of Irenæus lasts to all time. The special view of Marcion will be stated in the chapter on Tertullian.

As to Irenæus' theological position, we must note that the Catholic Church never taught abstruse dogmas by choice; she was forced into dogmatic positions by the attacks of rivals or heretics, who wanted to bring Christian truths within the logical limits of the human understanding. In this respect Gnosticism is the forerunner and type of most heresies. What Irenæus did, as Harnack explains,[1] was to establish a theology of facts; he did not enter into the deeper questions which occupied, say, Athanasius or Augustine, a century or two later. He laid down as facts: that God is One;

---

[1] *Outlines of History of Dogma*, ch. v. pp. 142, 148.

that the supreme God created the world out of nothing;
that God was the God of the Old Testament; that the
Old Testament was a revelation of the Most High;
that Evil arose out of the free-will of Man; that Christ
was the God-Man. He shows the unity of His Personality, the essential character of His Divinity, and the
reality of His Humanity; that there was nothing in
matter that was irredeemable; and finally he asserts
the resurrection of the entire man; in other words,
the resurrection of the body. Irenæus frees thought
from abstractions. God is not a creation of the mind,
but a living Unity, combining purity, holiness, glory,
intellect, love; and He is perceived by love, which
emanates from Him to us.

Four fragments of Irenæus were discovered in Turin
in 1715 and have since been lost. The first of them
contained a statement that the true Gnosis consists
not in controversial subtlety, but in divine wisdom and
imitation of Christ; the second contains one of the
Eucharistic quotations already given; the third was
a plea for Toleration; the fourth was on the object of
the Incarnation, in which he said Christ would return
to destroy all evil and reconcile all things, that there
may be an end of impurity. Elsewhere Irenæus made
another statement, that there would possibly be an
annihilation of the wicked—" they will deprive themselves of the privilege of continuing for ever." These
last two statements seem to suggest that he might modify
the belief in eternal punishment, which was apparently
contained in his creed; and to which must be added
the belief that Christ would come again and establish
a Millennium, a reign of Himself with the redeemed on
earth for a thousand years. This was generally held
by Christians of the first two centuries. There also
occurs for the first time an interesting antithesis between
Eve and the Blessed Virgin—interesting because Cardinal
Newman gives it as an instance of the early dawn of a

special reverence for the Virgin. Irenæus says, " The knot of Eve's disobedience received its solution by the obedience of Mary. For what the Virgin Eve bound by unbelief, that the Virgin Mary loosed by Faith." [1] He has generally been counted as a martyr, but there is no direct historical evidence of his martyrdom.

[1] *Hær.*, III. 22.

CHAPTER V

(Born very early in Second Century. Beheaded at Rome
A.D. 166)

THE Apologists seem to stand apart from the general history of Christian thought. The period of the Apologists proper extends through nearly the whole of the second century, the central figure being St. Justin; Tertullian, St. Clement of Alexandria and Origen, however, also wrote famous apologies, but were not primarily apologists. The rest are known chiefly through those few fragments of their works that have come down to us.

When Hadrian came to the throne, the mild character of the man and his interest in foreign religions seemed to present an opportunity to Christians to make a frank appeal at Rome for fair play. During his reign Quadratus and Aristides presented the earliest apologies, and the entire work of the latter was recovered in 1878. These apologies may have been actually read by the Emperors, or they may only have been published in the form of " open letters." In the reign of Antoninus Pius, about 140–150, Justin produced his first and most important apology; and in 164, under Marcus Aurelius, his second. His other chief work was the Dialogue with Trypho, stating the case of Christianity against the Jews.

The Apologists are not great theologians, though much may be learnt from Justin as to the beliefs of the time. The chief interest of their work lies in the pictures of Christian life and worship at that day

40

and in the fact that Christians, now make their first claim to State recognition.

Justin had to defend his religion in three quarters: (1) against the State authorities; (2) against popular prejudice; and (3) against the educated classes. The State indeed cared very little about the religious point of view, so long as no sedition was involved in it. No Christian was to be hunted out for punishment; but if informed against as revolutionary, he was put to the test of sacrificing to the State gods, or acknowledging the Genius of the Emperor; failing that, he was considered no good citizen and must meet his fate. But why was he an object of popular prejudice? Because in the popular mind he was licentious; he indulged in wild orgies; he fed on human flesh; and having no temple he was presumably an atheist. Further, he knew no distinction of rank, even between freeman and slave; and, from one cause or another, he held aloof from most of the social institutions of the time. So they summed him up by calling him the " enemy of the human race."

All these views therefore must be combated; by showing the State that the other kingdom he looked for was not of this world, and that his life, if true to his creed, was absolutely innocent, so that he was really the best of citizens; while to the populace was shown, instead of orgies, the Christian service, and the awful accusation of cannibalism was refuted by the Blessed Sacrament. Finally, he required no temple made with hands. Incidentally, therefore, in St. Justin we have the first account, so often quoted, of the manner of celebrating the Sacraments, and of Christian worship in general.

" All who are persuaded and believe that the things taught and affirmed by us are true and who promise to be able to live accordingly, are taught to pray and beg God with fasting to grant them forgiveness of their former sins, and we pray and fast with them. Then we bring them where there is water; and after the same manner of regeneration as we were regenerated ourselves, they are regenerated. For in the name of God the Father and Lord of all things and of our Saviour Jesus Christ, and of the Holy Ghost, they then receive the washing of water : for indeed Christ also said, ' Except ye be born again,' etc. . . . But after thus washing him who has professed and given his assent we bring him to those who are called brethren : where they are assembled together to offer prayers in common both for ourselves and for the person who has received illumination,[1] and all others everywhere with all our hearts that we might be vouchsafed, now that we have learnt the truth, by our works also to be found good citizens and keepers of the Commandments, that we may obtain everlasting salvation. We salute one another with a kiss when we have concluded the prayers; then is brought to the President bread and a cup of water and wine, which he receives; and offers up praise and glory to the Father of all things, through the name of His Son and of the Holy Ghost; and he returns thanks at length for our being vouchsafed these things by Him. When he has concluded the prayers and thanksgivings, all who are present express their assent by saying Amen. When the President has celebrated the Eucharist and all the people have assented, they whom we call deacons give to each of those who are present a portion of the Eucharistic bread and wine and water; and carry them to those who are absent. Now this food is called the Eucharist, of which no one is allowed to partake but he who believes the truth of our doctrines, and has been washed in the laver for forgiveness of sins and to regeneration, and who so lives as Christ hath directed. For we do not receive them as ordinary food or ordinary drink, but as by the

---

[1] " Illumination " was a common synonym for baptism.

Word of God Jesus Christ our Saviour was made flesh
and had both flesh and blood for our salvation, so also
the food which was blessed by the prayer of the Word
which proceeded from Him, and from which our flesh
and blood by assimilation receive nourishment, is, we
are taught, both the Flesh and Blood of that Jesus who
was made flesh.   For the Apostles have declared "
(Here follow the words of institution.)

Later on Justin says : " Now on the day that is
called Sunday there is an assembly in the same place
of all who live in cities or in country districts, and the
records of the apostles or the writings of the prophets
are read as long as we have time.   Then the reader
concludes, and the President verbally instructs and
exhorts us to the imitation of these excellent things.
Then we all together rise and offer up our prayers, and
as I said before " (Here follows a second similar account
of the Eucharist).

These famous extracts have been quoted by various
schools in defence of their own particular views.   For
instance, Freppel, Bishop of Angers in the middle of
the nineteenth century, who has written one of the
most learned works on Justin, sees in his description
of Baptism a full acceptance of the doctrine of original
Sin.[1]   What, however, Justin says, a little later than
the passage quoted, is, " since we were brought up in
evil customs and wicked training, (we were baptized)
in order that we might not remain the children of necessity and ignorance but of choice and knowledge and
obtain remission of sins formerly committed." [2]   Other
critics see in this a denial of original sin altogether.
The truth perhaps lies half-way—that Justin, who is
not an accurate theologian, only half understood the
doctrine.

Freppel, again, sees in his account of the Supper the
entire doctrine of the sacrifice of the Mass, the essentials

---

[1] *Apologists*, Book I. ch. xv.   [2] Ap., I. 61.

being Oblation, Consecration, Communion. He says the elements were evidently offered; and were consecrated during the long prayer. In the passage quoted, the offering is indeed only one of praise and thanksgiving and not of the elements; but elsewhere [1] he distinctly speaks of the " Bread of the Eucharist which Christ commanded us to offer in remembrance of His Passion ": and again, " Those sacrifices which are offered to Him in every place by the Gentiles, viz. of the Eucharistic Bread and equally of the Eucharistic Cup." It is impossible, therefore, to doubt that St. Justin taught some sort of Eucharistic Sacrifice, and also that the bread and the wine were the Body and Blood of the Lord. Freppel therefore claims Justin in defence of Transubstantiation; but Roman Catholics generally argue that the Real Presence *ipso facto* implies Transsubstantiation.

This account of the Sacraments was of course given to show what Christians were really doing at these secret meetings at dawn, when they were accused of licentiousness. He goes on to show that they had a higher standard of right and wrong than other people; that it was an essential of their religion that it should be so, especially owing to the belief in the Resurrection of the Body; for they believed they would be punished in the body for sins committed in the body. [2]

Justin was well qualified to make this defence, because he had been himself attracted to the Christians by the purity of their lives, by their fidelity to their creed and by their contempt of death. All these things had struck him as incompatible with the crimes alleged against them. Previous to that he had tested all the philosophic systems in his desire to find the truth— Pythagorean, Stoic, Epicurean, Platonic; and had given them all up in despair: when one day he met on the seashore an old Christian missionary who explained

[1] Trypho, 41. 70.   [2] Ap., I. 18.

to him the fulfilment of the Hebrew prophecies.[1] Having tested this by his own study, he adopted Christianity; and taught it, as he had other systems, in his philosopher's cloak. But he embraced it with all his heart, and finally about 166 gave his life for it.

St. Justin is not content in his apology to defend Christianity, but assumes a strong aggressive attitude against the popular superstitions. His attitude towards Polytheism is chiefly marked by his theory of the dæmons, but also by the toleration and kindly spirit which he showed towards the heathen. The whole question of the belief in dæmons, the conflict of Christianity with dæmons, dæmon possession, the exorcising of dæmons, the accusation against our Lord that He was possessed of a dæmon, is one of immense interest and mystery, and here we have in St. Justin some kind of theory on the subject.[2]

It was an idea common among famous Greek Philosophers, the best of whom always aimed at Monotheism, that between the Most High and mankind there were intermediate beings, and this idea was worked out by the Gnostics in their many fanciful theories of Æons. In earlier systems, however, it was held that they were a sort of semi-deities, whose actions were not perfectly holy, but who shared the frailties of men, and mingled too freely with them. Consequently that there was at least a basis of fact about many of the mythological stories.

Justin copied this idea by saying that in the order of existence evil angels were between God and the dæmons and that the dæmons were the offspring of the intercourse of the sons of God (the Evil angels) with the daughters of men, referred to in Genesis.[3] These dæmons were wholly evil, and had invented polytheism. Justin agrees that mythology was not always untrue; for it sometimes narrated the deeds of dæmons, which had

[1] Trypho, 3.　　[2] Ap. I, throughout.　　[3] Ibid., II. 6.

actually occurred. On the whole, however, these stories were machinations of the dæmons to beguile men from the truth. The dæmons knew Moses and the prophets, and invented stories similar to theirs to draw mankind away from their teaching; one way and another the dæmons enslaved humanity, terrifying it with fears and punishments, teaching false sacrifices, deluding it with magic, and sowing the seeds of murder, adultery, war and all impurity. The poets were, however, Justin thought, the principal ministers of the dæmons for the seduction of mankind, and therefore he sympathized with Plato in proposing to exclude Homer and Hesiod from his ideal community.[1]

Assuming this fantastic theory to be true, Justin had no choice but to be extremely sorry for Pagans, and refrains entirely from the invective of other Christian writers. He tries to lead them to the truth by showing them how eminently reasonable Christianity is, and how clearly it is proved by the fulfilment of Prophecy. This indeed is his main argument. The Old Testament having been appropriated by Christianity, he calls the prophets Christians, and claims that the Christian facts had been truly foretold long before *by Christians*. But he also calls to witness the mighty changes wrought on man's character by Christ; the fixing of the highest truths in the minds of the lowest; the excellence of his teaching; his miracles; and his clearly attested Resurrection. In order to help Pagans to come over, he shows them that even in their own mythology there were cases of the resurrection and ascension of the sons of Zeus, and even suggests that Mercury, as the expresser of the mind of Jove, bore some analogy to Christ as the Word of the true God.[2]

St. Justin attacked Polytheism, not so much because he thought it was based on any arguments worth refuting, but because it was necessary to oppose the

_____
[1] Ap., II. 10.   [2] *Ibid.*, I. 21-2.

violent prejudice of the mob by showing the folly of what they believed in, and the greater reasonableness and purity of Christianity. With the philosophers it was very different; their views St. Justin had learned to respect. Epicureanism indeed all Christians rejected utterly, not only as a materialistic system, but also on account of the effect it produced on the lives of men. The high morality of the Stoics, however, had impressed him favourably, but their theology ended in abstractions or Pantheism; their highest principle was at best a God of the head and not of the heart, leaving no room for a religion of love. This was indeed the fault of all the systems; still, with the exception of the Aristotelian, all of them aimed at knowledge as a means to an end—the saving of men's souls; only knowledge, they thought, could do this. The Gnostics especially proceeded on this fallacy; but we have no more in St. Justin's works than brief allusions to the Gnostics, because he had already dealt with them fully in a work that is lost.

Platonism had specially attracted him; when he first came across the Platonic theory of Ideas, his soul had " mounted upward as if on wings." [1] The philosophy of Plato attracted mankind to the contemplation of God, and tended to detach spirit from its material environments and to reveal it. Through the study of the Ideas man was to be led up to God. All this in Plato's philosophy was to the good with St. Justin; but it broke down through allowing that Matter as well as God had existed from all Eternity; consequently it ended in a Dualism, and gave no explanation of the origin of Evil. Christians, he said, were saved by the power of Jesus, [2] not by knowledge; their piety was the only true philosophy; this, he said, might seem absurd, but it was proved by results. Men like Plato had received much inspiration from the Logos, and so far were Christians; but they had received it indirectly

---

[1] Trypho, 2. [2] Ap., II. 10.

(through a study of Jewish lore, he strangely thought), while Christians had had the Logos living with them. Socrates was great and good; but who died for Socrates?[1] Plato certainly aimed at making men like God, and so far anticipated Christianity; men's souls were only injured, he thought, by doing wrong. Irenæus had much the same idea;[2] God was revealed that we might become gods, which Harnack calls an intoxicating thought.[3] Man was made in God's image, but through sin he had lost the image, and it had to be revealed to him again. Then, according to Justin, all the philosophers demolished one another; whereas the Prophets, in spite of great divergence of time and place, were entirely consistent.

To sum up, St. Justin thought philosophy, at any rate the Platonic, good, as far as it went, and thus he took a more liberal view than other Christians of his day, but he felt that it was imperfect and arrived at nothing. Why should Christians trouble themselves with speculations about the Logos, when they had the Incarnate Logos? It remained for St. Clement of Alexandria to use Plato constructively in his theological system.

In the last chapter it was shown that at the dawn of the Christian era there was among the educated classes an attitude of expectancy : a looking for something or for some one who should redeem the world and create a new order of things.[4] This feeling seems to have been shared by the Wise Men, who made their pilgrimage to Bethlehem. But the Jews also were further impressed with the idea that *about this time* the Messiah should come, a human prince, who would restore the Kingdom. " Art thou he that should come?" Simeon was waiting for (and expecting) the

---

[1] Ap., II. 10.   [2] *Hær.*, V. 6. 1, and 16, 21.
[3] *Outlines of History of Dogma*, p. 134.
[4] Cf. Blunt's *History of Christianity*, cap. vii.

consolation of Israel. Herod made anxious enquiries
about the Child : adventurers " boasting themselves to
be somebody " could always draw people after them.
So when Christ appeared, the people were ready to
receive Him, while the Scribes and Pharisees also
questioned Him closely. But they had no expectation
of a Divine Being; and when that claim was made,
there was a sharp recoil. When they saw His miracles,
they said " of a truth this is that Prophet that should
come into the world." But when He said He was the
Bread that came down from Heaven, they murmured.
At other times when He conveyed to them the thought
of His Divinity, they tried to stone Him for blasphemy.
And at the last, when the charge of blasphemy seemed
fairly brought home (" What need we any further
witnesses ? "), the mob that had cried " Hosanna " only
a few days before now cried " Crucify Him."

It was this perversion of all that the Jews had expected
which caused that violent hostility of the Jew against
the Christian, which continued during all these three
first centuries, evoking special treatises from Justin,
Tertullian, Origen, Cyprian. The Jew hated the Christian with a bitterer hate than the heathen, and from a
deeper cause. Had Christ been like those others claiming
to be somebody, they would have passed Him by with
contempt; but the overthrow of their worldly expectations, coupled with His Divine claim, was not to be
forgiven.

Obviously, then the line which men like Justin would
take would be to show the Jews that they had misunderstood their own books : and in the dialogue with
Trypho he argues that it was all a question of interpretation. The Jews interpreted literally : to him
Christ was the key. Christ accepted as the central
point, everything was explained in its true sense. Many
of his interpretations are of course familiar to all
instructed Christians; but he pushed his types and

E

prophecies to an extreme point, and so did his successors. Space does not allow us to quote many here, and the Dialogue is not long and can easily be read through. It is noteworthy, however, that he considered all the appearances of the Deity in the Old Testament to have been appearances of Christ; and this must have materially helped Christians themselves to realize His Divinity.[1]

The allusions also to types of the Cross are very striking. This scandal of the Cross was the crowning difficulty with the Jews. Even if they could otherwise have believed Him divine, that God should have suffered the death of a criminal was unthinkable: " to the Jews a stumbling-block, to the Greeks foolishness." Yet, said Justin, Moses assumed the attitude of the Cross, with his arms outstretched, while Joshua (or Jesus) led the armies of Israel.[2] The horns of the unicorns (Psalm xxii.); the brazen serpent on the pole; the mark of the blood on the lintel; the cruciform spit on which the lamb was roasted; all pointed to the Cross, as Jonah did to the tomb and the resurrection, and the 24th Psalm to the Ascension. Was it not to emphasize the glory of the Cross against Jew and Greek alike that the Christians placed the Cross everywhere (though never a crucifix;[3] for the Lord was not on the Cross now, but risen, and so they preferred to think of Him)? But the Cross was on their dress, in their houses, on their persons. Whatever they did, says Tertullian, even at their rising up and sitting down, they made the sign of the Cross.

[1] Trypho, 75.   [2] *Ibid.*, 90, and elsewhere.
[3] Cardinal Bona gave the following stages in the evolution of the crucifix—

    (1) Plain Cross, generally St. Andrew's.
    (2) Cross upright, with lamb at foot.
    (3) Christ on the Cross, hands uplifted, but not nailed.
    (4) Christ nailed, but living and eyes open.
    (5) Realism and agony.
    (6) Revolting realism rendered sublime by Italian art.

Another argument that St. Justin could bring effectually against the Jews, which many of the Apostles could not, was that with the fall of Jerusalem the sacrifices of the Temple were gone, and the ordinances of the Law could not any longer be fulfilled; to which Tertullian added that if the prophecies were not now fulfilled, many of them would never have a chance of fulfilment.[1]

In many respects St. Justin's theology is not clear; but in regard to the First and Second Persons of the Trinity [2] he is explicit. The Father is the Creator of the Universe, Unbegotten and Ineffable. " In the beginning, before all created things, God begat from Himself a certain Rational Power, who is called by the Holy Spirit the Glory of the Lord, sometimes the Son, sometimes Wisdom." The relation between Father and Son he illustrated by saying that if one fire is lighted from another it does not diminish the fire from which it is lighted.[3] The Rational Power was emitted that He might be the Father's Minister in the creation of the Universe. Whether the Son was co-eternal with the Father or begotten in time does not appear. The question probably never occurred to Justin, since it dates rather from the period of Arianism. His teaching as to the Holy Spirit is somewhat uncertain. Generally he calls Him the Spirit of Prophecy, or the Prophetic Spirit, and sometimes he speaks of Him as the Spirit of Christ, confusing somewhat the Logos and the Spirit. Yet he worships Him as God, and assigns to the Prophetic Spirit the third place.

One much-quoted passage occurs in which he seems to say that Christians worshipped the Angels.[4] " We worship and reverence the Father and the Son and the army of the other good messengers who follow

---

[1] v. Jews, 13.
[2] Definitions of the Trinity run all through his works.
[3] Trypho, 61.　　　　[4] Ap., I. 6.

Him and are like to Him, and the Prophetic Spirit."
Protestants have questioned whether the text has not
become corrupted; but for this there is no evidence.
The statement presents difficulty, and is not in accord
with Justin's clearly expressed views elsewhere. The
words are σεβόμεθα καὶ προσκυνοῦμεν, implying two
different grades of worship, which may perhaps carry
the solution. Possibly, however, it is only an instance
of inexact writing.

The Incarnation, according to Justin, was decided on [1]
before the Creation. The Humanity of Christ was real
and actual, and His Divine and Human nature were
united. The pre-existent Logos and the man Jesus
were one in all respects. " Jesus the Christ was Son
of God and Messenger, formerly being Logos, and He
had sometimes appeared in the form of fire, and sometimes in the image of incorporeal things [2] (? the manna
and the Rock that followed them), but now through
the will of God He had become Man for the human
race." He endured to suffer what the dæmons caused
Him to endure at the hands of the senseless Jews.[3]

As regards the Atonement, Donaldson says,[4] Justin
knew nothing of vicarious satisfaction : by dying Christ
destroyed the death that had been inflicted on man
for disobedience [5] and destroyed the power of the
seducing dæmons. His suffering was not merely on
the cross, but all that He endured by becoming man.[6]
St. Justin called Him the eternal priest of God, but
gave no account of His priestly functions.[7]

Free will was a fundamental theory in this writer's
theology. In the beginning God made the human race
with the power of thought, and capable of choosing
the truth and doing right, so that all men are without
apology before God, being born rational and contem-

---

[1] Trypho, 63. [2] Ap., I. 63. [3] Ibid., 63.
[4] Apologists, III. 14, and p. 39. [5] Trypho, 45.
[6] Ibid., 58; Ap., II. 13. [7] Trypho, 33.

plative.[1] But every man is born in ignorance and through necessity (viz. the act of his parents, in which he had no voice), and is brought up among evil customs and with wicked training; whereas by his baptism he becomes the child of choice and knowledge.[2] How far original sin is affirmed, or denied or kept open by this, is a moot question, as was already pointed out on p. 43. Bishop Kaye thought it was affirmed, but not traced to the fall of Adam.

Somewhat in this connection occurs the same antithesis between Eve and Mary which was given by Irenæus. " Eve when a virgin and undefiled conceived the word of the serpent and brought forth disobedience and death. But Mary the Virgin (receiving the angelic message) said, " Be it unto me according to thy word." [3]

As regards the Millennium Justin said that all the best-instructed Christians believed in it, but that many pious Christians, pure in doctrine, thought otherwise.[4]

The second apology is a spirited appeal, caused by an act of hardship in private life, but is not of the same importance or length as the first. St. Justin had at that time a serious dispute with Crescens the Cynic, and foretold that this Crescens would cause his death, as he shortly afterwards did, about 164–6. Martyrdom has always in a special sense been associated with St. Justin and the word Martyr has been almost incorporated in his name. He is also never portrayed without the martyr's crown.

There are several works which were at one time attributed to St. Justin, but are now considered spurious; such are a *Confutation of Aristotle ; Questions of Christians to the Gentiles and of Gentiles to Christians ; Answers to the Orthodox ; Exposition of the Trinity ; Epistles to Zenas and Serenus ;* and especially the *Epistle to*

---

[1] Ap., II. 7.　　　　　[2] *Ibid.*, I. 61.
[3] Trypho, 100.　　　　[4] *Ibid.*, 80.

Diognetus, the latter being a very interesting work, the author of which is entirely unknown. On the other hand, the Hortatory address to the Greeks (though it is doubted by Kaye) is considered genuine by Donaldson, as also a Discourse to the Greeks, and a fragment on the Resurrection.

Later apologists, with the approximate dates at which they wrote, were Tatian (160), a disciple of Justin, who composed a Harmony of the Gospels called the *Diatessaron*, and afterwards lapsed into heresy : Appollinaris (176); Athenagoras (177); Melito of Sardis (177); Hermias (180) and Theophilus (180); but as none of these are accounted Fathers, they do not come within the range of this work. The last-named was the first writer who used the Greek word, Trias, or Trinity.

CHAPTER VI

(A.D. 150 *to some time between* 220 *and* 240)

TERTULLIAN was one of the most powerful personalities in early Church History, and one of the most forcible and voluminous writers. He introduces us in Africa to an entirely new phase of Church life and thought, and was also the founder of Western Theology and of ecclesiastical Latin.

The influence of the African Church was great on Christianity generally, but especially on the West, till the fifth century; but when and by whom it was first planted no one knows; suddenly it comes into history, fully organized and under many bishops, towards the close of the second century.

Africa, as we must now consider it, was not the whole northern seaboard of Africa, but the Roman province of Africa, which in a general way corresponded with the modern seaboards of Tunis and Tripoli. The African Church, therefore, was distinct from the Church of Egypt, which centred at Alexandria and was Greek. The centre of the African Church was Carthage, which had been destroyed and ploughed up in 146 B.C., but was colonized afresh by Julius Cæsar in 46 B.C., and in the second and third centuries was a prosperous trading colony; without an aristocracy or a distinctive school of philosophy, and therefore with no great interest in the metaphysical questions which troubled the Eastern mind; eminently practical, and so far as it was Christianized, profoundly interested in' all that concerned the moral and spiritual welfare of mankind.

55

Tertullian, in his address to the Proconsul Scapula, warned him that if he extirpated the Christians, he would decimate the population; and therefore, unless he exaggerated, we must assume that 10 per cent. of the population had already been converted. This population was composed, as to its upper crust, of middle-class Romans; and below of a passionate, black-blooded African race. Nowhere was there any Greek element in it worth mentioning. Consequently the Christian literature developed at Carthage was from the outset Latin, instead of being, as at Rome itself, Greek. The blending of the characters of these two races produced the characteristics of the African Church; restless, energetic, passionate, ardent, benevolent, self-sacrificing, practical; yet narrow, schismatic and intolerant; a Church which has been said to have bred more martyrs than saints. The upper classes spoke Latin; the lower the old Punic, which was of the same Semitic family as Hebrew, although very unlike it. In Latin, therefore, Tertullian naturally wrote; and early in his lifetime also there appeared the first Latin Bishop of Rome, Victor.

For the Greek character of the Roman Church was now beginning to disappear. When Rome finally shed her Greek, it is difficult to fix; but we learn that when Athanasius visited Rome in 340, he had to learn Latin, in order to instruct the clergy in the controversy of the day.

To this African Church was attracted, somewhere between the ages of 35 and 45, Quintus Septimus Florens Tertullianus, son of a Roman centurion; a lawyer, a man thoroughly versed in the science, philosophy and general literature of his age, and in Greek, in which he wrote several treatises, now unfortunately lost; of whom St. Jerome said, " Who more learned or acute? " of whom St. Vincent of Lerins said, " As Origen among the Greeks, so Tertullian among the Latins is to be accounted far the first among all our writers." What especially attracted him we know not; probably the heroism of the martyrs. It was not likely to be the Bible; for, as he said himself, heathens knew nothing about it. Nor philosophy; for of that, at least after his conversion, he had a great contempt, calling philosophers the " patriarchs of heretics," and saying further, " We despise the learning of secular literature, which is reckoned as folly with God; " [1] so that he had no gratitude in that quarter, and would never admit, like St. Justin or St. Clement of Alexandria, that Philosophy paved the way for Christianity.

But when once converted, he embraced the Faith with all his heart. He began writing shortly afterwards, probably not later than 197, and was also ordained. The fact of his ordination rests on general tradition (especially the authority of St. Jerome) and on many remarks in his works. It is, however, somewhat questioned, because in one place he says, " Are not we laymen also priests? " [2] It is supposed, however, that he was then, when he had become a Montanist, ranging himself rhetorically on the side of the laity, whose priesthood he was defending, since otherwise it would be inconsistent with his other statements.

His writings were apologetic, doctrinal and practical; but throughout there is an entire absence of the calm judicial spirit of Clement of Rome, Irenæus, or Justin. He is usually a violent advocate; admitting nothing to the other side; thinking of nothing but enforcing his point with the most powerful language and even invective at his disposal. Thus his apology, instead of entreating like Justin's, defies, and was probably an incentive to persecution, doing at the time more harm than good, for it flung the gage into the enemy's camp. In his earlier works against heretics, no word is too bad for a heretic, nothing too pure and perfect for a

[1] Spect. 18. [2] Exhort. Cast. 7.

Catholic. Yet soon he grew dissatisfied with the Catholic Church, and joined the Montanists; then all is contempt for the simple Catholic; so that the value of his writings depends to some extent on whether he was writing as a Catholic or a Montanist. Not, however, when it is a question of Theology; for to the last he upheld Catholic Theology, even when he was opposed to Catholic practice.

He joined the Montanist sect in 202 or thereabout, and on this account his position is differently estimated by different religious schools. Thus the *Catholic Dictionary*, under the heading of " Fathers," does not count Tertullian as strictly among them. It says, " In a general sense the word includes some on whom there rests more or less the reproach of heterodox doctrine. Tertullian became an open apostate from the Catholic Church, yet his writings as a Catholic are among the most excellent and precious remains of antiquity." In point of fact, some of his most orthodox books, such as *Marcion* and *Praxeas*, were written as a Montanist, and to the end of his life he is believed never to have been out of communion with the Catholic Church. Pusey, again, from a middle or Anglican point of view, remarks that " to the right use of Tertullian more care and judgment are required than for other fathers." [1] On the Protestant side, however, De Pressensé sees nothing but good in him. " No influence in the early ages could equal that of Tertullian, and his writings breathe such a spirit of undying power that they can never grow old, and even now render living controversies which have been silent for fifteen centuries. . . . Never did a man more fully infuse his whole moral life into his books." [2]

What, then, was the Montanist sect which Tertullian joined ?

[1] Library of Fathers, Preface to *Tertullian*.
[2] *Martyrs and Apologists*, p. 368.

The gifts of prophesying and of tongues were among the earliest features of the Church; but what either exactly meant is involved in some obscurity. Prophesying was apparently a kind of extempore preaching; and those who had the gift formed something like an order, instruction and edifying being a work rather assigned to them than to the presbyters. That is, comparatively simple. The speaking in tongues is more difficult to understand; but what is most important to observe in it is that it was connected with ecstasy or trance. It was recognized by Irenæus, who says, "We have many brethren in the Church having prophetical gifts, and by the spirit speaking all kinds of tongues."[1] By the fourth century, however, the speaking with tongues had disappeared; for St. Chrysostom says of it, "This whole topic is very obscure; but the obscurity is produced by our ignorance of the facts described, which are such as then used to appear, but now no longer take place."[2] To some extent, however, it reappeared in the prophesyings of the fifteenth century, in Quietism in the seventeenth, among the Quakers in the seventeenth and eighteenth, and the Irvingites in the nineteenth.

Montanus, therefore, in the middle of the second century, when he began prophesying, was not striking out any new line; the innovation lay in the way he used his gift. He was himself a Phrygian, and had been a priest of Cybele, and was altogether a weak-minded person. After his conversion he commenced prophesying and associated with himself two deaconesses, Maximilla and Priscilla, who, like himself, gave utterances "in the spirit"; the essential condition being, that the mind was absolutely passive, and that the spirit swept over it, like the plectrum over the lyre— a condition, in fact, of trance or ecstasy. Montanus

[1] *Hær.*, VI. 6.
[2] Cf. Stanley on the *Epistles to the Corinthians*, p. 244.

called himself, and was called by his followers, the
Paraclete; not that he claimed to be the Holy Ghost
Incarnate, but that through him and his equally inspired
and spiritual followers the Spirit made fresh and supplementary revelations. In fact, it was in their view a
delusion that the faith was once for all delivered, for
there was to be a progressive revelation till the time
of the New Jerusalem, which, however, was not far off.
They held, as Neander puts it, " a gradual advance of
the Church, according to a general law of the developments of the kingdom of God.[1] St. Augustine tells us
that Montanus, Maximilla and Priscilla, claimed that
the coming of the Holy Ghost was more fully and
powerfully realized in themselves than in the Apostles.
Tertullian wrote six books on Ecstasy, which are unfortunately lost. St. Clement of Alexandria, however,
went so far as to call it a sign of apostasy.

Tertullian, writing as a Montanist, calls the Old
Testament dispensation Infancy, the New Youth, and
the days of the Paraclete Maturity. These parts of the
Christian dispensation, he teaches, which relate to the
life and conversation, admit of change and improve-
ment. On this very account our Lord sent the Paraclete, to the end that, as the weakness of man's nature
rendered him incapable of bearing the whole truth at
once, the Christian rule of life might be carried to
perfection by the Holy Spirit substituted in the place
of our Lord.[2] Here, then, is the first sign of the Roman
Catholic doctrine of development. Cardinal Newman
admits and in fact claims this, saying in his *Essay on
Development*, "The very foundation of Montanism was
development, though not of doctrine, yet of discipline
and conduct; " and Tertullian, he adds, " understood
even the process of it."[3] Again, Newman says, " Mon-

---

[1] *History of the Christian Religion*, II. p. 180.
[2] Virg. Vel. 1.
[3] *Essay on Development*, VI. p. 2.

tanism is a remarkable anticipation or presage of developments, which soon began to show themselves in doctrinal determinations, and the ecclesiastical usages of the middle ages are the true fulfilment of its self-willed and abortive attempts at precipitating the growth of the Church." And again, " The prophets of the Montanists prefigure the Doctors of the Church, their inspiration her infallibility, their revelations her developments." But if Montanism was a forerunner of development, it was also so of Puritanism, and Puritanism in its most extreme form. It tried to raise an impossible standard for humanity. Fasting was carried to an impracticable point. Marriage was undesirable. Second marriage, which the Church only discouraged, was adultery. Military service was barred. Amusement of all kind was sinful. Profane learning was forbidden. Only those who could realize these high ideals were true Christians, and these they called the Spiritales : the ordinary Catholics were only Psychichi, possessing souls, but not spirits; sometimes they were only Carnales, mere bodily existences. Rule in the Church depended on spiritual endowments and not on Church order. They exaggerated the idea of the priesthood of the laity. They distinguished between venial and mortal sins.

It was doubtful if any one, but God alone, could pardon mortal sin committed after baptism; if any one could, it was not a Bishop, but one of the Prophets, who were the true successors of the Apostles. As the Prophets were above the clergy, so the prophetic sayings were above Scripture.

No doubt they were confronted with a growing worldliness in the Church, and there was some good in their aim; but the effect on character was to produce gloominess, acerbity, and spiritual pride. This at any rate was the effect produced on Tertullian. They held firmly to orthodox doctrine; so did he. Indeed his most splendid doctrinal works were of the Montanist period. *Ad Praxeam* (in which he denounces that confusion of Persons, which produced Patripassianism, or the doctrine that the Father was crucified) was elicited by Praxeas' action in causing Victor of Rome to withdraw his recognition of Montanism. But if early works like *Ad Martyres* are compared with later ones like *De Pudicitia*, there is a distinct deterioration from a tone of humility and self-abasement to arrogance, coarseness and self-confidence. It is reported by St. Jerome that he was driven into revolt by the envy and contumely of the Roman clergy. He passed certainly into extreme Montanism, and at the end of his life founded a sect of his own, the Tertullianists, who had a Church near Rome late in the fourth century. St. Augustine a little later seems to have brought a remnant of them into the Catholic Church; about which time they died out. Montanism was so far like English dissent, that it accepted for the most part the doctrines of the Church, but repudiated her order.

His works might be classified either according to whether they are (1) Practical, (2) Controversial, (3) Apologetic; or whether written when he was a Catholic or a Montanist. Bishop Kaye gives the following classification—

Catholic.		Probably Montanist.
De Penitentia	De Resurrectione	Ad Valentinianum
De Oratione	Ad Praxeam	Ad Scapulam
De Baptismo	Scorpiace	De Spectaculis
Ad Uxorem	De Corona	De Idololatria
Ad Martyres	De Virginibus Velandis	De Cultu Mulierum
De Patientia	Exhortatio ad Casti-	
Ad Judæos	tatem	—
Præscriptio	De Fuga in Persecu-	
	tione	Period quite uncertain.
—	De Monogamia	Apologia
	De Modestia	Ad Nationes
Montanist.	De Jejuniis	De Testimonio Animæ
Ad Marcionem	De Carne Christi	De Pallio
De Anima	—	Contra Hermogenem

His style is everywhere most powerful and graphic; but the peculiarity is that he coins Latin words with the utmost freedom, when he does not find one suitable to his purpose, either because it is not strong enough, or because he has to translate a religious or scientific word hitherto only found in Greek. Naturally he also abounds in superlatives and compound words. Latin became henceforth an ecclesiastical language, and Tertullian was the founder of that peculiar form of it known much later as scholastic.

His relation to tradition is seen in the *Præscription of Heretics* written when a Catholic. Præscriptio was a legal term, putting the other side out of court before the case was tried; a sort of demurrer, or throwing out the bill by the Grand Jury; and Tertullian pleads that heretics have no claim to be heard, because they do not obey the Rule of Faith; which is that " which prescribes the belief that there is only one God : and that He is none other than the Creator of the world, who produced all things out of nothing through His own Word first of all sent forth : that the Word is called His Son, and under the name of God was seen in divers manners by the Patriarchs; heard at all times in the Prophets; at last brought down by the Spirit and Power of the Father into the Virgin Mary; was made flesh in her Womb, and being born of her went forth as Jesus Christ; thenceforth preached the new law and the new promise of the Kingdom of Heaven, and worked miracles. Having been crucified, He rose again the third day : then having been caught away into the heavens, He sat at the right hand of the Father; sent in His place the Power of the Holy Ghost to lead such as believe; will come with glory to take the saints to the enjoyment of eternal life and the heavenly promises, and to condemn the wicked to eternal fire, after the resurrection of both these classes shall have happened together with the restoration of their flesh. This rule, as it will be proved, was taught by Christ." [1]

[1] Præscr. 13.

This is again substantially the Apostles Creed, as stated by Irenæus, but now in quite different words, and it is the essential truth of the early Catholic Church. If heretics differed in any respect from this traditional rule, it was useless to argue with them; they were not Christians. Freedom of enquiry was only allowed on non-essentials. He goes on to say that Christ appointed twelve Apostles to teach the nations. They founded Apostolic Churches, and others became the offspring of Apostolic Churches. If Christ sent Apostles to preach, then others are not to be counted as preachers. All teaching which agrees with the Apostolic Churches must be reckoned as truth, since it contains without doubt that which the Churches received from the Apostles and the Apostles from Christ. " How happy," he adds, " is that Church (Rome) on which Apostles poured forth all their teaching along with their blood; where Peter suffered in like manner as his Master, and Paul won his crown by a death like John the Baptist." [1] Tertullian, however, while thus upholding Tradition, places Scripture alongside of it as the Scripta Traditio,[2] and acts continually in accordance with this idea. Indeed the Scriptures were the very words and letters of God.[3]

The psychology of Tertullian [4] is very interesting. In the *De Anima* he gives his account of the human soul, dealing (1) with the nature of the soul; (2) the origin of the individual soul; (3) its relation to evil; and (4) its state after death. The soul derives its origin from the breath of God : the mind is its servant. The soul is immortal, corporeal, has figure, is simple in substance, possesses within itself the principle of intelligence, is endowed with free will, is affected by externals, which produce a great variety of talents and disposi-

---

[1] Præscr. 36.   [2] Cor. 3.   [3] Apol. 31.
[4] See Bishop Kaye's *Ecclesiastical History of the Second and Third Centuries*, illustrated from writings of Tertullian.

tions, is rational, is intended to rule the whole man, has an insight into futurity, thinks, wills and disposes: to carry out its designs, it needs the help of the body as the medium of sensation; the body therefore must rise again. Further, all souls proceed from the soul of Adam. Evil is taught to the soul by the dæmons; and he agrees with St. Justin that the dæmons were the offspring of the sons of God with the daughters of men. Souls do not return to earth; this is a delusion of the dæmons. In dealing with the soul after death he certainly implies that in his view some sort of purifying process takes place.

This treatise must not be confused with the *Testimony of the Soul,* which deals not so much with the nature of the soul as the natural evidence of the soul to the existence of one God; of right and wrong; judgment and a future state; and shows that, in spite of the evil adhering to man's nature and his need of redemption, there is a natural alliance between the human and the divine. "Come forth, O soul; [1] I want thee, not, as tutored in libraries and academies thou utterest wisdom; I want thee in thy rude ignorant state, as thou art in those who have thee alone. I want thee pure as thou comest from the highway and workshop. I want thy inexperience, for no one has any confidence in thy experience." However much, he argues, men follow polytheism, yet they say " Good God," [2] " If God will," " God bless you." If God is good, man is evil. The fear of death witnesses to judgment and the future. After a close argument he ends, " You proclaimed God, but sought Him not; evil spirits you hated and yet worshipped; the judgment of God you appealed to, yet doubted its existence; the tortures of Hell you foresaw, yet did not guard against; you recognized the Christian name, and yet persecuted the Christian."

As regards Tertullian's general doctrinal position: in

---

[1] *Test. ani.* 1.　　　　[2] *Ibid.,* 2.

F

the *Ad Praxeam* are throughout remarkable, almost Nicean,[1] definitions of the Trinity; and in the Apology we find " God of God, Light of Light." " For though They are Three,[2] They are so not in condition but in degree; not in substance but in form; not in power but in species; being of one substance, condition and power : because there is one God, from whom those three degrees, forms and species, in the names of Father, Son and Holy Ghost, are derived. Father and Son are two, not by division of substance, but *ex dispositione*. The Three Persons stand together in the relation of root, shrub and fruit; of fountain, river, and cut from the river; of the sun, the ray, and the terminating point of the ray. In the *Hermogenes*,[3] though he describes the Son as pre-existent and consubstantial, he seems to imply that there was when He was not. But he was writing before Arianism had appeared, and would therefore be less careful in his statements. As regards the Holy Spirit, there is a clear conception of His Personality in many passages; but Tertullian is sometimes confusing in his language, owing to the various meanings of the Latin word Spiritus. In Tertullian's view there seems to have been a progressive emanation of the Trinity; the Son proceeding from the Father at the Creation, the Spirit proceeding from the Word at the Ascension.

On the Atonement he says that Christ is the " Propitiator of the Father, and offers His own Soul for the salvation of the world." [4] " The death of Christ is the chief (Summum) foundation of the Gospel and of our salvation." [5] " He came, that being Himself pure and holy He might endure all things for sinners." [6]

On the Eucharist he says, " Taking Bread He made it His Body." " Our Lord in the Gospel showed bread,

making it His Body, in order that you might thence
understand Him to have given the bread the figure of
His Body," not apparently meaning that it was a
symbol of an absent Body.[1] " In the bread is understood His Body." [2] " He feeds on the richness of the
Lord's Body." [3] He also tells us that offerings of the
Eucharist were made for the dead on their anniversaries, or birthdays. Also that great care was taken
not to spill the elements.[4]

He expresses himself clearly on original [5] sin—that
all are infected from the sin of Adam. The soul is
partly rational and partly irrational. At first it was
rational, but the irrational element has been so thoroughly introduced by the dæmons as to become part
of the original character. But he makes this reserva-
tion : that there has been no total corruption. What
was derived from God is rather obscured than destroyed.
In the worst there is some good. No one born into the
world is exempt from sin, till born again by water and
the Spirit. Yet in one place he suggests the deferring
of the baptism of infants till they have passed the age
of innocence.

As regards Free Will and Grace, Adam was created
free : otherwise a law would not have been given him
which it was death to break; but now that man has
fallen, before he can repent and do good, his will must
be subjected to the Grace of God. No controversy had
as yet arisen as to Justification; but he speaks of
repentance as justified by faith; [6] and from the context
it is clear that repentance acquires its merit from
Christ's sacrifice.

On the Intermediate state he believes that there are
two places—the Inferi and Abraham's bosom (although
both are sometimes included under the former name),
to which spirits go till the Judgment; when the con-

---

[1] Marc. 20 and 40.   [2] Or. 6.   [3] Pudic. 9.
[4] Cor. 3.   [5] Kaye's *Tertullian.*   [6] Marc. IV. 18.

demned will pass from the Inferi to Gehenna, and the good from Abraham's bosom to Paradise. But the martyrs and saints go at once to Paradise. For the rest, neither can the full reward of the good, nor the full punishment of the wicked be conferred, until soul and body are reunited at the Judgment.[1]

Here are a few famous sayings of Tertullian—

"What greater pleasure is there than to despise pleasure?"[2]

"The blood of the martyrs is the seed of the Church."[3]

"A Christian must be made, not born."[4]

"Christ is truth, not custom."[5]

"It is contrary to religion to compel religion."[6]

"Credo quia absurdum. Certum est quia impossibile."[7]

The writings of Tertullian are so voluminous, that it is impossible to describe them all. The contrast between the earliest and latest should be noticed. One of the first is a letter *to the Martyrs* in prison, which is simple, humble, affectionate. He warns them not to disagree. "Grieve not the Holy Spirit, who hath entered with you into prison." "Though the body be imprisoned, all is open to the spirit. Walk to and fro, thou Spirit; not setting before thee shady walks or long cloisters, but that way which leadeth unto God."

Another early work was *On Baptism*, in reply to a woman, who thought the ceremony useless, where there was no faith. The following is a short summary : Any sort of water will do—an angel presides—anointing follows the triple immersion in name of the Trinity; then the laying on of hands; all the Apostles, except Paul, were baptized with the baptism of John; baptism necessary by Christ's command; one God, one Church, one Baptism; heretic baptism invalid; the second baptism is that of blood; only clergy may baptize

---

[1] Res. Car. 42.   [2] Spect. 29.
[3] Apol. 50.   [4] Ap. 18. 4.
[5] Virg. Vel. 1. 5   [6] Scap. 2.   [7] Carn. Chr. 5.

except in case of necessity, but in that case a great responsibility rests on the layman; the rite not to be given unadvisedly; better not to baptize adults till they marry or are proof against impurity; Easter to Pentecost the best time; preparation by fasting, prayer, confession.[1]

The *De Oratione* is, as to the first half, a commentary on the Lord's Prayer; it also opposes formalism, such as doffing the cloak or washing the hands before praying; it teaches that the Eucharist must not be abstained from because it is a fast day; that women should dress modestly, and unmarried women should not go abroad unveiled (a subject which he treats at length in *De Virginibus Velandis*); that they should not kneel at Easter and Pentecost, etc.; and at the close is a powerful passage : " Under arms in prayer guard the standard of your General. The angels pray : every creature prays : the cattle and wild beasts bend their knees and pray : nay, the birds rising up from their nests upraise themselves heavenward, and instead of hands, expand the cross of their wings, and sing something that seems like prayer."

In the work *On Patience*, which he commences with grief at his own impatience, he says, " Patience sits on the throne of that calmest and gentlest Spirit, Who is not found in the roll of the whirlwind, nor in the leaden hue of the cloud; but is a Spirit of soft serenity, open and simple. For where God is, there too is His foster-child, Patience. When God's Spirit descends, then Patience accompanies Him inseparably. If we do not admit her along with the Spirit, will He always tarry with us? " *Penitence* is another work in which Tertullian, as in all his early practical works, writes tenderly.

With these appear in strong contrast the three most violent and bitter works of the Montanist period : *Modesty, Fasting, Monogamy;* of which the style is

[1] This analysis is from Fleury's *History of Christianity*.

rigid and the expression coarse, with often forced
interpretations of Scripture.

On Flight from Persecution falls in the same period;
denouncing the practice of " flying to another city "
in time of persecution. *Modesty (De Pudicitia)* commences with a violent attack on the Bishop of Rome
for offering absolution for sins against the flesh after
proper repentance and penance. There is a difference
of opinion as to whether this Bishop was Victor, Zephyrinus, or Callixtus; but he addresses him with the utmost
scorn as a " bishop of bishops," a title which the Roman
Bishops at once, or very shortly afterwards, adopted.
A malicious suggestion is made that the offer to absolve
should not be posted up in Church, but on the gates of
houses of ill-fame. In this work occurs a passage,
that Peter was the rock, and to him personally were
given the keys, but that they descended not to any
mere Bishops, but to the spiritual men—in fact to
Montanists. In other words, the power of absolving
depends not on ordination but on character—a most
mischievous theory. In this work also is a passage,
which is used as an argument against the doctrine of
" Superfluous Merit." Addressing a departed saint,
he says : " If you are a sinner yourself, how can the oil
out of your cruse suffice for both you and me? "[1]

Among other interesting practical works are the
De Spectaculis and *De Idololatria.* In the former the
cruelty of the public shows is considered of less importance than their connection with idolatry, and a good
deal of learning is displayed as to their origin : the
stage plays, 'for instance, being traced to the worship
of Venus, and games to sacrifices to the dead, whose
souls were appeased by gifts of blood. It ends with a
lurid picture of judgment, and the delight which the
author will feel at the damnation of the idolators;
which is quite in his later manner; for although Neander

[1] Pudic. 22

places this work among his earlier writings, Kaye considers it probably of the Montanist period.

The *De Idololatria* is historically interesting, as showing the enormous number of trades from which Christians were debarred, owing to their connection with idolatry; such as, image-making, sale of incense, astrology, to some extent education, building of temples, beating out gold leaf, etc. The refusal to join in these trades, and indeed their condemnation of them, would all tend to persecution. A fine passage occurs in this work : " Amid these rocks and bays, these shoals and straits of Idolatry, Faith, wafted onwards by the Spirit of God, holdeth her course; safe while on her guard, secure while in amazement. But for those who are cast overboard, there is an abyss whence none can swim; for those who strike on a rock, there is a wreck whence none can escape; for those who are swallowed up, there is in idolatry a whirlpool, where none can breathe; every wave of it choketh; every eddy sucketh down to hell." [1]

The most important of his works against heretics are : (1) *The Præscriptio*, of which the main position has already been stated; (2) *Ad Praxeam*, which has also been quoted as an Exposition of the Trinity against Patripassianism. In this he makes a very useful statement : " Never shall the name of two Gods proceed from my mouth; not that the Father is not God, the Son God, and the Holy Ghost God, but because the Son is called God only through His union with the Father. Therefore I shall imitate the Apostle; and when I have to speak of Father and Son together, I shall call the Father God, and the Son our Lord Jesus Christ. When I speak of Christ alone, I shall call Him God." [2] Praxeas having relied on the words " My Father and I are one," he replies that Christ said " are " and not " am," and that " one " was neuter, " one

---

[1] Idol. 24.   [2] Prax. 13.

thing "; not masculine, " one Person." Also that
Christ said " I am in the Father," not " I am the
Father." [1]   (3) and (4) *On the Flesh of Christ* and *On
the Resurrection of the Flesh*, both written against the
Docetic view.   In the first of these occurs again the
antithesis between the virgin Eve and the Virgin Mary,
and also the celebrated paradox, " Credo quia absurdum :
certum est quia impossibile." The argument is like
this : " a crucified God, a dead God, a risen God, may
seem to Marcion a foolish impossibility ; its very foolishness is the triumph of my faith ; in its transcendence of
human reason lies its certainty." His other treatises
against Gnostics are against *Valentinian* and *Marcion*.

The latter name has already repeatedly appeared,
and as Tertullian was his principal refuter, some account
must be given of him ; since, however much we may
doubt whether the other Gnostics were heretics, or simply
teachers of a rival philosophy, Marcion, the son of a
Bishop of Sinope, started entirely from a Christian
standpoint ; always sought to be restored to communion ; founded a Church of his own, which claimed
to be Christian in the fullest sense ; but to explain
his own peculiar views borrowed largely from the
Gnostics. He was indeed a heretic, and the most
dangerous of the Gnostics ; therefore Polycarp called
him " the firstborn of Satan." Irenæus gave less
attention to Marcion than to Valentinian, because the
system of the latter was more comprehensive, and he
thought in answering him exhaustively he replied to
all the Gnostics ; but he also noticed Marcion, and
promised to deal with him later on. Tertullian, however,
devoted five books to him. Marcion came to Rome to
promulgate his views, but the Roman Church refused
him communion. By this time all the heretical teachers
had invaded Rome. However free Rome might have
been from corrupt teaching in the time of Ignatius,

[1] Prax. 22.

and St. Clement of Alexandria says that no heresies
appeared in Rome till the time of Trajan, yet now the
words of Tacitus might be adapted, that " Rome was
a sink into which flowed all the crimes and baseness of
the world."

When Marcion was refused communion, he asked
the meaning of " putting new wine into old bottles ";
and made this the keynote of his teaching. The New
Testament was not a completion or fulfilment of the
Old, but antagonistic to it. The Old Testament was
to be entirely repudiated, and so much of the New as
well, as did not support his own view; which was that
Christ was not the Jewish Messiah, who had yet to
appear, but the Son of the supreme God, who came to
redeem the world from the imperfect deity of the Old
Testament—the Demiurge in fact. He said that
Christ never came in the flesh at all, but only as a
Spirit : so he is Docetic—indeed more than all of
them.

Marcion's theology was a Dualism. There was a
good God and a just God, meaning by just, inexorable
(eye for eye, tooth for tooth); the latter did not emanate
from the former, but was a separate First Principle;
consequently the system of Æons became superfluous,
and so he rejected it. Matter indeed was with him,
as with Plato, another first principle; but he did not
trouble himself much about that, as it did not bear
on his main subject, the relation of the Old to the
New Dispensation. His just God was opposed to his
good God, not as evil to good, but as imperfection to
perfection. He accepted just so much of the New
Testament as he could conveniently argue from; ten
of St. Paul's Epistles, and a mutilated edition of St.
Luke (as St. Paul's companion), arranged by himself
to suit the requirements of what he thought was the
Gospel according to St. Paul, whom he recognized as
his great master, but whose teaching he twisted and

exaggerated. The rest of the New Testament he considered was written by Judaizers.

Tertullian replied to the dualism of Marcion; that if both his Gods were equal, possessing supreme power, duration, and self-existence, they were really one; if unequal, only the higher was God at all; and if two, why not thirty? How could material things be evil, or the work of imperfect deity, if Christ used them in His Sacraments? Since Christ has now come, why is Matter still allowed to continue? Why was Christ's redemption so long delayed? Why was all this unknown till Marcion discovered it?

The antagonism between the Testaments he refuted from St. Paul's writings, which Marcion had embodied in his doctored Bible. The cavils against the Old Testament were met by showing, partly that he had misrepresented facts, partly that he had drawn wrong inferences. For instance, Marcion said that God created Adam and then allowed him to fall, being either unable or unwilling to prevent him. Tertullian replies that he fell through the exercise of man's highest gift, Free Will. But especially Tertullian established the important truth, that man's incapacity of conceiving God makes it necessary to speak of divine things in language adapted to human understanding. Tertullian is said to have trampled on Gnosticism, as later St. Athanasius did on Arianism. Yet Marcionism dragged on some sort of existence till the seventh century.

Tertullian's leading apologetic works are : (1) *The Apology*, (2) *Ad Nationes*, (3) *Adversus Judæos*, and (4) *Ad Scapulam*. The most important is the first, which was addressed not to the Emperor, but to the Governor of proconsular Africa. Christianity, he says, courts publicity; do not condemn us unheard. Try us as criminals, not because we carry the name of Christian. We are not atheists, just because we refuse to worship gods who are only dead men deified and bad men at that; not even men like Scipio, Cato, Pompey or Cicero. The heathen are as irreverent towards these gods as the Christians; actors and philosophers laugh at them. The worship of a cross has already appeared in many of the heathen rites. The Bible is accessible to all; study it. It is the oldest book in the world. Moses lived 1000 years before the siege of Troy, and the latest prophets are as old as the earliest philosophers. Has- Rome risen to greatness through her gods? War, endless war made Rome. Her power was established before her religion. Christians are loyal; they pray for the Emperor but refuse to deify him. The worship of the Cæsars is hypocritical. Christians do not retaliate; yet though a people of yesterday they fill cities, camps, in fact every place but the temples. They are not a faction, and should be left alone, like the Epicureans. Their social life, worship and charities are described. They are not unprofitable citizens, but employ themselves only in useful and innocent trades. Philosophers are not compelled to sacrifice: why then Christians, whose lives are far better? Yet philosophers derive the best of what they know from Jewish mysteries. Even if Christian doctrines are false, they are at least moral.

The *Ad Nationes* resembles the *Apology* in a shorter form, so that it has sometimes been thought to be a first draft of it; it is, however, addressed to the populace, instead of to the authorities. The style is in some places very gross, satirizing the accusations levelled against Christians.

In the treatise *against the Jews*, he points out forcibly that the Jewish sacrifices are necessarily at an end, because they could only be offered at Jerusalem; whereas Malachi had foretold the world-wide sacrifice. There is an interesting statement, showing how widespread was the Gospel at this date: it had reached " the Getulians, the Moors, all Spain, parts of Britain which were inaccessible to the Romans, the Sarmatians, Dacians, Germans, Scythians, and many islands and places unknown to the Romans."

Tertullian lived to extreme old age, but the exact date of his death is unknown. He was the first of the marvellous triumvirate which the African Church produced, and of which Cyprian and Augustine were the other two members. Cyprian was contemporary with his old age, and always regarded him as " the master." Augustine, however, belongs to another century. Of the tenets of the Tertullianists, whether they held an extreme or modified form of Montanism, we know not. Let us hope the latter, and that old age tempered Tertullian's severity.

CHAPTER VII

(Presbyter ; and Head of the ˇCatechetical School,
A.D. 190–202)

" Christianity is the heir of all past time and the interpreter
of the future."
" Philosophy also is a creation of Divine Providence."
" The true Gnostic makes all philosophy his own, because it
is the Divine preparation for the Gospel : he uses and studies
the world because the world leads him to God."

THESE sentences of his form suitable mottoes for a
chapter on St. Clement, since they express exactly the
position taken up under his influence by the Christian
school of Alexandria, in advance of St. Justin, and in
direct opposition to Tertullian. It is at last recognized
that God was educating the world before the coming
of Christ, and that not by Judaism alone. The truth
is now established that reason as well as revelation is
a gift of God ; and being so established, Christian teachers
have no longer any hesitation in using existing philosophic methods, and working over such philosophic
doctrines the Christian theology.

For a thousand years the great city of Alexandria was
the centre of all learning ; and never, except in Athens
at her best period, was there such a brilliant home of
culture. Founded in 322 B.C. by Alexander the Great,
fifteen years after the death of Plato, it at once assumed a
literary importance, and on Alexander's death the Ptolemies nobly carried out the founder's intention. The
first of them established a library with 50,000 rolls or
books, the number of books gradually increasing to

500,000 or according to one account 700,000. It was
to the Ptolemies also that the Jews owed the Septuagint.
The library was in two buildings—the Museum and the
Temple of Serapis. Of these, the former was partially
destroyed by fire in the time of Julius Cæsar, but re-
plenished by Cleopatra's present of the Pergamus collection to Mark Antony. The Temple of Serapis was
destroyed in a Christian riot in A.D. 391; and soon after
that time both the learning and the Christianity of
Alexandria began to decay, until both alike were swept
away by Mahommedanism in the seventh century.

When Hadrian visited Alexandria, he wrote that " no
one was idle—not even the blind, the lame, or the
crippled; " also that the people were " fickle, uncertain,
blown about by every gust of rumour." The fact was
that the Alexandrians were eclectic and critical. The
special feature of the Alexandrian thought, Christian,
Jewish, and Pagan alike, was that it tried to absorb the
best of everything; the feature of the Alexandrian
himself was to criticize everything and be satisfied with
nothing. Thus when Origen, the great successor of
St. Clement, attended the lectures of the Neo-Platonists,
over the door of the school were the opening verses of
St. John's Gospel; while Numenius, a Pagan, said that
Plato was only Moses speaking Greek. But there was
also a strong imaginative sentiment in all the schools,
which had " a tendency to evaporate religion into
allegory, and philosophy into dreamy speculation,
while the critical spirit marred the creative power." [1]
Thus Alexandria, as De Pressensé says, " with her learning and subtlety gathered together and fused all the
elements of the old world, and created in her own manner
a sort of universalism, vague rather than broad, in which
the religions of East and West were alike deprived of their
exclusive character, Judaism itself being made to enter
into alliance with the polytheistic religions, which it had

[1] Plummer's *Church of Early Fathers*

so long proscribed. Born of this heterogeneous union, the Alexandrian mind rose above all national divergences, but it also rose above reality and above history, to the cloudy summits of speculation, and was utterly wanting in the historic sense. Strong in its allegorical method, it sported with facts; and its philosophical theories were at once aspiring and unsubstantial." [1]

The great proportion of Jews in Alexandria was remarkable. A considerable number were imported by Alexander himself into the City, and another forced importation was afterwards made in the time of Ptolemy Soter. By the time of Clement the natural capacity for trading of the Jewish nation had increased their numbers to about 100,000 out of a total population of 300,000 besides the slaves; and they occupied two out of the five quarters into which the City was divided. No wonder then that the influence of Jewish upon Alexandrian thought was very considerable. But the reverse was also the case. Even earlier than our Lord's time, there were many Jewish teachers in Alexandria, who had caught the allegorizing spirit, and applied it widely to the Old Testament. At the same time they had to some extent transformed the Jewish idea of Jehovah into the Platonic idea of God, or possibly his " Idea of the Good." Against this tendency, Philo, the principal Jewish-Alexandrine, who was a contemporary of our Lord, raised a partial protest; partial, because he was himself carried away by the allegorizing tendency to a great extent. But while he admitted that much of the less essential parts of the Old Testament were full of allegory, there was always, he taught, an irreducible minimum, which was not only exactly and literally true, but of Divine revelation; and accordance with this revelation must be the test of the truth of all other philosophies. The Jews were, in his view, priests and prophets for all mankind.

[1] *Martyrs and Apologists*, p. 283.

Here, then, were two important facts which paved the way for the acceptance of Christianity. There had been a distinct revelation from God which established *authority :* there was a revealed message from God to *all mankind.* But when it came to metaphysics, Philo adapted himself to Platonic views; as, for instance, the Divine apathy— that the First Cause was behind all thought and feeling, passionless; also that Matter was Eternal. But again, as Thought and Power must necessarily precede Creation, he accepted a theory of Personalities, something like the Æons of the Gnostics. Thought and Power were among them; but the chief of these forces was the Logos, the Mind of God declaring itself, but a personal Mind, and also essentially God. Here, then, were the two schools of thought with which Christianity had to contend, and which she finally vanquished : the one an Eclectic Pagan school, which was founded mainly on Plato, but had incorporated material from all the other philosophic systems of the world; the other a Jewish school following to some extent the same lines but with a foundation of Revelation, a message to mankind, and a literature which Christianity had already annexed. The Greeks had an opinion (πίστις) : the Jews a practical conviction (γνῶσις).

According to a tradition which Lightfoot considers may be accepted, the Alexandrian Church was founded by St. Mark, probably as early as A.D. 40. Hence it was often called the Evangelical See. It is probable also that St. Mark was the emissary of St. Peter. The Catechetical School, which became so celebrated later on, may have been also founded by St. Mark, as tradition records. For a long time, however, it was only a training school for catechumens. The correctness of the list of early Alexandrine bishops is very doubtful, nor were any of them prominent characters till towards the end of the third century. The head of the Catechetical School, who was appointed by the bishop, but not neces- sarily even in orders, was a much more important personage. The first of these who attracts attention is Pantænus, the predecessor of Clement, who called him " the Sicilian bee, gathering spoils from the flowers of the prophetic and apostolic meadow, who engendered in the souls of his hearers a deathless element of knowledge," [1] and who, when the Indians called for a Christian missionary, went' straight from his professorship at Alexandria to the Far East, and is said to have found there a copy of St. Matthew in Aramaic. Though not much is known of the teaching of Pantænus, except that he was a man of great power, learning and eloquence, he seems to have seen more clearly than Justin the unity of the Divine plan, in spite of the various nationalities and the apparent confusion of events.[2] At any rate he was the great instructor of Clement, who found complete satisfaction in his teaching after seeking it from a great variety of masters.

One strange anomaly in the Alexandrian Church must be mentioned as a matter of history. It is possible that till the fourth century the bishops were ordained by their presbyters. Apparently there was till towards the middle of the third century only one bishop in Egypt, although Christianity had spread far up the Nile. Neale in his *History of the Eastern Church* contends, and Waterman in his *Post-Apostolic Age*, thinks it likely that the twelve presbyters, whose duty it was to elect one of their number on a vacancy, were really an Episcopal College. Waterman supports this view by saying that as in A.D. 250 there were forty-six priests in the Roman Church, there must have been more than twelve in the Alexandrian; and that the twelve who elected must therefore have had a higher function. But of this there is no distinct evidence, although it is possible that these twelve may have been bishops without dioceses. Bright thinks it exceedingly improbable that the twelve presbyters did more than elect.

[1] Str. 1.　　[2] De Pressensé, *Martyrs and Apologists*, p. 271.

G

St. Clement was probably born about the middle of the second century, since we find him succeeding to the chair of Pantænus in 190, and continuing in it till the persecution under Severus in 202, when he left Alexandria; not certainly through any want of courage, for he afterwards undertook a perilous errand for his pupil Alexander, subsequently Bishop of Jerusalem and a celebrated friend of Origen. His death is generally given as in 212, but after 202 little is known of his movements. The expression " Chair of Pantænus " does not imply that there was any recognized meeting-place of the Catechetical School, or building. It was conducted at this time in the most primitive way, usually in the private house of its head, although it afterwards became the leading university of the Empire.

St. Clement represents in three different ways a transitional period in Christian History : a transition from oral tradition to written definitions; from a study of the main points of revelation to that of the whole realm of human experience; and a taking over of the whole life as an object of Christian discipline.[1] His works are full of learning, and contain quotations from 500 other authors. He quotes from nearly all the books of the Bible, and also from many uncanonical books, as if they were Scripture. Like his predecessors, and his contemporary Tertullian, he recognizes the " tradition of the blessed doctrine derived directly from the holy apostles." But the chief point in all his teaching is his claim, as stated at the opening of this chapter, that the world's education was on a Divine plan; and that if the Law was a schoolmaster to lead the Jews to Christ, Philosophy was the schoolmaster to lead the Greek mind there. His sympathy with Platonism seems sometimes to lead him to an extravagant appreciation of knowledge, and like Philo, to allegorize overmuch. As to the first, he says, " Right conduct must depend on right know-

[1] *Dictionary of Christian Biography.*

ledge;" which sounds rather a dangerous statement,
though often repeated in modern times. Instances of
the second occur continually. The serpent in Eden
symbolized Pleasure, which creeps on the belly like
earthly vice. Lot's wife becoming a pillar of salt meant
that she lost all sensation in looking back on vice and
was for the future salt, to salt or preserve those who
have spiritual discernment. To the third day on which
Abraham lifted up his eyes and saw the place afar off
is assigned more than one fantastic meaning. Joseph's
coat of many colours signified his various knowledge,
which his brothers envied. The number ten of the
Commandments has several figurative meanings, and
even the meaning of the Commandments is allegorized
most fancifully. Scripture, however, had always a
literal sense as well : it had three altogether, the literal,
the moral and the mystical. Clement's quotations from
Scripture seem generally made from memory, and are
often inaccurate; or the right sense is expressed in different words; or sometimes two different passages are
mixed up. He differs philosophically from Philo,
mainly in denying the separate existence of matter as
eternal evil, and in asserting strongly Free Will; which
was an unpopular doctrine in Alexandria.

As regards the general position of the Christian school
in Alexandria, and therefore of Clement, who is for us
its founder, since we know so little of Pantænus, Harnack
says, " In Alexandria the entire Hellenic science was
adapted to the service of the Gospel. . . . Christianity
is the doctrine of the creation, education and perfecting
of the human race through the Logos, whose work
reaches its climax in the perfect Gnostic; and the perfect
Gnostic has made use of two means, the Old Testament
and the Hellenic philosophy. An attempt was made to
fuse the aim of the Gospel at making us rich in God, and
gaining from Him power and life, with the ideal of the
Platonic philosophy to raise oneself as a free spirit above

the world into God; and then to bind together the instructions pertaining to a blessed life which are found in both."

Faith (πίστις) and knowledge (γνῶσις) are sharply contrasted by Clement; and knowledge is the higher. Faith is the foundation; knowledge the superstructure.[1] Faith (the belief in God, the desire for God) is natural to every man: if he has it not, he is abnormal. But to attain to the knowledge of the true Gnosis is not so given; it is an accomplishment to be acquired. Nor is the knowledge to be offered to every one. There are two grades in the Christian life; the lower one of faith, the higher one of knowledge. Faith is not an arbitrary opinion, but a practical assent, arising from the apprehension of truth implanted in man, and the natural disposition to believe in a truth that reveals itself. When you come to act up to your faith, then the higher knowledge follows, not as a matter of speculation, but as a light that arises in the soul through obedience and a righteous life. This knowledge is the subjective Gnosis; there is also the objective Gnosis, Scripture. To arrive at a complete understanding of the latter, learned preparation is required.

Early Platonic associations probably caused Clement to treat with some disdain the simple faith, as a carnal faith useful only for the repression of evil; the higher knowledge being requisite to arrive at a real sanctification of the heart. He held also that it was not good to cast pearls before swine; that some could only be fed with milk, not meat. Out of this idea came the Disciplina Arcani (Discipline of the Secret), the holding back a reserve of religious thought and teaching, which was only to be imparted to the highly trained Christian and withheld from his simpler brother. On the other hand, the test of admission to the reserved doctrine was purely a moral and not an intellectual one. St. Clement

[1] Str. VI. 26

summed up this view by saying that " the man of faith acts from fear and hope and is blessed, but a child : the Gnostic acts from love, and is a man." Again, " The Gnostic, who is the master of the fountain of truth, will incur a penalty if he gives cause for offence, by causing one who is still only conversant with minor points to be swallowed up by the magnitude of what he delivers, and by transferring one who is only an operative to the region of speculation. We must therefore be chary of imparting the higher knowledge to those who are incapable of receiving it, lest it lead them astray." [1] But it must be always borne in mind, when considering this subject of the Discipline of the Secret, that St. Clement had to move most cautiously in trying to lead Christians to the pursuit of human learning. For at this time when Gnosticism was at its height, Christians had a great dread of philosophic studies, fearing they would lead them astray, and it was about the same time that Tertullian was denouncing them utterly. Christian Alexandria was almost as nervous as Carthage in this respect.

The three principal works of St. Clement give the main points of his teaching in progressive form. The first, the *Exhortation to the Heathen*, points out the sins and errors of Paganism in scathing language, and sets in contrast with it the truth and beauty of Christianity. In this work there is an enormous number of quotations from heathen authors. The second, the *Pædagogue*, or *Tutor*, assumes that the Pagan has been converted, and it is an exposition of the Christian life. The tutor, who is our Saviour, the Incarnate Logos, led the Jews by fear, and leads the Christians by love; but He is always the same, whether showing justice or mercy. The Christian life consists of faith, which is submission to the sovereign reason, and in the practice of virtue; and the minutest regulations are given as to the daily round of conduct all day and all night. What to eat

[1] Str. 5.

and drink; how to eat and drink; about going into society; the cultivation of art; good manners; dress; hours of sleep; private prayer; the relation of husband to wife; of master to servant; frugality; exercise; the bath; and many other topics are dwelt on. In consequence it is a fair account of how Christians lived, or were expected to live, in the second century; since Clement had too much good sense to enjoin a standard that was quite impracticable. The *Tutor* being completed, the third work is the *Stromata*, or *Miscellanies*, which are mainly philosophical, and in which most of the higher teaching of Clement will be found. They are rightly called Miscellanies, as there is no regular sequence of thought in them. Although they doubtless represent mainly the learning and original thought of St. Clement, he modestly speaks of them as memories which he has stored up from the teaching of his masters; and he also professes to have often veiled the truth, that it might not be too readily understood by the unworthy. The irregularity of the ideas may perhaps be caused through their being taken from notes of extempore lectures. Book I shows the usefulness of human philosophy as a preparation for the Gospel. Book II compares Faith and Knowledge. Book III is on Marriage and purity of life. Book IV is on Martyrdom, arguing against the alleged injustice of God in permitting it. It also shows that a knowledge of God would be a higher aim than eternal salvation, if the two ideas could be separated. This was the foundation of Fénelon's argument against Bossuet. The fifth book give his account of God; the sixth and seventh the description of the True Gnostic, portraying the highest flights to which a Christian can in this world attain; and the eighth book is on Philosophical methods. This last is quite unconnected with the others, and seems to be some other work substituted for a lost original eighth book. There were also eight books of Hypotyposes, expounding Scripture, of which only a few choice fragments remain. Several other works, now entirely lost, are known to have existed, and besides these, he mentions several more, which he either had written or intended to write.

The only other complete work extant is the treatise *Who is the rich man to be saved?* (in Latin, *quis dives salvetur?*), showing that the clue to salvation is rather a right disposition of soul, than the mere handing over of this world's goods. This treatise is also interesting as being one of the earliest examples of sermon or homily making. The *Second Epistle to the Corinthians*, wrongly attributed to St. Clement of Rome, was perhaps the first. Tertullian's work on the Lord's Prayer is practically a homily, that is, an exposition of Scripture verse by verse, which allowed a very free treatment of the subject. But the Western Church was more inclined to sermons than homilies, the real home of homilies being the Eastern, and one of the greatest homily makers Origen. The *Rich man saved* consists practically of three discourses : on the young rich man; on the good Samaritan; and on Penitence.[1]

There were certain hymns usually bound up with St. Clement's works which may have been written by him, but were more probably written by a follower and admirer of his. They have a certain interest as character istic of the time, and as specimens of the earliest hymns. The most famous is " To God the Saviour," and another is " To the Tutor." The first, which is in the original a long string of adoring expressions, is very freely translated into English, and amplified so as to resemble a modern hymn, in the Ante-Nicene Library. The first verse is as follows, and gives a general idea of it :—

" Bridle of colts untamed,
   Over our wills presiding;
 Wing of unwandering birds,
   Our flight securely guiding :
 Rudder of youth unbending
   Firm against adverse shock :

---

[1] Bishop Freppel.

> Shepherd with wisdom tending
>   Lambs of the royal flock :
> Thy simple children bring
>   In one, that they may sing
> In solemn lays their hymns of praise
> With guileless lips to Christ their King."

As regards St. Clement's theology,[1] his view was that it was impossible to give any written account of God, that He was raised above all speech and thought[2] and therefore undemonstrable; so that He could not be the object of science; and he even speaks of Him as an Abyss, which seems to show the influence of Plato, especially as once he speaks of Him as exempt from wants and passions and form :[3] when we apply to Him hands, eyes, and feet, some holy allegory is hidden under these names.[4] Yet God is completely known through the Son, (Logos) who is wisdom, truth, science, and everything of the same order. Thus He is the demonstration and explanation of truth, and the Incarnation of the Logos is the crown and consummation of the history of the world. Many passages imply the close union between Father and Son, the latter being often described as God. The Word has in various ways instructed man from the first foundation of the world and perfected him. -In Str. 7 is a long description of all the attributes and functions of the Word (Logos), which includes all the attributes of the Godhead; but when spoken of as the Son, the relation implies a certain subordination. Of the Trinity St. Clement says : " The Father of the Universe is one : the Word of the Universe is one : the Holy Spirit is one and the same everywhere "[5]; yet " God is one, and beyond one and beyond the Monad." As regards the Atonement, " Christians are redeemed from corruption by the blood of the Lord "[6]; " The Lord gave Himself as a Victim for us [7] "; " Salvation is offered to all who

---

[1] See Bishop Kaye, *Some Account of the Life and Writings of St. Clement of Alexandria*.

[2] Str. 5.	[3] *Ibid.*, 2.	[4] *Ibid.*, 5.
[5] T. 1.	[6] *Ibid.*, 1. 5.	[7] *Ibid.*, 1. 11.

believe in Christ " [1]; " Faith is the rational assent of a soul free to choose." [2]   As regards Justification, he says that " Abraham was justified not by works but by faith; wherefore good works are of no avail after life, unless those who do them also have faith " [3]; " It is not enough that an act is right, its aim must also be right " [4]; " An act, to be right, must be done from love of God." [5] But on the other hand he also says, " When we read in - the Gospel ' Your faith hath saved you,' we are not to imagine that all who believe are saved, unless good works follow."   As regards Grace, he says that " we stand in need of Divine Grace, and right instruction, and pure affection, and we require that the Father should draw us unto Himself." [6]   As regards Baptism, he says that " Christ forms man out of dust, regenerates him with water, and causes him to grow by the Spirit " [7]; again, that it is a sovereign medicine, by which we are cleansed from all our sins and cease at once to be wicked.   It is also an eternal adjustment of the vision, which is now able to see the light, since like loves like.[8]   Sins after baptism were to be purged by discipline, of which a part was public confession.   This discipline is so necessary, that if not completed here, it must be after death, and it is then effected by a fire which pervades the soul, which is not destructive, but discriminating.[9]   In Eucharistic doctrine St. Clement is rather deficient, and he seems rather to tend to symbolic teaching.   Thus, " The Lord in the Gospel brought this out by symbols, when He said Eat my flesh and drink my blood, describing exactly by metaphors the drinkable properties of faith and the promise." [10] This is so unlike most of the Patristic teaching, that one cannot help feeling that he was carried away by his tendency to allegorize.   Elsewhere he says, however, " The vine bears wine, as the Word bears blood; both are drunk

---

[1] T. 1. 6.   [2] Str. 5.   [3] Ibid., 2.
[4] Ibid., 6.   [5] Ibid., 3.   [6] Ibid., 5.
[7] T. 1.   [8] Ibid., 1. 6.   [9] Str. 7.   [10] T. 1.

by men · into salvation; the wine bodily, the Blood spiritually." [1]

The Christian school of Alexandria, and consequently St. Clement, exhibited complete loyalty to the Creed, as handed down by apostolic tradition. But beyond that, they held themselves free to speculate and teach. Scripture also was inspired, but the Platonic doctrine that nothing should be believed which was unworthy of God, made Reason for them the interpreter of Revelation. The letter of Scripture was interpreted therefore allegoric-ally, when it came into conflict with science, as in the story of the Creation. But they were far from being wholly rationalist; on the contrary they were as alive, as was St. Irenæus, to the mystic and the supernatural. They tried, however, to show that neither reason without faith, nor faith without reason could realize the highest results; only by a combination of both could the Chris-tian grow to the stature of the perfect man, in whom the saint and the thinker are blended together in the unity of the Divine Love.[2] And indeed, what is here true of religion is true also of science, where first principles are known by an intuition which corresponds to faith in religion.

St. Clement did not confine himself to Plato as a philosophic guide. With the exception of the Epicureans, he respected all the schools and quoted them freely, he also borrowed to some extent from Stoicism, especially in treating of pure Reason. But Plato seemed to him to be more adaptable than any of them to the service of Christianity: in his monotheism; in the Idea of the Good; in the belief in immortality and in future rewards and punishments; in that belief in the World-soul (Logos), which emanated from God and yet was God, and which paved the way for the Christian Trinity; in the necessity of Divine help (i. e. grace); and in likeness

[1] T. 1.
[2] Biggs, *Christian Platonists in Alexandria*, p. 51.

to God being the chief aim of man. But besides all this, Platonism was more of a religion than any other Greek system. It is true that we find hymns to the glory of God by Cleanthes the Stoic, Epictetus and others, and that even in Sophocles and Æschylus there is deep religious feeling; but to Plato alone belongs that aspiration for the Beatific Vision, which carries philosophy into a realm in which Christian thought is at home. Witness the account of the Ideal Beauty in the discussion on Love in the Symposium—" Suppose it were possible to one to behold the Beautiful itself, clear and pure and unalloyed, the Divine Beauty as it really is in its simplicity, do you think it would be an ignoble life that one should gaze thereon and ever contemplate that Beauty and hold communion therewith? Do you not rather believe that in this communion only will it be possible for a man, beholding the Beautiful with the organ with which alone it can be seen, to become the friend of God and attain to immortality?" [1]

But what is " the organ "? Bussell, in *Plato and his School*,[2] implies that it was " the unifying principle of love, admiration and hope." Yet, as Professor Adam points out,[3] " the Ideal Beauty must be found by an intellectual operation, a certain method known as Dialectic. In Plato's mind there is no real distinction between the enthusiasm of religion and the enthusiasm of science. The lover of knowledge in Plato inevitably becomes a seeker after God." Conversely, however, the seeker after God is immersed in intellectual speculations. " Socrates inspired boundless friendship and esteem : but the inspiration of reason and conscience is the one inspiration that comes from him, and impels us to live righteously as he did; a penetrating enthusiasm of love, sympathy, pity and adoration, reinforcing the inspiration

[1] The quotation is very much abbreviated.
[2] p. 274.
[3] *Religious Teachers of Greece*, p. 396.

of reason and duty, does not belong to Socrates." [1] Yet even in this connection, we cannot forget Plato's description of the perfectly righteous man, who, in order to manifest his righteousness to his fellow-men, would endure calumny and the scourge, and even humble himself to the death on the cross; for Plato almost uses these words.

St. Clement's resemblance to Plato is found, (1) in his method, his analysis of philosophic terms, and the general structure of his philosophy; (2) in his idea of God, who transcends all human thought, and explanation, and is beyond all feeling, as men understand feeling; in fact, passionless. So that the idea of Fatherhood seems quite lost. And yet it is not lost, for he continually speaks of it and fully realizes it. Plato, however, also recognizes the idea of Providence, the good will of God to mankind : and St. Clement enlarges the Platonic conception to this extent; that while, with Plato, the goodness of God is like a ray from the sun warming and illuminating mankind generally, with St. Clement God cares for each individual soul and corrects it by pain; and His supreme occupation is the salvation of humanity. (3) In the highest aim of man being likeness to God, which had been a leading thought of Plato but had hardly been formulated by Christian teaching hitherto, though Irenæus and Justin touched on it. In the apostolic writings it was rather likeness to the human nature of Christ. As regards the likeness to God, Clement frankly claimed that Plato borrowed this idea from the Bible : " Let us make man in our own image and likeness." (4) In the comprehension of an ideal transcendent science of the things that are knowable (νόητα) actual (ὄντα) those things which St. Paul said were unseen and eternal. (5) In the idea of a sort of aristocracy among Christians; that the higher truths were not to be revealed to simple souls.

[1] Matthew Arnold, *St. Paul and Protestantism*, p. 53.

St. Clement adopts the word Gnostic for Christians as he claimed the only right Gnosis was Christianity.

Yet in spite of the division of Christians into classes, and the consequent separation of the simple believer from the Gnostic or advanced thinker, the man, in fact, who had acquired the knowledge, it is in his description of the Higher Life, as followed by the true Gnostic, that St. Clement is at his best. Disdaining elsewhere what he calls tricks of style as being meretricious, he rises here into an altogether higher sphere, and in the seventh book of the *Stromata* will be found writing of a very rhetorical and beautiful character. For by the side of knowledge St. Clement assures us there is always Love: Love is, in fact, the *organ* by which the knowledge is grasped. It is Love that supports the Gnostic in suffering and bad fortune. It is Love that steels his courage. It is for Love that he submits to torture and martyrdom, the love of the Church and of his brothers. And it is Love that raises him above all earthly passions, makes him, in fact, a partaker of the Divine Apathy, and in close communion with God. So near is he to God that he *is* a god, and God is always present to him. " Holding festival in our whole life, persuaded that God is everywhere present, we cultivate our fields praising : we sail the sea hymning." " The Gnostic is very closely allied to God, being at once grave and cheerful in all things : grave on account of the bent of his soul towards Divinity and cheerful on account of the Blessings of Humanity." " Prayer is converse with God. Though whispering and not opening the lips we speak in silence, yet we cry inwardly. For God hears continually all the inward converse." " Prayer may be uttered without the voice by concentrating the whole spiritual nature within one expression by the mind, in undistracted turning towards God." " The Gnostic is always pure for prayer. He also prays in the company of angels, being already of the angelic rank, and he is never out of their keeping;

although he prays alone, he has always the choir of the blessed praying with him." The true Gnostic is an unrealizable ideal and St. Clement acknowledged it; unless perhaps the blessed apostles had attained to it. But so was Christ's standard, "Be ye perfect, even as my Father in heaven is perfect." The division between the "simple souls" and the Gnostics, the democracy and aristocracy of Christianity, after all exemplified another of the sayings of the Master: "If any man will do His will, he shall know of the doctrine." The faith first: the dogma and the theology afterwards.

Titus Flavius Clemens, who carried the same name as St. Clement of Rome, was honoured on December 4 as a Saint until the seventeenth century, when Benedict XIV struck him off the list on the ground that little was known of his life, that there was no evidence of any cult of him in early times, and that his orthodoxy was somewhat suspected. But the French Church has always retained his name in the calendar, although Bishop Freppel, in obedience to the dictates of Rome, refuses to acknowledge him as a Saint.

CHAPTER VIII

ORIGEN

(A.D. 186–253. *Ordained Priest at Cæsarea in* 228)

At last we come to a Father of the Church whose whole life is on record. Of those of his predecessors we know hardly anything, except what we gather from their writings and a little scrappy information. Even in the case of Tertullian it is difficult to decide to which period of his career certain writings are to be assigned; but we see Origen in his childhood, maturity and old age, and he is one of the most interesting, and perhaps the most fascinating, personalities of the Early Church. He was also, next to St. Augustine, the most voluminous writer, though much of his work is lost.

Origines Adamantius was born at Alexandria in A.D. 186, and was the son of a devout Christian, Leonidas, who was either an Egyptian or a Greek, and was martyred in 202. Origen, who was then a boy of sixteen, encouraged his father, and entreated him not to be deterred from martyrdom by his affection for his wife and child. Indeed, it was only by hiding his clothes that his mother prevented the boy from offering himself as well. There is a touching story that when Origen was a child his father used to kiss his breast as he lay in bed, regarding it as the temple of the Holy Ghost. So that from childhood Origen was dedicated to the Church, which he served unceasingly and with never-flagging enthusiasm and industry till his death. From his father he received an excellent all-round education, which enabled him at eighteen to succeed St. Clement as the head of the Catechetical School. In his youth he is said to have been seized by a mob, carried to the temple of Serapis, dressed as a priest, and ordered to distribute palms to the people; whereupon he distributed them boldly, not in the name of an idol, but of their true Lord, Jesus Christ.

On his father's death, his mother being in poverty, he was patronized by a rich Alexandrian lady, and gave lessons in grammar, collecting at the same time a library; but as he wished to be independent, he shortly afterwards sold the library for an annuity of the equivalent of sixpence a day, resolving to teach gratuitously in future. At the same time he led a completely ascetic life, sleeping on bare boards, and following literally the instruction in St. Matthew not to have two coats, or to wear shoes. He seems to have been always working or praying, for he prayed into the middle of the night. He is also said to have become an eunuch " for the Kingdom of Heaven's sake "; although Dean Farrar throws some doubt on this. But his asceticism never made him austere in his relation to others. From 204 till 215 he retained his position as Catechist, that is, till twenty-nine years of age. During this period he was assisted by Heracles, who in time succeeded him as head of the school, and was subsequently Bishop of Alexandria : he also converted Plutarch, and accompanied him to his martyr's death. Indeed, he always made a point of cheering and encouraging the martyrs, and as a born Christian seems to have been in less danger than the converts. In the year 211 he attended the lectures of the Neo-Platonist, Ammonius Saccus, so as to be able to meet his pupils' intellectual difficulties.

In A.D. 215 Origen fled from Alexandria on the occasion of a persecution of literary men by Caracalla, in revenge for some satirical writing; and about this time visited Rome. He also paid a visit by request to Arabia to give religious instruction, and also to Julia Mammæa

at Antioch, the mother of Alexander Severus, afterwards
Emperor. Dates at this point are a little uncertain,
but it was presumably on his way to Antioch that his
friends, Theotistus, Bishop of Cæsarea, and Alexander
of Jerusalem (who had been his fellow-pupil under
Clement) ordered him to preach before them, to the
great indignation of Demetrius, Bishop of Alexandria.
The attitude of Demetrius towards Origen at this period
is rather strange, since at an earlier date he had given
him his unqualified approval. He seems, however, to
have considered lay-preaching before a bishop a dangerous innovation, although the Asiatic bishops produced
precedents, and he therefore (in 213) recalled Origen to
Alexandria.

The next ten years were spent less in teaching than
in writing. During this period he was financed by
Ambrosius, formerly a Valentinian Gnostic, whom he
had converted. This useful friend provided him with
seven shorthand clerks, seven transcribers, and a
number of girls who were skilled in caligraphy. Then in
228 (aged forty-two) he went to Greece by invitation
for controversial purposes. On the way, probably to
strengthen his position, the Bishops of Cæsarea and
Jerusalem, or rather one of them, ordained him, and this
finally turned Demetrius against him, so that when he
returned to Alexandria in 231, he found his position
intolerable. The complaint against him was that he
had committed a breach of Church order in receiving
ordination from any other than his own bishop; possibly
also that his self-mutilation disqualified him. There is
no evidence that his views were questioned, although this
is possible, as the *Periarchon*, which contained views
questioned after his death, was by that time written.
At any rate Demetrius called a local Synod, which
forbade Origen to teach, but refused to depose him.
He therefore left Alexandria for Cæsarea. A little later
Demetrius called together three other bishops, who

H

excommunicated and banished him. Where he got these bishops from is not explained, for in the last chapter it was shown that there was only one in Egypt. This may, however, tend to prove that the twelve presbyters of Alexandria had episcopal ordination. Notice was given to the Church at large of this action, and the Roman Church is believed to have concurred in it.

The Eastern bishops, however, remained Origen's firm friends. On his way to Cæsarea he preached in Jerusalem on Psalm 1. 16, 17, and is said to have wept bitterly on giving out the text. In 235 he retired, owing to a persecution, to Cappadocia, where he was sheltered by a learned Christian lady, Juliana. This lady possessed a valuable library, which was of great use to him, especially as it included Symmachus' translation of the Old Testament, which he was thus enabled to include in the *Hexapla*. On that marvellous work of textual criticism he was engaged for twenty-eight years. He returned to Palestine in 238. Finally we find him at Tyre, where in 251 he was put to the torture in prison, from the effect of which he never recovered. His death at Tyre occurred in 253 or 254; the last work of his life being the *Contra Celsum*, which was the crowning Christian apology, and directed against the most powerful of all Pagan attacks on Christianity.

One of the most famous pupils of Origen at Cæsarea was Gregory, afterwards Bishop of Neo-Cæsarea, and generally known as the Wonder-worker (Thaumaturgus). On leaving the class he wrote a letter of thanks to his master as a tribute of his devotion, from which we gather an account of Origen's charm and fascination, of his skill in training individual minds, and the progressive method of education that he adopted. First he aimed at exactness of definition, and a just appreciation of the scope of an argument. When his pupils' minds had thus been prepared, they were next taught to. study Nature, and to have a reasonable admiration for it, instead of an unreasoning wonder. Geometry and Astronomy were subservient to this branch of the course. Then followed practical Ethics, the main virtues being Wisdom, Justice, Self-restraint and Courage. The highest teaching of philosophy came next, with an encouragement to read authors of all schools except the Epicureans. Finally, as the crown of all, came Theology. Gregory writes as if heartbroken at leaving the class, and says he is like Adam leaving Paradise; and the same marvellous fascination was felt by most of the leading spirits of his time.

Indeed, it was extended to subsequent generations. St. Jerome, who differed strongly from him on the disputed points of his theology, called him " the greatest master of the Church after the Apostles; " St. Augustine, " that great man; " St. Basil, St. Hilary, St. Ambrose, St. Gregory of Nyssa, St. Gregory of Nazianzus and St. Vincent of Lerins all warmly admired him. In our own day Cardinal Newman said, " I love the name of Origen; " and elsewhere he spoke of " the sweet soul of Origen." Bishop Westcott said " his whole life was one unbroken prayer,[1] one ceaseless effort after close fellowship with the Unseen and Eternal." Dean Farrar said, " The influence of Origen on the History of the Church is the watershed of multitudes of different streams of thought." During his lifetime he was the one great teacher to whom all turned for inspiration and advice. Yet after his death this great champion of Catholic orthodoxy, who may be said to have first systematized Christian Theology, became a by-word of heresy.

There is no clear evidence that any action was taken against Origen during his life for erroneous teaching; and, as Bishop Freppel says, a man cannot be more of a heretic after his death than he was when he was alive.

[1] Origen's own definition of what life should be.

But early in the fourth century Methodius attacked his speculations on the Creation, the relation of the soul to the body, the resurrection and free will. From that time until the middle of the sixth century an endless controversy ranged round the memory of Origen, till finally his name was included among a number of heretics by the Fifth General Council. His name, however, appears last on the list and out of chronological order. It may therefore be an interpolation. There is no trace that his views were *discussed* except by a Home Synod of Bishops from the neighbourhood of Constantinople.

The four points in Origen's *Periarchon* that were generally objected to were: (1) That souls had existed in a previous state, and that the present life in the body was a punishment for sins committed in that state; (2) That the *human soul* of Christ had been united to the Father before the Incarnation; (3) That material bodies will some time or other be dissolved into ethereal spirits; (4) That there will be a final restoration of all spirits, when even the Devil will be saved. Of these the first two were in the region of pure speculation, but the last two were practical theology; No. 3 seeming to deny the immortality of the risen body, and No. 4 eternal punishment. Besides all this, the somewhat excessive subordination that Origen seemed to ascribe to the Son caused Arius to claim him as an authority, although no one more emphatically proclaimed the " eternal generation of the Logos " than Origen. But this last charge may be at once dismissed, because no less an authority than St. Athanasius defended his orthodoxy on the Trinity in detail. As regards 3 and 4, Origen may have made mistakes, but to use a modern phrase, he submitted himself in all things to the judgment of the Church, and was at any rate never an intentional heretic, still less an obstinate one. Outside what he considered the Apostolic Tradition, he claimed the

utmost freedom for speculation, and in such speculations
he expressed himself always modestly, as " I think,"
" It is my opinion," etc.

As regards the Tradition he says : " Seeing there
are many who think they hold the opinion of Christ,
and yet some of them think differently from their
predecessors; yet as the teaching of the Church, transmitted in orderly succession from the Apostles and
remaining in the Churches to the present day, is still
preserved, that alone is to be accepted as truth, which
differs in no respect from ecclesiastical and apostolic
tradition." This is in the Preface to the *Peri Archon*,
and is at the base of the argument of the whole work.
He then goes on to say that " the holy Apostles delivered
themselves with the utmost clearness on certain necessary
points, leaving the grounds of their statements to be
examined into by those who should deserve the excellent
gifts of the Spirit, *i. e.* gifts of language, wisdom and
knowledge." But there were also, he thought, many
points which were left entirely open to private speculation.

The creed which follows is essentially, as with his
predecessors, the Apostles' Creed; but with certain
amplifications. For instance, " the Holy Ghost is
associated in honour and dignity with the Father and
the Son, but it is not clearly distinguished (*i. e.* by the
Apostolic tradition) whether innate or born, and whether
a Son of God or not." A definition of the Soul is also
given, as having substance and life, and to be rewarded
or blessed in the future; but the origin of the soul was
not stated in the Tradition. Our author feels, therefore,
justified in giving his own modest views about the
origin of the soul. The Resurrection of the Body is also
according to Tradition, and he repeatedly confirms his
belief in this doctrine; but as to the nature of the risen
body, he expresses his individual view, that the chemical
particles will not be those of the body that died. Bishop

Freppel says, " Neither in the third century nor at any subsequent date has the Church defined in what consists the identity of the risen with the mortal body." [1]   In this, as on many other points, Origen anticipated the arguments and conclusions of Modern Science.   But he also believed, or perhaps hoped, that there would come a time, after countless ages, when bodies would become unnecessary.   For bodies were given us as instruments with which to struggle against the devil and his angels; so Origen said, " We think, indeed, that the goodness of God, through His Christ, may recall all His creatures to one end, even His enemies being conquered and subdued." [2]   But he added : " For the multitude it is sufficient to know that the sinner will be punished." Thus Origen, in holding out the " wider hope " that all men at last would be reconciled to God, nay, even the Devil himself, so that God should be all in all (although he thought that only the advanced Christian should be taught this), saw no further need for bodies.   Perhaps his Platonic environment caused him to doubt the possibility of perfection, so long as the body remained. In St. Jerome's letter to Avitus, Origen's view is quoted thus : " We shall perhaps at some future time live without bodies, when we have been completely subjected to Christ.   If all have been subjected to Him, then all will lay aside their bodies.   The need of bodies will cease, because, apparently, bodies are only given us to wrestle with evil." [3]

The alleged heresies of Origen were thus connected entirely with questions on which the Church had not pronounced judgment.   Nor was he alone in his view of the ultimate future.   Whatever was the exact meaning of the Greek word in the New Testament for " eternal," the earliest Fathers must have used that word

[1] Origen (cours d'éloquence sacrée), XXI. p. 43.
[2] Per. I. 6. 2.
[3] The question is discussed in Periarch, II. 2. 1.

in the same sense. Justin and Irenæus, however, both used expressions signifying ultimate redemption or else total extinction. Clement hinted at the ultimate amendment of every evil nature.[1] Gregory of Nyssa believed that the soul, having an affinity to God, must ultimately return to God; that all evil would ultimately disappear; that all punishment was remedial.[2] Athanasius only mildly reproved Origen for his view, while Ambrose supported it.[3] Augustine treated the question as one of free opinion, not of faith, though he took an opposite view. The first four Councils refrained from dogmatizing on the subject, though it was discussed.

In connection with this question, Clement spoke of the discriminating ($\varphi\varrho\acute{o}\nu\iota\mu o\nu$) fire, and Origen of the purifying ($\varkappa\alpha\theta\acute{\alpha}\varrho\sigma\iota o\nu$) fire, through which all must pass : the ordinary sinners till they are purged. It was a baptism of fire for those who had not been sufficiently purified by the baptism of the Spirit; it was, in fact, remorse for remembered sin. From Alexandria therefore came probably the doctrine of Purgatory, although the Roman Catholic Church bases it on 1 Cor. iii. 13, 15, the " fire that shall try every man's work."

For a long time no action was taken against Origen's books; but when party spirit ran high between his admirers and opponents, many personal animosities being involved in it, judgment was given against him by two Popes, Anastasius and Gelasius, and possibly, though by no means certainly, by the Fifth General Council.

The complete Godhead of each of the Persons in the Trinity was fully realized and expounded by Origen, and he taught that in their essence they were absolutely equal. Thus he was the first to use the expression " eternal generation of the Son," and also the " God-Man." But in their person and office and their relation

---

[1] Str. I. 17.   [2] See Ch. XVI.
[3] Ps. xxxv. 15 and cxix. 153.

to man they were quite different. The Father was the one fount of the Godhead. The Father, holding all things together, reaches to each being, imparting being to each from that which is His own, for He exists absolutely. The Son is less than the Father, reaching only to rational beings; and further, the Holy Ghost is less still, extending only to the Saints. So that in this sense the power of the Father is greater in comparison with the other two, and that of the Son greater than that of the Holy Ghost.[1] The human soul that Christ took was the only one that had remained perfectly pure in a previous existence.

This doctrine of previous existence comes into conflict with the orthodox doctrine of the Fall, for the world, according to Origen, was created to receive in their bodies the spirits who had already sinned.[2] Yet in commenting on St. John i. 22, and Romans v. 1, he fully admits the Fall. But again in *Celsus* I. 4, quite at the close of his life, he reverts to the theory of pre-existence; and in Matt. xv. 35, also at a late period, he makes the story of Adam an allegory, and Paradise the previous existence. But throughout Origen's writings there are continually found inconsistencies of this kind; his philosophical speculations carrying him into high flights in one direction, while his desire for orthodoxy and his reverence for Scripture are drawing him towards another. Besides this, the enormous amount that the man wrote (two thousand works, according to St. Jerome), makes it impossible that he should always be consistent. He regretted himself the rapidity with which his work had been done, and also complained that it had often been tampered with by heretics.

Whatever was his view of the Fall, he expressed himself quite clearly about Free Will. " Every rational creature is capable of earning praise or blame—praise, if, in accordance with that reason which it possesses,

---

[1] Peri. I. 3.   [2] *Ibid.*, III. 4

it advances to better things; blame, if it falls away from the right course." [1] Grace, too, is necessary, and grace is offered to all; but it is like the sunshine, which melts wax, but hardens clay.[2] The Incarnation had a two-fold object : to be a pattern (to restore the image) and also an expiation. The "likeness to God" is achieved by the unceasing action of the Trinity towards us, which will enable us some day to look on the holy and blessed life. God creates us; Christ gives us our rational nature; the Holy Ghost holiness. He also claimed that the Church taught the doctrine of original sin and Baptismal Regeneration; for "if there were nothing in little children to call for remission and indulgence, the grace of baptism would seem superfluous." [3]

As regards the Eucharist, Origen was always so ready for symbolism and allegory, that he used occasionally expressions which imply a merely symbolic view. For instance, he speaks of "the typical and symbolical body." [4] But he has many other passages which give quite the Catholic view. Thus, " The manna was a symbolic food : to-day the flesh of the Word of God is a true nourishment." [5] "He is Himself the Bread, and He eats with us; He is Himself the Wine, and drinks with us." [6] If these last two quotations might be taken either way, here is a stronger one. " We eat with prayer and thanksgiving the bread which we offer, which becomes by prayer a Holy Body." [7] Waterman [8] thinks that to Origen's mind the elements were in some quite literal sense the Body and Blood, and there simple believers might rest; but that every material fact, even the Body of the Lord, was also a symbol of some spiritual idea. And this seems further probable from the fact that he taught that good and bad alike partook of it; and in commenting on Exodus xiii.,

[1] Peri. I. 5.　　　　　　　　　　　[2] *Ibid.*, III. 11.
[3] On St. Luke viii. 3.　[4] On St. Matt. xi.　[5] On Num. vii.
[6] On St. Matt. viii. 6.　　　　　　[7] Cels. 8. 33
[8] *The Post-Apostolic Age,* p. 343.

he refers to the fear lest the least fragment of the consecrated gift should fall to the ground. Possibly also the Discipline of the Secret may have deterred him from unveiling too much the sacramental doctrine; for on Lev. ix. he says, " He who is initiated into the mysteries recognizes the Flesh and the Blood. Let us not dwell longer on a subject which is clear to those who know, but a closed book to those who are ignorant." This is something like the saying of the Saxon Ælfric, that the elements seem one thing to the understanding mind, but cry quite another thing to the believing soul.

The idea of Predestination was fraught with much difficulty to Origen, whose leading thought was the Fatherhood and absolute love of God. He explained it thus [1]: If God predestinated only those whom He foreknew, it follows that He does not foreknow those whom He does not predestinate. But this is absurd. He explains " know " therefore as " love," and God loves only the good. These therefore he predestinates according to (their own) purpose; or, if according to God's purpose, then because He knew they desired it. Man is free in such a complete sense, that God Himself does not know what he will do.

In connection with the position of Origen, a contrast is drawn by Fairweather [2] between the Latin and Greek theologies in their general tendencies. The Greeks better understood the Immanence of God, but for this very reason were brought dangerously near to Pantheism. To the Latins, God was far away in Heaven. The old difference between the Paganism of the two races may have prepared them for this. The Greek gods had always been gracious beings moving amongst men; the Latin deities were cold abstractions. Again, the Incarnation was the leading thought to the Greek, and he stood by the cradle. The Latin thought constantly

[1] Rom. viii. 29.
[2] *Origen and the Greek Patristic Theology*, ch. x.

of the Atonement, and he stood under the Cross. The Greek's mind was full of the Fatherhood of God and His love, and he thought of Him as good rather than just; the Latin mind dwelt much more on sin, justice, propitiation.

The *Periarchon* (περὶ ἀρχῶν: *De Principiis*), which was written in a comparatively early period of Origen's life, contains his general philosophic scheme; and it was presumably to this that Erasmus referred, when he said that he learnt more Christian philosophy from one page of Origen than from ten of St. Augustine. It was written, however, entirely for the learned, and never intended as a text-book for simple believers. In this work most of his questionable tenets appear. To gather his views on topics of modern controversy it is better to study his Commentaries on the Bible. The *Periarchon* deals in Book I with God and the Spirit; in Book II with this world and man; in Book III with Sin and Redemption; in Book IV with Scripture.

This is the first time that the position of Scripture in the Christian scheme is exhaustively dealt with, and it is an important feature in Origen's work. The divine writings were, according to his view, unquestionably the word of God. They were composed by the inspiration of the Holy Ghost, agreeably to the Will of the Father expressed through Christ. But the writers were not mere mechanical instruments. The impulse to write came from God; the writers conveyed the message in their own words. The inspiration was proved by the effect produced by Scripture on man; by the fulfilment of prophecy; by the superhuman power that watched over the work of the Apostles. Scripture was a mine of speculative truth, and every word was true.

But Origen held with Clement that there were three sorts of truth—three meanings: the literal, the moral, the spiritual. Sometimes all three would be found,

sometimes only two, or even one.   Only love and faith
in Christ gave the power to find the spiritual meaning.
Of course it was difficult; for " he who believes the
Scriptures to have proceeded from the Author of Nature,
may well expect to find the same sort of difficulties in
them which he finds in Nature." [1] (This was Bishop
Butler's famous argument from Origen.)   Many texts
of Scripture were not to be taken literally at all, as being
physically impossible.   For instance, that there could
be a morning and evening before the sun was created.
Others again were morally impossible; as that you
should not possess two coats; although Origen had
taken this very literally in his youth.   The things,
however, that were not literally true were often those
which possessed the deepest spiritual meaning; their
obvious impossibility stirring the mind to look deeper.
An instance of the allegorical interpretations of Origen
will be found in the account of the sons of Aaron
wrapping the Tabernacle and its vessels, while the
other sons of Kohath were only allowed to carry them.
Only Aaron's sons, the men of spiritual insight, says
Origen, were allowed to gaze on the holy things unveiled.
In this one of course sees also an allusion to the Discipline
of the Secret.

The immense work which Origen did in connection
with the Bible, writing commentaries on almost every
book, and also criticizing various texts in his *Hexapla*,
calls for a note here on the New Testament Canon.
Until the period of the Councils, no authoritative
declaration was made by the Church as to the limits
of the New Testament, or what books were to be considered inspired and what apocryphal.   Books like the
Shepherd of Hermas, the *Epistle of Barnabas*, possibly
the *Epistle of Clement of Rome*, and many others,
were treated as almost, if not quite, Scripture; and the

[1] Philocal. 23.   [2] On Num. iv. 15
[3] See Westcott on the Canon.

views of the different Churches varied. But in the third century these apocryphal books had almost entirely lost their hold, and all the New Testament books were firmly established, except Hebrews, St. James, 2 and 3 St. John, 2 St. Peter and St. Jude. About these there was still a difference of opinion.

Origen, as representing the Church of Alexandria, accepted generally all the New Testament, but spoke with caution of the disputed books; he thought 2 St. Peter doubtful, also 2 and 3 St. John. He once also admitted some doubt as to the authenticity of St. Jude. He also spoke of " the Epistle in circulation under the name [1] of James." As regards Hebrews he says: " I should say that the thoughts are the Apostle's, but the diction and composition that of some one who recorded from memory the Apostle's teaching, and, as it were, illustrates with a brief commentary the sayings of his master. . . . The men of old time handed it down as Paul's; but who it was that wrote it, God alone knows certainly.[2] Some say Clement, while others assign it to Luke." His successor, Dionysius, accepted St. James and also Hebrews as Pauline, but threw doubt on the Apocalypse as emanating from St. John. In this, however, he stood practically alone. Apparently no Alexandrian, except Origen, accepted 2 St. Peter.

The Carthaginian Church ignored Hebrews; Tertullian accepted St. Jude, but appears not to have known St. James, 2 and 3 St. John, or 2 St. Peter.

The Roman Church did not accept Hebrews as Pauline. In Asia Minor there was no trace of St. Jude and St. James; 2 St. Peter very uncertain.

In the Church of Antioch the Canon seems to have been complete about A.D. 300.

The Muratorian Canon gives the earliest list extant. It was published in 1740 from a MS. in Milan, which had been transcribed in the seventh or eighth century

---

[1] On St. John xix 6. [2] Hom. on Hebrews.

from a previous MS. of about A.D. 170. This omits St. James, 2 St. Peter, and Hebrews. The following books, therefore, Hebrews, St. James, 2 St. Peter, 2 and 3 St. John, and St. Jude are called by Roman Catholics *deutero-canonical*, as having been accepted later.

The chief of Origen's practical works are those on Prayer and Martyrdom. In the first he teaches that Divine foreknowledge does not release men from responsibility : that the moral attitude of prayer is in itself a sufficient blessing; that it establishes an active communion between Christ and the angels. The duty of prayer is proved by the example of Christ and the Saints. It must be addressed to the Father through the Son. The proper disposition, place, attitude and topics of prayer are discussed, and the sympathy of the dead with the living is enforced. It is best, according to Origen, to pray standing, with eyes and hands uplifted. The Tract on Martyrdom is also a beautiful work, in which he reminds the Martyrs that they are surrounded by hosts of unseen spiritual witnesses.

The philosophy of Origen is to be found, as already said, in the *Periarchon*, the leading thought of which, according to Bishop Westcott,[1] is that " All Being is one throughout, answering to the absolutely perfect Will of God, and man makes an onward progress from sphere to sphere, from lower to higher phenomena." The Biblical work appears mainly in the Tomi, or Commentaries on nearly every work in Scripture, which have come down to us in a very imperfect state; in the *Homilies*, and in the *Scholia*, of which last there are only extant some fragments. We have also fragments of the *Stromata*, originally written in ten books, and four fragments of his treatise on the Resurrection. Large fragments remain of the *Philocalia*, which were extracts from his works made by St. Basil and St. Gregory Nazianzen. The *Hexapla* was a comparison

[1] *Contemporary Review*, May 1870.

in six parallel columns of six editions of the Old Testament: the Hebrew; the same in Greek letters; the Septuagint; and the translations respectively of Aquila, Symmachus and Theodotion. It took twenty-eight years to complete, and was in fifty great parchment rolls. At Origen's death it was removed to the library at Cæsarea, and is supposed to have been burnt by the Arabs in 653. Fragments remain which were published in Paris in the eighteenth and at Oxford in the nineteenth century. Eusebius and Pamphilus copied out the Septuagint column with Origen's marginal notes.

The crowning work of Origen, written at the close of his life, when his views were thoroughly matured, was the *Contra Celsum*, which is admitted to be the finest of all the Christian Apologies. Celsus had, about eighty-five years before, published a most scathing attack on Christianity both on moral and intellectual grounds. The book is lost, but can be almost reconstructed, as Origen quotes him and answers him point by-point. The arguments of Celsus would satisfy a rationalist of the nineteenth or twentieth century. He first contended that Christianity was repudiated by Judaism, of which it was an offshoot; next, that it was a revolutionary system, based on incredible legends; a religion of threats and bribes, unworthy of good or wise men. Origen replied with a history of Christianity, and a description of its character, and its relation to philosophy, paganism and life. The argument of Celsus generally was: "Christ has failed and yet you believe Him." The reply of Origen: "He has not failed, *because* we believe Him." In other words, Origen's defence was on a moral and historical basis. "Jesus hath both risen Himself, and led His disciples to believe in His Resurrection, and so thoroughly persuaded them of its truth, that they show to all men by their sufferings how they are able to laugh at all the troubles of life, beholding the Life Eternal and the Resurrection clearly demonstrated to them both in word and deed." [1]

The close connection of both Clement and Origen with Bishop Alexander of Jerusalem suggests a passing note on the early history of the Mother Church. The first Bishop was, of course, James " the brother of the Lord." Then Simeon, son of Clopas, who was martyred in 107. After him followed Jewish Bishops till the revolt of Barcochba in 136, when the city was rebuilt as Ælia Capitolina. The Christians had been persecuted by the Jews during the revolt, because they sided with Rome : Hadrian recognized this, and allowed them to remain, while expelling the Jews. From this date we find Gentile Bishops in the Holy City, of whom the most important was Narcissus. He died in 216, aged 120, and was therefore actually born in the first century. The Metropolitan See passed to the Metropolitan city, Cæsarea, though Ælia gradually recovered the name of Jerusalem, and at the Council of Nicæa was given a precedency of honour, but without prejudice to the Metropolitan rights of Cæsarea. Narcissus in extreme old age appointed Alexander, then a Cappadocian bishop, his coadjutor, who afterwards succeeded him and created the famous library, dying as a confessor in the Decian persecution (251).

It is hardly necessary to deal with the Platonism of Origen, as it was founded on that of St. Clement : and although Origen did a far greater work for the Church than Clement, yet the latter is a more prominent landmark in the history of Christian thought. The services rendered to Christianity by the Alexandrines were magnificent. They met in battle and conquered the most highly cultivated minds of the age : and the reasoning of Origen was so modern, that it serves as a basis for Christian apologetics for all time. They lived before the age of accurate definitions, and had therefore

[1] Cels. II. 77.

a freer hand than the writers of subsequent centuries. Even in their own time they needed a highly educated city like Alexandria to fully appreciate them. In the next century only the great leaders of the Church could sympathize with them. With all their large-heartedness and liberalism, they taught the supreme importance of what Clement called Knowledge and Origen Wisdom. The men of the next century began defining knowledge very accurately, and as St. Clement said right conduct depended on right knowledge, theological error soon became damnable heresy. So Origen was condemned, because his views were on some points not as theirs; and centuries afterwards we find men, chiefly monks, who were neither capable of understanding him, nor worthy of touching the hem of his garment, writing wearisome treatises on whether or not the soul of that uncanonized saint of saints was eternally lost.

CHAPTER IX

(Bishop of Carthage, A.D. 248–258)

IT is not so much as a theologian or writer that we have to regard St. Cyprian, but as a great administrator; the greatest in fact that the Church had known since St. Paul. Under him the power of the Episcopate was thoroughly consolidated, and what is known as monarchical Episcopacy, in contrast to the presidential Episcopacy attributed to earlier times, became an established and permanent fact. He was essentially an organizer and a statesman. Under him we find the Church going forth as an organized body of active workers to relieve suffering. From him we get an account of the diseased state of the body politic and of the attitude the Church should take towards social questions. By him the essential unity of the Church was emphasized, and the importance of the sacramental system as a bond of that union.

Thascius Cyprianus was born probably about the beginning of the third century; for he was certainly in advanced middle life, when, in 246, being at that time a lawyer, man of property and cultivated gentleman of Carthage, he was converted to Christianity by Cæcilianus, whose name he took at his baptism. In the following year he was ordained priest, and in the second of his Christian life he became by popular acclamation Bishop or Pope of Carthage, and so head of the great African Church.

For his Theology he relied on Tertullian, whom he

always referred to as his master.   Many of his works were on the same subjects which Tertullian had treated, and bore the same or similar titles.   But Cyprian was a refined scholar, and he conducted into " smooth channels the turbid waters of his master's eloquence."   His first literary work was called *That Idols are not gods;* dealing, after the accustomed manner, with Polytheism by showing in contrast to it the Unity of God; and explaining the position of Judaism.   This essay is generally known as *De Vanitate idolorum,* but the other title is in accordance with the MSS.   Shortly after his baptism, he wrote to a fellow-convert, Donatus (who must not be confused with another Donatus, then Bishop of Carthage, or with the founder of Donatism), the *Ad Donatum,* on the contrast between the miseries of the Pagan life around them and the peace of the Christian.   This work is remarkable for the attention called in it to the signs of the times; the accumulations of locked up capital, the disappearance of arable land, and of an independent labouring class, and the weakened sense of obligation between rich and poor.   In this respect he practised what he preached, for no sooner was he ordained than he sold his property and distributed the proceeds.   He would have parted in the same way with his gardens in Carthage, had not his friends insisted on buying them in. His third work, also written before he became Bishop, was the *Ad Quirinum,* commonly known as *Testimonies against the Jews.* Only the first book, however, deals with the Jews; the second with the " Mystery or Sacrament of Christ "; while the third is a collection of texts from Scripture for daily use.

During the first two years of his Episcopate he was engaged in peaceful organization, which was not made easier by the factious opposition of " the Five Presbyters," and the party that followed them, most of whom, however, were won over in time.   At first the opposition was strong against a bishop who was so recent a convert.

The forty years of rest, which the Church had practically enjoyed since the persecution of Septimus Severus in 202, had caused a good deal of laxity.   Even bishops were found immoral; engaged in agriculture and tradé, even illicit trades; too ignorant to instruct catechumens; indifferent as to heresy; and when, subsequently, persecutions arose, too ready to lapse.   One can imagine, therefore, what had befallen the presbytery and the laity. It is evident that persecution was as effectual as the Apostolic Tradition in holding the Primitive Church together, and it now required the strong hand of Cyprian to restore order and discipline.   The deterioration of the African Church at this date may possibly be some justification for the stern views of Tertullian and the Puritan Montanists half a century earlier, for perhaps they foresaw what would happen.   Among many other irregularities of the time were those of the Virgins— women who had vowed celibacy, but were unable to take advantage of conventional restrictions, because no convents as yet existed, and were therefore living secular lives, and not always without scandal.   This subject is dealt with in the *De habitu Virginum.*

The title of Pope which was usually given to Cyprian, rather than Bishop, is not without interest.   In the Early Church the two titles were often interchangeable, Pope giving the idea of Father in God.   It was found in many French Sees; at Jerusalem, Alexandria and elsewhere; generally, however, in important Sees.   It is rather strange that it does not appear in the Catacombs till about 300, although it was evidently the formal mode of addressing Cyprian in 250.   Rome, therefore, was rather late in adopting the title, and not till 1073 did Gregory VII forbid any other See to use it, although about 400 the Bishop of Rome began to be known as *the* Pope.

Early in 250 the storm of the Decian persecution fell on the Church throughout the Empire.   Nothing like it had been known before. Hitherto Christianity had been unlawful, but Emperors had generally discouraged persecution or punishment where it could be legally avoided. The persecutions were generally local, and it is doubtful whether they came seriously under the notice of the Emperors in most cases. Magistrates had been incited to punish by the populace; now it was the Magistrates that incited the mob. For Decius, in his desire to restore ancient Rome, and to follow out the ideal of Trajan, found that "Pagan society was in the meshes of a net, whose steadily increasing strength and extent had baffled all attempts to destroy it."[1] For the next sixty years, therefore, there is a "fight to the finish" between the organized forces of the Empire and the Church, instituted by the powers at Rome, and ending in 313 with the final triumph of the Church.

Orders were now given everywhere to attack the Bishops. Cyprian prudently retired from Carthage, and ruled his Church from a distance, preferring to choose his own time for martyrdom. During the whole of this year there was no Bishop of Rome at all; Fabian was martyred in January, and it was thought prudent to leave the See vacant. The presbyters who temporarily governed the Roman Church wrote two simultaneous letters to Cyprian; one describing the death of Fabian, which he warmly acknowledged; the other hinting that Cyprian would do well to follow his example; which Cyprian in his reply trusted might be a forgery, as it had neither authentication, nor address, nor style. This gentle irony brought the Roman clergy, with whom Rivington says, "the aroma of infallibility lingered,"[2] to a truer appreciation of Cyprian's position.

At Carthage, while many of the Christians, the Stantes, or Standfasts, behaved splendidly, enduring both torture and martyrdom, the numbers of the Lapsed were far

---

[1] Plummer's *Church of Early Fathers*, p. 162.
[2] *Primitive Church and See of Peter*, p. 52.

greater than Cyprian had expected, even among the
clergy, most of whom deserted or lapsed; one country
bishop carrying most of his flock over to Paganism.   But
this principally happened during the initial panic.   The
passion for martyrdom soon began to spread, and alongside of it the heartbroken remorse of the Lapsed, who
had excommunicated themselves and sought restoration.
The Lapsed were divided into three classes : the Sacrifi-
cati, who had actually joined in the Pagan sacrifices;
the Thurificati, who had thrown incense on the Altar; the
Libellatici, who had received certificates, or *Libelli* of
Paganism.   The word *libellus* sometimes referred to the
certifying document received, and sometimes to the
written statement they presented.   It came to the same
thing.

But there was another libellus, the *libellus pacis*, which
caused great trouble. A custom arose, comparatively
innocent at first, for the martyrs and confessors to give a
letter, or *libellus pacis*, to a lapsed friend, which he was
to take to the bishop, entreating restoration on their
intercession and through the merit of their martyrdom
or confession.   This rapidly grew into a right to absolve
the Lapsed, and eventuated in a general absolution by
those in prison of all the Lapsed outside.   The result, of
course, was the complete dissolution of discipline.

The statesmanship of Cyprian was pre-eminently
displayed in the way he dealt with this difficulty in the
first three Councils of Carthage.   But from this custom
dates, in history at any rate, the whole Roman Catholic
theory of Superfluous Merit, Supererogation and Indul-
gences; the Treasury of the Merits of the Saints, which
the Church on earth can apply.   In a modified form the
practice had existed in Tertullian's time,[1] but it is only
from now that it becomes a serious question.

In the early part of 251 Decius left Rome to fight the
Goths, and the persecution almost ceased in Carthage.

---

[1] Ch. vii.

Cyprian returned, and a number of bishops assembled at Carthage to hold a Council. The Romans also ventured to elect a Bishop, Cornelius; a man of gentle character, inclined to forgiveness, and therefore too mild for the Puritan party at Rome, who considered apostasy a crime that men could never absolve. This Puritan party set up a rival Bishop, Novatian, who in a short time managed to plant schismatic Bishops, following his lead, throughout the Empire.

The first act of the Council of Carthage was to repudiate Novatian, with the result that a little later a Puritan anti-bishop, Maximus, was set up at Carthage as well. The Episcopal successions of Novatian did not die out till the sixth century. In dealing with the question of the Lapsed, the Council modified considerably the plan proposed by Cyprian, who loyally accepted theirs; showing that when he had convoked a Council, however autocratic his views of the bishop's office may have been, he recognized the Church Council as the superior authority. Cyprian's plan during the heat of the Persecution had been that the cases of all the Lapsed, whether holding *libelli pacis* or not, should be deferred till a Council could he held : after that, they should be heard by bishop, clergy and laity, restoration being given after full confession. But he conceded to the martyrs' prerogative, that if any one holding a libellus were on the point of death, he might be restored. The Council, however, ignored the prerogative altogether, and made four rules : (1) That the motives as well as the acts of the Libellatici should be duly considered, many having asked for certificates to save their wives and children, and some having received them through misunderstanding. (2) That those who had sacrificed, if they continued penitent, should be restored at the point of death. (3) That the Lapsed, who had not sacrificed, should be restored after a long penance. (4) That those who had refused penance and confession till the hour of death should not then be received. Thus the Council dealt successfully with two questions : the schism, in which connection Cyprian wrote his leading work, *De Unitate ;* and the Lapsed, about whose case he wrote the *De Lapsis.* Both were read to the Council. A second Council was called in the following year, 252, which considerably modified the action of the first, by granting a general and immediate amnesty to all who had so far continued steadfast in penance.

Allied to Novatian in Rome had been Novatus of Carthage, the leader of the Five Presbyters, who opposed Cyprian. This man, although he was on the side of laxity and the general acceptance of *libelli pacis,* had gone to Rome, partly because a prosecution was hanging over him at home, and partly, as it seems, with the direct intention of supporting the independence of the presbyterate, wherever he found an opportunity. Cyprian, about this time, found himself confronted with two rival Bishops : Maximus, representing Novatian and the policy of severity to the lapsed; and Fortunatus, representing the party of extreme laxity, with Novatus as wire-puller. The latter party, however, found practically no support. It is important to observe that the *De Unitate* was written at this period, when Cyprian was in the most cordial relations with Cornelius, Bishop of Rome; and not a year or two later, when he was in violent opposition to Stephen, the Bishop next but one after Cornelius, Lucius occupying the See in the interim for a few months.

The most important of Cyprian's writings, the *De Unitate,* is the text-book for all supporters of Episcopacy, and is also claimed by Rome as a leading support of the Papacy. Round this treatise, in fact, ranges the whole controversy between Rome and England. What was the meaning and result of our Lord's commission to Peter? Where is the Unity of the Church? The situation was entirely new. Never before had a schism arisen on a mere question of discipline, in which the seceders had elected an opposition Bishop, and professed to unchurch the Catholic Church. The Montanists had always claimed to remain in the fold. Now this phenomenon presented itself at Rome, the centre of the whole Church. Cyprian's argument then was based on the commission to St. Peter. Christ founded the Church on one, that its Unity might be recognized; he afterwards renewed the commission to all the Apostles, that they might be all on the same level, " pari consortio prædeti et honoris et potestatis, sed exordium ex unitate proficiscitur." [1] Each bishop holds, as Archbishop Benson translated it, " a tenure on a totality." (Episcopatus unus est cujus a singulis in solidum pars tenetur.) [2]

The main chapter (IV) reads, so far as it is essential, as follows : the Scriptural quotations are abridged : the brackets explained presently.

" The Lord said to Peter, ' Thou art Peter, etc. . . . shall be loosed in Heaven.' (And to the same He says after His Resurrection, ' Feed my sheep '). He builds (His) Church upon (that) one (and to him entrusts His sheep to be fed); and although after His Resurrection, He assigns equal powers to all His Apostles, saying, ' As the Father hath sent Me, so send I you, etc. . . . whosesoever sins ye retain, they are retained,' nevertheless, in order to make the unity manifest, He (established one chair and) by His own authority appointed the origin of that same unity beginning from one. Certainly the rest of the Apostles were that which Peter (also) was, endued with equal partnership both of honour and office, but the beginning sets out from unity (and primacy is given to Peter, that one Church of Christ and one chair may be pointed out; and all are shepherds and one flock is shown, to be fed by all the Apostles with one-hearted accord), that one Church of Christ may be pointed out."
After quoting from the Song of Solomon, Cyprian adds :

" He that holds not this unity, does he believe that he holds the faith ?   He who strives and rebels against the Church (he who deserts the Chair of Peter on which the Church was founded) does he trust that he is in the Church ? "

In Chap. V is the quotation, " tenure on a totality," given above, and in Chap. VI follows a famous description of the Church by analogies from nature, which, if Chap. IV is to be read Roman-wise, may be used against the Anglican body most effectively.   For instance, " Pluck a ray away from the sun's body : unity admits no division of light.   Break a bough off a tree : once broken it will bud no more.   Cut a rill off from the spring : the rill dries up."   Overwhelming evidence is, however, produced by Benson that all the bracketed words in Chap. IV are interpolations.   They do not appear in a single MS. earlier than the tenth century, although seven earlier MSS. are extant; and a French scholar of the eighteenth century, Baluze, witnesses to having seen twenty-seven MSS. without them.   There is also clear evidence that the words were put in, and that the later Roman Church forbade the editing of any MSS. which omitted them.   It will be seen that the whole chapter reads smoothly without them.   Father Rivington, an English Roman Catholic controversialist, dispenses with them and reads Roman Catholic views into the text apart from them : in which case it is hard to see why so much trouble was taken to maintain them, or why the bracketed portions were ever interpolated at all.

On the whole question of the claims of Rome in the first five centuries two books can be usefully studied; *Primitive Saints and the See of Rome,* by F. W. Puller (a Cowley Father) on the Anglican side; and *The Primitive Church and the See of Peter,* by L. Rivington, on the Roman. The second is in answer to the first.   Previous to Cyprian, Clement of Rome, Irenæus and Victor are called as witnesses by both sides.   In case the question may have in previous chapters been stated unfairly on the Anglican side, Father Rivington's book is recommended, and some of his arguments are here given.

As regards Clement of Rome (see Chap. II) it has been shown that in his Epistle to the Corinthians his name, as Bishop, never appears, and there is no personal element. Rivington replies that this was not necessary; according to the Roman Catholic theory, the personality of the Pope is merged in the Church. His name was probably omitted through prudence, in time of persecution; just as St. Peter called Rome Babylon. The letter was written in answer to an appeal, as shown by the apology for delay in answering; and the fact of the appeal, as well as the authoritative tone of the letter, which Bishop Lightfoot admits to be " imperious," justifies a belief that Clement was " setting the type " of Roman Supremacy.

As proof that St. Peter was Bishop of Rome, Rivington quotes Eusebius : [1] " Peter, after founding the Church at Antioch, set out for Rome, and there preached the gospel, and stayed there as prelate of the Church for twenty years." This is in the Greek version, but it is confirmed by St. Jerome's Latin version; also that although Irenæus said that Peter and Paul founded the Church and jointly consecrated Linus, he also must have counted Peter as first Bishop, since he twice counts Hyginus as ninth, who otherwise would only be eighth.[2]

As regards Irenæus' statement of " the necessity of all Churches agreeing with, or having recourse to Rome " (Chap. V), Rivington claims that they both mean the same thing : also that the necessary recourse, not of all people to Rome, but of all Churches to the Roman Church, implies ecclesiastical supremacy. In regard to Victor's excommunicating the Churches of Asia : Riving-

[1] The Chronicle, II. 150, not the History.
[2] *Hær.* I. 27. 1, and III. 4. 3

ton says that a measure of separation from Rome was
not intended to involve separation from the whole body.
That Victor failed owing to the passionate tenacity
with which the Asiatics wrongly adhered to a national
custom.   It was not a matter of faith, and so he showed
his wisdom in waiving the point.[1]

As regards Cyprian's written views, Rivington quotes :
" from St. Peter the ordination of Bishops and the
ordering of the Church runs down along the course of
time, and the line of succession." [2]   Therefore he claims
that if Peter had a supremacy, his successors in his own
See would also have it.   That the *De Unitate* was not
dealing with the Papal question, but of the right of each
Bishop to govern his own See.   That in Ep. lix, he
speaks of " the principal Church (Tertullian having
defined *principalis* as something that was ' set over ')
and the Chair of Peter, whence episcopal unity arose."

But apart from the writings of Cyprian, we have also
on this question to consider his acts : (1) in regard to
two celebrated appeals, and (2) in regard to the baptism
of heretics—if we are to understand his attitude towards
Rome.

In 253, Cornelius of Rome, with whom Cyprian had
always been in complete accord, was exiled and died.
Stephen, after Lucius had ruled for a few months,
succeeded to the Chair of Peter in May 254.   Meanwhile
Cyprian had held the Third Council of Carthage, which
is not of much importance.   In 254, two Spanish Bishops,
who had lapsed and lost their Sees in consequence, fresh
Bishops being appointed, after an interval appealed to
Stephen, and by means of some falsehood induced him
to recognize them as the lawful bishops.   The Spanish
Churches appealed to Cyprian, who called the Fourth
Council of Carthage of thirty-seven bishops.   This
Council reversed the Roman decision on the ground that

---

[1] Tertullian says (Prax. 1) that Victor insisted on the authority
of his predecessors.   [2] Ep. 33.

Stephen had been imposed upon, and advised the Spaniards to have nothing to do with their lapsed and degraded Bishops. Rivington says about this, that the Spanish appeal to Cyprian was for advice, and in no way disputed the Pope's authority as a matter of principle, though there might be some restriction on his claim to exact obedience. This, however, seems to be rather a large concession.

The other appeal was from the French Bishops, headed by Faustinus of Lyons, against Marcian of Arles. Marcian was an extreme Novatianist, who had executed the harshest sentences of excommunication against penitents and also refused to communicate with his brother bishops. The appeal was made first both to Rome and Carthage. When Stephen refused to take any action, a second appeal was made to Cyprian, who in strong terms remonstrated with Stephen, and plainly told him his duty (Epist. 68). He addresses him as " my dearest brother "; says " it is *our* duty to remedy this," and that Stephen must advise the French bishops not to let Marcian insult *our* Episcopal College. The bishops are knit fast with the glue of mutual concord, and if any make a heresy, the rest are to come to the rescue. The Gallic Bishops are to excommunicate Marcian, and with the help of clergy and laity elect a new bishop. Stephen is to tell Cyprian who is the new bishop. Benson's point of view here is that there was a peculiar relationship between Gaul and Rome, as appeared in the time of Irenæus, when Lyons was the only See in Gaul. But that apart from that, Cyprian undoubtedly regarded Rome as holding a primacy of honour, *primus inter pares*, and the Roman bishop as the natural one to take the lead. On the other hand, he was open to the severest criticism by other bishops; for though there was one flock, there were several shepherds. The Roman Catholic divines read into this letter the fullest recognition of the Papal claims. The Roman Bishop, says

Peters,[1] is shown to have "ordinary and immediate jurisdiction over the whole Church." Rivington only says that at any rate Cyprian recognized the Pope as the right man to move.

But the real struggle between Cyprian and Rome was on heretic baptism. There is no question as to whether, on doctrinal grounds, Cyprian or Stephen was right. Rome was undoubtedly right in declaring that all baptism in the name of the Trinity was valid, whatever might be the views of the baptizer; Cyprian wrong in saying there could only be one baptism, that of the orthodox Catholic. As the English Church says, "The unworthiness of the Minister hinders not the effect of the Sacrament"; [2] for Christ is the real minister. This Rome claimed to be of Apostolic tradition, and the greater part of the Church agreed with her. But Africa and a considerable part of Asia Minor held the opposite view, and three Councils were held in Carthage during 255 and 256 on the subject, eliciting a good deal of bitterness. As not long afterwards, the whole Church quietly dropped into the Roman custom, the controversy has now little doctrinal importance; but historically it has a good deal.

For it is very difficult for us to believe that the leading Churchmen of that day could have had any conception of the Papacy as found in either modern or mediæval times, when we read what they wrote to Rome and about Rome. Cyprian himself, addressing the Third Council on Baptism, says, "There is none of us who constitutes himself Bishop of Bishops (the title adopted by Rome), or pushes his colleagues with a tyrannous terror to the necessity of compliance : since every Bishop according to the scope of the liberty and office which belongs to him has his decision in his own hands, and can no more be judged by another than he can himself judge his neighbour, but we await one and all the judgment of our Lord Jesus Christ, who one and alone has the power both to *prefer*

---

[1] *Cyprian von Karthago*, p. 479.   [2] Article 26.

us in the governing of His Church, and to *judge* our conduct
therein." This is explained by various Roman Catholic
Commentators in quite contradictory ways, though the
intent seems clear.

Then, again, Firmilian, Bishop of Cæsarea in Cappadocia, wrote a long letter on re-baptism to Cyprian,
in which he compared the action of Stephen to the
kiss of Judas, but made no allusion to any Roman
claim to authority; showing apparently that he had
never heard of it. When Stephen excommunicated the
Churches that disagreed with him, Firmilian wrote to
him that the only bishop he had excommunicated was
himself. The Church, in fact, would go on just the same,
whether he withdrew from communion with Africa and
Asia or not. That, at any rate, was Firmilian's view.

Undoubtedly Cyprian took a very high sacerdotal
view of the episcopal office. It is often alleged against
him that he innovated in this respect, and that he was
actuated by policy. But we find his theory clearly
enunciated in his very first Epistle, and in the Testimonies, one of his earliest books; so that he was taught
it, or at any rate conceived it, with his first impressions
of Christianity. Again his monarchical view was tempered by modifications. The bishop was only rightly
elected with the full concurrence of the laity. While
bishop, his duty was at all times to consult his clergy as
assessors. When a bishop gravely misconducted himself, the laity had the right to desert him, " to separate
themselves from a sinful prelate." [1]

Again, as regards the Church : he is accused of limiting
it, and of confining it within the bounds of a rigid
orthodoxy and episcopacy. Certainly he used the famous
expression, " outside the Church there is no salvation."
But this also was tempered by an equally famous phrase,
" salvo jure communionis diversa sentire "; [2] difference
of views are not inconsistent with intercommunion. The

[1] Ep. 67.   [2] Quoted by St. Augustine, *Baptism*, VI. 7.

Church must be one body, and there must be no setting up of altar against altar; but within that body freedom of opinion is to be allowed on non-essentials. It was something like Archbishop Temple's dictum, that there should be uniformity in worship along with difference of opinion.

His language seems sometimes harsh and intolerant; as when he speaks of " the cancer of heresy, the anger of damnation, the witchery of error ";[1] " the false and wicked baptism of heretics, from whose mouth is expressed poison, not life ";[2] and of heretic baptism, " as stained with the contagion of adulterous water."[3] Novatus he accused (perhaps justly) of robbing widows and orphans, embezzling Church funds, kicking his wife, and leaving his father's dead body in the street.[4] Yet St. Augustine, though he differed entirely from him on the Baptismal question, had an immense veneration for Cyprian, and his " heart of overflowing love." To Augustine " his whole life was a sanctification." Once he says of him,[5] " Praise be to Him who made this man what he was, to set before His Church the greatness of the evils with which Charity was to do battle, and the greatness of the goodnesses over which Charity was to have precedence, and the worthlessness of the Charity of any Christian who would not keep the Unity of Christ."

A few years earlier than this, in 252, Cyprian had organized two great works of active benevolence. One was on the occasion of the Berber raid, a great incursion of Barbarians from the south, when the Church community subscribed the equivalent of £800 for the redemption of captives, the money being to a great extent collected from poor donors. The other was in a time of plague. Cyprian called all his people together, and invited them in a memorable sermon to witness to their eternal sonship

---

[1] See Eps. 70 and following.   [2] *Ibid.*
[3] *Ibid.*   [4] Ep. 52.   [5] Serm. 312.

in God by responding to their birthright (*respondere natalibus*). They were to nurse the sick and bury the dead, independently of creed. This is the first instance on record of the Christian community organizing itself for its fellow-men, Christian and heathen alike, in time of a great public calamity.

The persecution of Decius soon passed away, and from 253–60 Valerian was on the throne. At first he acted with much toleration, but later he was induced to change his policy. The Decian attack on the bishops had been found fruitless. Either the bishops disappeared as missionaries to another field, or they actively governed their Dioceses from hiding-places; or, if they were killed, fresh bishops immediately took their place. In 258, therefore, orders were issued for the destruction of all the clergy; and it was in this persecution that Cyprian fell. In the previous year he had been exiled to Curubis, a town about fifty miles away. Here he had a dream of martyrdom, in which he foresaw the manner in which it was to take place, and which therefore he regarded as an intimation that his time was come. A year after he had gone into exile a new proconsul, Galerius, sent for him; but being ill at Utica, told him to remain in his own house at Carthage. Shortly afterwards he ordered him to come to Utica; but Cyprian, determined to die among his own people, disappeared. So soon as Galerius reappeared in Carthage, Cyprian was at home again. After a short trial, he was condemned to be beheaded. Very full details of the martyrdom will be found in Archbishop Benson's *Life of Cyprian*.

Few saints have attained such a high place in the memory of the Church as St. Cyprian, both in the West and the East. He is the only Latin Father really recognized by the East; and he is the only saint commemorated in the Roman Mass by name, who was neither a member of the Roman Church nor martyred at Rome. And this is the more wonderful, because apparently he

K

died excommunicated by Rome.   Modern Roman Catholic writers dispute this, saying that Stephen never proceeded beyond a threat.   But the famous letter of Firmilian to Stephen already quoted seems to prove the opposite.   He writes, " For mark this : it is only thyself thou *hast* cut off."   If the excommunication of those who refused the baptism of heretics was so carried out, Cyprian was of course among them, and there is not the least evidence that he ever was restored or changed his practice in regard to Baptism.   It therefore would be the strongest argument that communion with Rome was not at that time held to be synonymous with membership in the Catholic Church if one, who died outside that communion, was raised to the highest honours.   He is commemorated in the Roman Calendar along with his ally, Cornelius, Bishop of Rome, on September 14.   At the Reformation the English Church transposed his date to the 26th.

As St. Cyprian is the last great Father before the close of the period of persecution, it will be useful to give here a short summary of the remaining persecutions.

Gallienus (260–8) in effect, though not formally, made Christianity a lawful religion.   Aurelian (270–5) not only left Christians alone, but decided a lawsuit about Church property in their favour.   He was, however, on the point of initiating a new persecution when he was murdered.   Diocletian (284–305), like his predecessors, Decius and Trajan, made a grand attempt to restore old Rome by a reconstitution of the Empire, and therefore desired a national religion.   He was naturally averse from bloodshed, but persecution became necessary to his plan.   At the Feast of the Terminalia in 303, a concerted attempt was made to destroy all churches, and especially all copies of the Scripture.   Those who gave up copies were called Traditores, and at this time many old and independent MSS. were lost.   All clergy were to be imprisoned and held as hostages.   At last came an edict that Christians were everywhere to be exterminated, unless they sacrificed, and Christian virgins sent to houses of ill-fame. This was probably the most terrible period of all, and known as The Tenth Wave. But it was the last that counted. In 311 Galerius issued a curious edict of toleration. Christians were reviled as obstinate dissenters; but persecution having failed, they were to be tolerated, if they did not break the discipline and would pray for the Imperial house. In 312 and 313 came at last the Edicts of Constantine for universal toleration of all religions.

Of six treatises of St. Cyprian mention has already been made : *That Idols are not Gods, To Donatus, To Quirinus, On the Dress of Virgins, On the Lapsed,* and *On the Unity of the Church.* During the plague year he wrote, *On Work and Almsgiving, To Demetrianus, On Mortality,* and *On the Lord's Prayer.* All these are earnest and spiritual discourses but do not bring forward much doctrine that is new. In the first there is a slight tendency to teach that a man's alms are a sort of satisfaction for his sins. The second is a Christian apology somewhat like Tertullian's *To Scapula.* It was addressed to an unusually cruel magistrate, and Cyprian is even more severe for once than his master. It was a direct challenge to Paganism to show which was the most responsible, Paganism or Christianity, for the physical and political troubles which were at that time distressing the Empire. There occurs also in it a suggestion that Cyprian at any rate believed in everlasting punishment, without any further purgation beyond this life.[1] The *On Mortality* is an attempt to meet that greatest of difficulties, the mystery of sorrow. Christians had complained of the injustice of death from plague when they were looking for the crown of martyrdom. It points out that all pain is probationary and purifying, and that it affords an

[1] Dem. 26

opportunity for self-sacrifice and attention to the wants
of others. " It is not the martyr's blood, but his faith
that God asks for." [1] In the *Lord's Prayer* he works
very freely on the lines of Tertullian, adapting many of
his thoughts and even words. The *Martyrdom* is a
collection of thirteen texts from Scripture, with short
notes, intended as a manual for martyrs and confessors.
The remaining essays are *On Patience*, and *On
Jealousy and Envy*. The chief historical interest will
probably be found in Cyprian's Epistles, eighty-one in
number, from which the whole of his life as a Christian
can be traced.

Note.—This chapter is based on Archbishop Benson's *Cyprian ;
his Life, his Times, his Work.* No one has more thoroughly
studied the subject, to which he devoted all the leisure he had
during thirty years. He is generally admitted to be the leading
authority.

SUPPLEMENTARY

Note on St. Hippolytus of Portus

In the closing years of the second century a prominent
personality, Hippolytus, moved in the Christian society of
Rome, who was bishop of Portus, and had attended the lectures
of St. Irenæus. Where this Portus was is a little uncertain,
but it was probably the port at the mouth of the Tiber, and
inhabited chiefly by Greeks. If Hippolytus derived his title
from this port, it is again uncertain whether he was a regular
diocesan bishop, or a coadjutor bishop of Rome, or the first
anti-pope. What we do know is that he was in violent collision
with two successive Roman bishops, Zephyrinus and Callistus,
whom he accused of heresy for inclining towards Patripassianism
—the view that as there was only one God, the Father
must have suffered on the cross. About these bishops he used
very strong language. The former was " a weak and venal
dunce "; the latter was " a cheat, sacrilegious, a swindler, and
heresiarch." In the sixteenth century his statue was dug up
in Rome, and at some time or other he became accounted a
saint, probably because of his great dogmatic work, the *Philo-
sophoumena*. This had generally been attributed to him,
though sometimes to Origen, who reproduced the first book.
Altogether the work consisted of ten books; and a MS. of most
of it was discovered in 1843, which proves that Hippolytus was the

---

[1] Mort. 8. 17.

author. The second, third, and part of the fourth and tenth books are still missing. The discovery of this great work has opened up a field of interesting historical criticism. In one of the persecutions Hippolytus was deported to the mines; but although this usually meant a speedy death, he lived on till nearly the middle of the third century, and was always held in honour by the early Church as a theologian.

Note on St. Dionysius of Alexandria

Dionysius "the great" was another most influential bishop of the third century, who would probably rank as one of the great Fathers, did we possess anything more than fragments of his writings. Born in 195, he was converted by the study of St. Paul's epistles, and became a pupil of Origen. When Heraclas, who succeeded Origen at the Catechetical School, became bishop of Alexandria, Dionysius took on the school (233), and subsequently became himself bishop (248). He was a great reader of all sorts of literature, having been told in a vision to read the books of all schools, that he might show himself a good money-changer. His studies and the Alexandrian environment together made him a humble and exceedingly liberal Christian, as well as a man of sound common sense: and his advice was sought by all the Churches. In the controversy about re-baptism he supported the re-baptizers on the ground that they were acting according to their conscience, in spite of the fact that he did not himself adopt their practice; for, as he said, he was a strong advocate of the mercy of Christ. Like Cyprian, he organized, during the plague epidemic at Alexandria, a staff of Parabolani (district visitors?) to bury all at all risks, independently of creed. On one occasion he was severely questioned by his namesake, Dionysius of Rome, for a statement which seemed to imply that the Second Person was a created Being, but cleared himself entirely by explaining the sense in which he had used certain words. A truly great, wise, and large-hearted bishop and a leader of his own age!

Note on Eusebius the Historian

Eusebius of Cæsarea, in his political and historical aspect, belongs chiefly to the fourth century; but he is the historian of the first three, and a historian of considerable merit. He was chamberlain to Constantine and the head of the "Conservative party" at the Nicene Council, and subsequently a leading representative of the middle or Semi-Arian party till his death in 339. He was born about 263, perhaps a little earlier, in Palestine, and was a great friend of Pamphilus, a celebrated Origenistic teacher at Cæsarea. Most of his life seems to have been spent in that city, of which in due course he became bishop and therefore metropolitan of Palestine. So far as facts are concerned, at any rate in regard to the Eastern Church, he is generally proved by modern research to be right, and he therefore becomes an important authority. His information about Western affairs was not so ample : but in dealing with the East he had access to the celebrated library of Jerusalem; to the history, entirely lost to us, of Hegesippus; to the records of the synods; to the catalogues of bishops; to State papers; and he quotes from many Jewish and Pagan writers. He begins his history by promising to track the episcopal succession in all the Churches, which is in itself of great value. Throughout he displays great carefulness and caution in dealing with statements of which he lacks absolute proof; but while his facts are generally correct, his inferences from them are often injudicious and unreliable. He is also addicted to slurring over or even suppressing anything which is discreditable to the Imperial family, or for that matter to the Church. Still he is the first Church historian whose works have come down to us, and the services he rendered deserve our gratitude.

CHAPTER X

313. *Edict of Milan.* Toleration of all Creeds by Constantine and his brother-in-law, Licinius, Emperors. Constantine summons a synod of Bishops to deal with the Donatist schism at Carthage : Donatists, dissatisfied with the decision, induce him to call,

314. *The Council of Arles.* A purely Western Council, including three British Bishops (London, York and Lincoln ?), which confirms Cæcilian as Catholic Bishop of Carthage against Donatists, finally settles the Easter question, and decrees that all baptisms in the name of the Trinity are valid.

315–320. Licinius, through jealousy of Constantine, gradually revives persecution in the East.

323. Constantine attacks Licinius and executes him.

324. Toleration of all creeds enforced, but Pagans are strongly advised by the Emperor to adopt Christianity.

319. Arius, Priest of the Bacaulis Church in Alexandria, begins preaching that the Son was not Eternal but created.

320. Arius, Secundus (bishop) and Theonas (bishop) and twelve clergy excommunicated by a synod at Alexandria. Arius retires to Palestine, and enlists the sympathy of many Eastern Bishops, notably the two Eusebii (Cæsarea and Nicomedia). Also publishes his scurrilous ballads and the Thalia. Rise of Athanasius as deacon of Bishop Alexander of Alexandria. Within a few years the whole East is infected with

Arianism. Alexandria the home of orthodoxy. Constantine, under influence of Eusebius of Nicomedia, writes a vexed letter to Alexander that the Church was rent over a foolish question, and finally consents to a Council of the whole Church.

325. *The Council of Nicæa.* Establishment of the Catholic Creed, and the Homo-ousion ("being of the same substance or essence with the Father"). Secundus, Theonas and Arius exiled.

326. Constantine summons Arius to argue before him. Death of Alexander. Athanasius, bishop, or archbishop, of Alexandria. Supposed discovery of the Sepulchre and Cross by Helena, Mother of Constantine.

328. Constantine designs Constantinople.

329. Eusebius of Nicomedia in Court favour, a decided Arian. Growth of Semi-Arian party under Eusebius of Cæsarea who hold the Homo-ousion (of like substance). An Arian synod at Antioch slanders Eustathius, the Catholic Bishop, at Court, and he is deposed. Split of the Church of Antioch.

331. Arius returns to Alexandria. Athanasius rejects him. All sorts of trumpery charges raised against Athanasius; that he had taxed the Egyptian to provide linen vestments; that he had sent a box of gold to a rebel; that he had broken the chalice and spilt the Elements of an Arian Eucharist; that he had murdered Arsenius, a monk, and used his dead hand for magic, etc. He is summoned to Court, and all charges refuted. Eusebius of Nicomedia demands a Council, which is held at Tyre; at which Athanasius produces Arsenius with both hands on. A commission appointed which collects evidence in Egypt from Jews, Pagans and Catechumens. Evidence of Catholics not accepted. Athanasius

stops the cavalcade of Constantine in Constantinople and demands justice. The Council at Tyre condemns Athanasius on the evidence of the Commission.

333. Dedication of the Church of the Holy Sepulchre at Jerusalem, and adjournment thither of the Bishops from Tyre. Constantine orders them all to Court. All charges against Athanasius dropped, and a new one raised, that he had tried to stop the corn-ships.

335. Constantine in despair sends *Athanasius to Treves.*

335–8. Arius at Constantinople. Bishop Alexander refuses him communion; Arius threatens to enforce it. Alexander prays that either Arius or himself may die, rather than this happen. Arius dies suddenly on his way to church. Death of Alexander in 336. His Catholic successor, Paul, deposed, and an Arian appointed. The East generally is now Arian: the West, Catholic.

337. *Death of Constantine.* His sons succeed :—
    Constans at Rome.
    Constantine II extreme West.
    Constantius, East.
Constantine, assuming the consent of Constantius, reinstates Athanasius.

338. *First return of Athanasius.* Athanasius accused of appropriating charities; protest against his resuming his See after being deposed by the recent Council. He appeals to Bishop Julius of Rome. Eusebius of Nicomedia Bishop of Constantinople.

340. Gregory (Arian) intruded into See of Alexandria by the State with a guard of soldiers. Riot and persecution of Catholics. Athanasius goes to Rome with two monks. First appearance of Monks at Rome. Death of Eusebius of Cæsarea.

341. Julius invites the Arians to a Council at Rome.

After making all sorts of excuses, especially that Christianity started in the East and not in Rome, they hold a Council of their own at Antioch, on the occasion of the Dedication of the Golden Church.

The Dedication Council. This was Semi-Arian, but was called by St. Hilary of Poitiers a synod of holy men, and its canons are still respected in the East. It confirmed the deposition of Athanasius on the basis of the twenty-eighth Apostolic Canon, which was also afterwards used against Chrysostom. It also issued a Creed based on that of Lucian of Antioch, generally Catholic, but refusing the word Homo-ousion. The Trinity Three in Person, One in Concord. Julius calls a Council of fifty Westerns, who acquit Athanasius.

342. Constans now rules in the West alone. Death of Eusebius of Nicomedia. Semi-Arians present a creed to Constans, which condemns the Arian position : " There was a *time* when He was not " (*i.e.* it was before time). Creed rejected.

343. Athanasius retires from Rome to Milan. *The Council of Sardica.* One hundred and seventy Bishops with a small Western majority came. Easterns refuse to act with them and adjourn to Philippopolis, where they hold one of their own, which they call " of Sardica." The West refuses to alter or add to the Nicene Creed.

344. Much Eastern persecution of Catholics. Scandalous treachery of Stephen, Arian Bishop of Antioch, who is deposed. This, followed by Western deputation to Constantius, supported by Constans, causes former to recall Athanasius. The long Macrostich Creed offered to the West, but rejected.

346. *Second return of Athanasius,* followed by his ten years of " deep and wondrous peace." About

this time a temporary reconciliation of Donatists at Carthage.

350. Death of Constans. Constantius, after a struggle with Magnentius, becomes sole Emperor. Under his influence, the West, and even Italy, is infected with Arianism : and from this point there is a steady fall in the Catholic fortunes for ten years. Paul of Constantinople exiled for second time, and Constantinople the stronghold of Arianism for thirty years.

352. Liberius Pope.

353. Athanasius sends envoys to the Emperor, who refuses to receive them, and orders him to Milan.

Councils of the Westerns at Arles. Nearly all the West gives up Athanasius on condition that the East abandons its heresy, which condition entirely fails. Liberius in disgust disowns the Council, and calls for another. Eusebius of Vercellæ and Lucifer of Cagliari in Sardinia become the two strongest supporters of orthodoxy.

355. *Council at Milan* (300 Westerns and a few Easterns). In spite of a bold stand by a small minority against the Emperor, the Council condemns Athanasius, and agrees to communion with Arians. Lucifer, Eusebius of Vercellæ and Dionysius of Milan exiled. Hilary, for calling it " a synagogue of malignants " is scourged. General persecution. Liberius and Hosius exiled. Felix, Anti-Pope. Hilary writes his first book to Constantius, being a defence of religious freedom of opinion.

356. An Arian Council at Beziers refuses to hear him, and he is banished to Phrygia, where he writes his book on the Trinity. State officials attack Church of Theonas at Alexandria during Service. Athanasius, smuggled away by the monks, escapes to the Egyptian monasteries, where he

writes the Arian history, and the Discourses against the Arians. George intruded in his place. Persecution of Catholics.

357. *Council of Sirmium* (called the third). The Blasphemia Creed. "Subjection of the Son in common with all the things which the Father hath made subject to Himself." Hosius in prison and exile, and over one hundred years old, is induced to sign it,[1] but afterwards bitterly repents and refuses to abjure Catholicism.

358. Fall of Pope Liberius, who owns communion with leading Arians, and is therefore reinstated at Rome.

St. Cyril of Jerusalem becomes very influential about now. He had been consecrated in 351, and was reputed a great saint, although he disliked the word Homo-ousion. Semi-Arians ask for a General Council; but it is decided to hold a Western Council at Ariminum, and Eastern Council at Seleucia. Hilary writes *On the Faith of the Easterns*, an attempt to establish mutual concessions between Catholics and Semi-Arians. *The Dated Creed* prepared at Court to be presented for acceptance at both Councils. It was generally Catholic, but omitted all mention of Ousia.

359. *Ariminum and Seleucia.* Before the Dated Creed arrived at Ariminum, the West had strongly declared for the Nicene. There were 320 Catholics and 80 Arians present, and each side sent reports to Court. Meanwhile at Seleucia the Dedication (Semi-Arian) Creed was confirmed. The Catholic Envoys to Court were made to sign a Homæan Creed and take it back to Ariminum; where the Council first disowned it, but were subsequently coerced into it.

---

[1] It is doubtful what Creed, if any, Hosius and Liberius signed. They, at any rate, agreed to communicate with Arians.

360. This is the lowest point touched by Catholicism, and the time at which St. Jerome said, "The world groaned and was astonished to find itself Arian." Liberius refused to sign the new creed.

A Council at Paris votes strongly for the Homoousion, and encourages a recovery of Catholicism. Meletius appointed Bishop of Antioch, and in spite of Semi-Arian antecedents takes a strong Catholic position.

361–363. *Reign of Julian the Apostate.* Unsuccessful attempt to rebuild the Temple. All exiled Bishops allowed by Julian to return, in order to cause confusion in the Church.

362. *Third Return of Athanasius.* Small Council at Alexandria, at which Hypostasis is understood by some to mean Essence and by some Person. Much difficulty is removed and a great step made towards drawing parties together. Julian at Antioch discovers the faded reputation of the Daphne. Translation of the remains of St. Babylas. Julian tries to attack Athanasius, "the despicable little mannikin." Athanasius says the cloud will soon pass, and Julian, though a young man, shortly after dies.

363. *Jovian,* Emperor for only a few months; a Catholic who receives instruction in the Faith from Athanasius.

364. *Valentinian,* Emperor in West (Catholic).

Valens, Emperor in East (Arian).

St. Hilary banished for his attack on Auxentius, Arian Bishop of Milan.

The Alexandrian Council also had tried to deal with the schism at Antioch; with help of Lucifer, who goes there to try and mend matters. He finds the Eustathians (strict Catholics) in schism against Meletius, and foolishly consecrates Paulinus, their chief. Rome supports Paulinus, and excommunicates Meletius.

370. Athanasius very reluctantly follows Rome, and narrowly escapes a quarrel with *St. Basil,* who becomes Bishop of Cæsarea in Cappadocia from now to 379 and is a great friend of Meletius.

371. Great persecution of Catholics by Valens. Rise about this time of the Macedonian heresy, that the Holy Ghost was created.

373. Death of St. Athanasius. St. Basil in the East and St. Ambrose in the West become now the principal Church leaders.

SUCCESSION OF EMPERORS FROM A.D. 364–395

364. Valentinian (Catholic) in West; Valens (Arian) in East.

375. Death of Valentinian (who had associated with himself in West his son Gratian, a child of nine years old).

375. Gratian associates with himself in West his half-brother, a child, Valentinian II.

375–378. Gratian and Valentinian (Catholics) in West; Valens in East (Arian).

378. Death of Valens at Battle of Hadrianople against Goths.

379. Gratian associates with Valentinian and himself Theodosius in the East.

383. Gratian murdered.

383–388. Maximus usurps the Empire of the extreme West (Gaul, Britain, etc.), but is at last defeated by Theodosius.

388–392. Valentinian (West); Theodosius (East); but influence of the latter supreme over the whole Empire.

392. Valentinian murdered. Brief usurpation of West by Eugenius.

395. Death of Theodosius. His two sons succeed— Honorius in West, Arcadius in East.

CHAPTER XI

(Born 297; Archbishop of Alexandria 328–373)

WITH the early years of the fourth century the history of the Church passes into an entirely new phase. No longer is she persecuted by outsiders; the persecution of the future is to be practised by Christians on each other, except during the two years' interlude covered by the reign of Julian the Apostate. In 313 the Edict of Milan decreed absolute toleration for all creeds; but not long afterwards Constantine advised all persons to become Christians. Consequently, although the struggle between Christian and Pagan modes of thought and systems of morality had still to be fought for many a year, not only was the opposition of the Roman Government withdrawn, but Christianity actually became the religion of the Court. Naturally, therefore, the world poured into the Church, and to a corresponding extent the Church was corrupted. The depravation of character was reflected in that depravation of creed, which was known as Arianism. From 319 to 381 the main interest in Church, and to a very large extent in Roman, History is bound up with the Arian struggle, and for half a century that struggle centred round the person of Athanasius. It was on that account that when an unknown author compiled a century or two afterwards (no one exactly knows when) a statement of the doctrine of the Trinity, which the Western Church accepted as a creed, he called it Athanasian, as a word almost synonymous with Catholic; although to one important statement in it, at any rate, the Procession

143

of the Holy Ghost from the Father and the Son, Athanasius would probably not have subscribed, nor has the Eastern Church at any period of her history.

Nobody can tell to what extent the conversion of Constantine was influenced by conviction or by motives of State policy; to some extent it was probably influenced by both. For a long time past the attitude of the Emperors towards the Church had been gradually changing, as the chances of suppressing Christianity became more and more hopeless. Since the time of Trajan several Emperors had appeared on the scene who desired to restore old Rome, and with this view recognized the necessity of a State religion. Naturally they would turn first to the old gods of Rome. But the Empire included distant races, who knew not the Roman gods, but had other gods of their own. Then came the idea of the divinity of the Cæsars. Here was a cult, of the head of the Empire, in which all classes throughout the Empire might join. But the ever-spreading religion of Christ opposed this cult more strenuously even than the other, and it was found by long experience that to suppress Christianity was impossible. The question then would naturally arise—Cannot this new religion, which extends its branches everywhere, be made the religion of the Empire, and hold the Empire together in the way we desire? No doubt Constantine was to a great extent influenced by this motive. At the same time, though he always regarded the Church from outside, deferring baptism till he was at the point of death; though he could never understand the importance of the controversial questions; though he so far failed to imbibe the Christian spirit as to be guilty of horrible murders, and even on his death-bed to order the execution of members of the Imperial family, whom he suspected of poisoning him; yet it is clear that he had a great reverence and admiration for the Church, to which on the whole he was a true friend. The Edict of Toleration

was soon followed by important acts; for the observance
of Sunday; for the institution of public prayers in the
Army; for the abolition of crucifixion; for the encouragement of the emancipation of slaves; for the suppression
of infanticide; for the prohibition of private divinations,
licentious and cruel rites and gladiatorial games. He
also curiously showed his zeal by preaching. His
favourite subjects were—the general system of Christianity, the follies of paganism, the unity and providence
of God, redemption, judgment. Besides all this, he
seems firmly to have believed that his armies had been
led by the Christians' God, and he was duly grateful.
But his great disappointment, against which he constantly struggled, was the discovery that this marvellous instrument for effecting the cohesion of the
Empire, was itself rent by internal dissensions; of
which he had to confront at first Donatism, and afterwards, and more especially, Arianism.

What, then, was Arianism?

In the year 319, when Alexander was Bishop of
Alexandria, and Athanasius his deacon (or arch-deacon),
one Arius, priest of the Bacaulis Church in that city,
began preaching to this effect : If the Son is a real Son,
then a Father must exist before a Son; therefore the
Divine Father must have existed before the Divine
Son. Therefore there was when the Son did not exist.
Therefore He is a creature; the greatest indeed and the
eldest of all creatures and Himself a God, but still
created; therefore, like all creatures, of an essence
(Ousia) which previously had not existed. And he
added that any other statement confounded the Persons,
by making the Son only a self-manifestation of the
Father, which was the Sabellian heresy. For the Sabellians said that God was the Monad and extended Himself
into the Trinity, the Persons being only like stage
characters assumed on different occasions to represent
the Deity to Man.

This was the first position of Arianism. Later on it assumed various phases; but one idea runs through them all. It was not by any means a denial of the Trinity, or of our Lord's Divinity. It was an exaggeration of the Trinity at the expense of the Unity, as Sabellianism was the reverse. It did not by any means go so far as the heresy which preceded it by half a century at Antioch, when Paul of Samosata had taught that the Impersonal Logos temporarily resided in Jesus, who " by moral advancement " became the Son of God.

The counter-position of Alexander and Athanasius was that the keynote of Christianity was the Incarnation of Almighty God. This must be stated, they said, quite simply. It was not of a secondary or created God, but the One God Himself; that the difference between the Persons was something that transcended all human logic, and could not be explained by it; and that this was the traditional faith of the Church. Further, they said the standpoint of Arius was polytheistic, and struck at the roots of the Faith. " We are fighting," said Athanasius later, " for our all." So Arius, with two bishops, Secundas and Theonas, and twelve other clergy were excommunicated. Arius went to Cæsarea, and enlisted the sympathy of Eusebius of Cæsarea; then to other Eastern Bishops, and finally to Eusebius of Nicomedia, in which city he published certain scurrilous poems, of which the worst was the Thalia. Everywhere he roused considerable sympathy on the ground that he was protesting against Sabellianism. The result of all this was the Council of Nicæa.

Now here it is important to observe that it was not Athanasius, or the Catholic party, that commenced dogmatizing in this controversy. The Arians at one time or another produced ten different creeds, all endeavouring to get away by different dogmatic statements from the one simple statement of the Catholics that the Father and Son were essentially the same.

It was hardly to be expected that Constantine, an outsider, could appreciate the minute difference, one of words only, as it seemed to him, by which the Church was divided; and as he was under the influence of both the Eusebii, he expressed his vexation chiefly against the Alexandrian Church. The position of these two Eusebii must be distinguished. Eusebius of Nicomedia was distinctly a courtier before everything. Later he became a decided Arian; was at one time Bishop of Constantinople; and all through he exercised a thoroughly bad influence. Eusebius of Cæsarea on the contrary was first a Churchman and an historian, though he also held a Court appointment. The position from which he started was moderating and conservative, and from him therefore sprang the Semi-Arian party. Constantine gladly assented to the proposal for a general council, which gave him just what he wanted, viz. the drawing together from all parts of his Empire of the representatives of this new Imperial religion, with himself as the presiding genius.

The first act of the Emperor was remarkable. He had received a great number of letters from bishops making accusations against their colleagues; and these he had carefully folded into one packet, which he burnt in their presence, as unworthy of them, before proceeding to business. The next question was, how to begin. As was natural, several bishops produced the creeds of their own Churches, and suggested them as a starting point. Among them was the creed of Cæsarea, the metropolitan Church of Palestine, produced by Eusebius, than which nothing seemed more appropriate. It may, in fact, be taken as a representative Ante-Nicene document, and ran thus : " We believe in One God the Father Almighty, Maker of all things visible and invisible, And in One Lord Jesus Christ, Word of God,

God from God, Light from Light, Life from Life, Son only-begotten, first-born of every Creature, before all the ages begotten of the Father, by Whom also all things were made." The remaining clauses do not affect the controversy, but it ended, " believing each of these to be and to exist, the Father truly Father, the Son truly Son, the Holy Ghost truly Holy Ghost." A great advantage claimed for this Creed was that it included no new terminology which went beyond Scripture. Yet although it said " begotten before all ages " it did not explicitly state the eternal generation of the Son; and " first-born of every creature " was liable to misconstruction. But it might have passed, had not the watchful Athanasius discovered that it was being interpreted by many as covering the Arian view. A determined stand was therefore made for the introduction of the essential identity of Father and Son, even though it necessitated the use of a technical term which went beyond the Scripture : for if Scripture was interpreted in different ways, the Church must explain Scripture by a term outside it.

In the course of discussion, Eusebius of Nicomedia objected that to call the Son uncreated, would imply that He was Homo-ousios (of the same essence) with the Father; and that word had formerly been condemned as materialistic. But now it was eagerly taken up as being just the word wanted : and from that moment it became the watchword and symbol of the Catholic party. The Creed was then fixed as follows, which is the original Nicene Creed.

" We believe in One God the Father Almighty, Maker of all things visible and invisible. And in One Lord Jesus Christ the Son of God, Begotten of the Father, only-begotten, that is from the essence (ousia) of the Father, God from God, Light from Light, Very God from Very God, Being of one Essence with the Father, by whom all things were made, both in heaven and earth;

Who for us men and for our salvation came down, was incarnate, and made man, suffered and rose again the third day, ascended into heaven, and shall come again to judge the quick and the dead ; and in the Holy Spirit." On the doctrine of the Holy Spirit there was as yet no controversy.[1] Then followed certain anathemas, on those who say, " There was a time when He was not "; or, " Before He was begotten He was not "; or, " He came into existence out of what was not "; or, " He was of· a different essence "; or, " He was created, or was capable of change."

This, then, was the settlement of Nicæa, which was signed by all the 318 present, except Theonas and Secundus, who, along with Arius,. were exiled. Here, let us note, was the first act of Christian persecution; and it proceeded from the Catholic side; although most of the persecution afterwards came from the other side. Exile was a civil punishment pronounced by the State with the concurrence of the Council. Pressure of public opinion seems to have carried away a great number· of bishops, like Eusebius of Nicomedia, who were certainly unconvinced; but from the explanatory letter sent by the other Eusebius to his Church, it seems doubtful whether even he quite realized all that was implied; and doubtless many others were like him, who afterwards formed the Semi-Arian or Eusebian party. But for the moment everything seemed satisfactorily settled; although really it was· exactly the reverse, for Nicæa was only the preface to the great Arian struggle, which was to last for fifty-six years.

The chronological sketch in the last chapter should be closely followed both for the history of Arianism and the life of Athanasius. Although the Nicene, like all the great Councils, was Eastern, the Creed itself being originally in Greek, the greater part of the East was

---

[1] It will be observed that no mention is made of the Virgin birth. Yet no one doubted it.

dissatisfied, and before long the East generally became Arian or Semi-Arian, though there was everywhere a Catholic minority. On the other hand, the West, with whom went Alexandria, was during most of the time Catholic, although for a short time under Court influence it went astray, and even a Pope lapsed. The three grades of Arianism were :—

(1) The Eusebians; or as they were called later, Semi-Arians; or as Gwatkin, in his *History of the Arians,* calls them, Conservatives. On the whole their views were honest. They wished to maintain the old Catholic Creeds, and considered the word Homo-ousion as a dangerous innovation, not warranted by Scripture, and likely to be misconstrued. They wished to insert instead the word Homo*i*-ousios (of *like* essence with the Father), and this became their watchword. Bright denies their conservatism, saying that the early Church believed Christ to be entirely and utterly God, and that any attempt to limit His Divinity was an innovation.

(2) The *Anomœan* (Unlike) party, the later development of pure Arianism, who were generally content to say that Christ was unlike essentially to the Father. The founder of this school was Aetius, and they were the real successors of Arius.

(3) Quite late in the day an *Homœan* party was formed, which theologically was a party of despair : proposing, as it were, to compromise the matter by leaving out all reference to Essence, and simply saying that the Son was like the Father. But really it was a political attempt, in the reign of Constantius, to combine the whole Church by a vague expression, and then bring it under State control.

Against all these parties the Catholics, under the lead of St. Athanasius, supported mainly by St. Hilary of Poitiers, Eusebius of Vercellæ, Lucifer of Cagliari in Sardinia, St. Cyril of Jerusalem, and at the end St. Basil and the Gregories, firmly stood; upholding always

against the various Arian proposals the Nicene Creed
and generally the Homo-ousion. Towards the close of
Athanasius' life, the Semi-Arians grew alarmed, and
drew nearer to the Catholics, influenced in great measure
by the diplomacy of Athanasius, who at a synod at
Alexandria offered to sacrifice words, so long as he could
retain meanings.[1] The words which caused the difficulty were Ousia (Essence) and especially Hypostasis
or Substantia, the Greek and Latin respectively for
Substance. Athanasius found that some, in using the
word Substance, meant Essence, and some meant
Person. Thus we speak now in our Creed of "one
substance with the Father" because the Latin Theologians came to use Substantia where the Greeks used
Ousia, or Essential Being, as meaning the same thing.

It is easy to smile at the immense importance which
the theologians of the fourth century attached to
differences of dogma on the inexplicable mystery of the
Trinity; but we have the verdict of such an impartial
modern critic as Carlyle, that if Arianism had not been
conquered, Christianity would in time have dwindled
into a legend. If anything short of the full Catholic
position had been conceded, then it must be admitted
that the complete revelation of God to man had never
been made, for the Son was something short of the
Supreme and so the Supreme was inaccessible to man.
Indeed the Arians said that Christ did not perfectly
know the Father; how then could He reveal Him?
The idea of the inaccessibility of the Supreme God was
a concession to Platonism; the idea of a secondary
God a concession to Gnosticism; the idea of the Trinity
without the Unity a concession to Polytheism. In
short, the worship of Christ would be idolatry, if He
were only a creature.

Athanasius, who is commonly thought of as a typical
dogmatist, was in fact much more a man of action.

[1] Partly also because they were included in the persecution

He would have been quite content to leave dogmas alone, and teach a simple traditional Faith, if the other side would have allowed him. His life was full of intensely dramatic incidents. As a child he attracted the notice of Bishop Alexander by " playing at Church " on the sea-shore. The Bishop found that he had been baptizing other children, and decided after careful enquiry that the baptisms were valid. So he took him into his house and trained him for the ministry. Born in 297, he was only twenty-eight when he exercised such a strong influence at the Nicene Council, and it was probably five years before that, that he composed his famous treatise on the *Incarnation of the Word*. In the year after the Council, he succeeded to the bishopric, and almost immediately he became so identified with the Catholic cause, that the way to attack the cause was to attack him personally. The most ridiculous charges were brought against him; that he had taxed the Egyptians to supply linen vestments; that he had appropriated charity funds; that he had broken the chalice at an Arian Eucharist; that he was immoral and addicted to magic; that he had killed a monk, Arsenius, and used his dead hand for magic; that he had aided a rebel with money; that he had tried to stop the corn supplies; all of which charges he repeatedly disproved. One of the dramatic incidents of his life was producing Arsenius at the Council of Tyre muffled up, and unveiling him at a critical moment in a debate, alive and with both hands on ! Another dramatic scene was his suddenly appearing in Constantinople and barring the way of Constantine and his retinue with a demand for a just enquiry into his case, which the Emperor reluctantly conceded. Bright compares it to the appearance of Elijah before Ahab, as the " troubler of Israel." On another occasion the Church at Alexandria in which he was enthroned, was attacked during the service by the soldiers of Constantine : yet he ordered the service to proceed, and the choir continued to chant "For His Mercy endureth for ever," till the soldiers reached the chancel; when he was smuggled away by the monks and mysteriously disappeared. For some years he was in hiding among the monasteries in the Egyptian desert, ruling his diocese all the time. Once, coming down stream, he met his pursuers sailing up the Nile. Not recognizing him they asked him where Athanasius was. "Not far away," he replied; and glided past them into Alexandria. He is described as a little man, with an auburn beard, and a very beautiful face. "Despicable little mannikin," Julian the Apostate called him; yet Gibbon, who had a profound admiration for him, said that he was much better qualified to rule the Empire than Constantius. No doubt for a long period his was the most important personality in the Empire.

The various returns of Athanasius to his See mark the different periods of his career, the first period coinciding within a year with the death of Constantine. Soon after Nicæa, Constantine seems to have concluded that the only solution of the difficulty would be the abandonment of the Homo-ousion, and he was therefore inclined to support the Eusebians, while giving all respectful consideration to Athanasius. At last, for the peace, as he thought, of the Church, he removed him to an honourable retirement at Treves; but Constantine II, on his succession to the West, reinstated him. This was his First Return (338).

But two years afterwards, when the Arian Gregory was intruded into his See, Athanasius went to Rome, to obtain the assistance of Julius of Rome, and generally to strengthen the brethren in orthodoxy. In 346, Constantius being somewhat alarmed at the Western opposition to his Arianism, and the deposition of Stephen, Arian Bishop of Antioch, permitted Athanasius' return. This, then, was his Second Return.

From 346 to 356, he enjoyed in Alexandria what he called ten years of deep and wondrous peace, although the storm raged all round him, and at one time he was abandoned by almost the entire Western Church. The culmination of this period was the attack on the Church from which he mysteriously disappeared. Then followed the period of hiding in the Egyptian desert till in 361 Julian the Apostate allowed all bishops to return. Then came his Third Return.

From 361 to his death in 373 he was practically left undisturbed.

His treatise on the *Incarnation of the Word of God*, though written quite early in his life, and before the rise of Arianism, is the best example of his theology, and is of special interest in modern times from its breadth of view and thoroughly philosophical standpoint. It is well worthy of his Alexandrian training and traditions. The Incarnation, he teaches, culminating in the death on the Cross, was not primarily a propitiation or the averting of a penalty. What is known as the " forensic " theory Athanasius avoided. It was rather a restoration from death to life. Human nature through sin was in corruption, and must be healed, restored, re-created. A true theory of Creation is given, in opposition to the views of the Epicureans, the Platonists and the Gnostics. Men were created above all the rest, in God's image, with even a portion of His own Word, so that having a sort of reflexion of the Word, and being in fact made rational ($\lambda o \gamma \iota \kappa \delta \iota$), they might be able to abide for ever in blessedness (c. 3). But if they did not obey His laws, they were to fall into and remain in death and corruption—a negative state; for what is good is, what is evil is not; evil is the negation of good, death of life, etc. Man turning to the evil partook of negative things, evil, corruption, death, and remained in them : he lost the image, and lost the life in correspondence with God (c. 5). The handiwork of God was in process of dissolution (6). God could not justly prevent this, seeing that He made the law, nor could He leave man to the current of corruption, and watch His work being spoilt. Even repentance by itself was useless (7), for it did not alter the nature, or stay the corruption. Only He could restore or recreate, Who had created. " For being Word of the Father and above all, He alone of natural fitness was both able to recreate everything and worthy to suffer on behalf of all, and to be ambassador for all with the Father." The Word therefore took a body, and lived and died, that all might be counted as having lived and died in Him (8), being united in His Body, and therefore sharing His incorruptibility and resurrection. Further (11) man by his corruption had lost the knowledge of God and fallen into idolatry, magic, astrology, although (12) without excuse, for the image was never wholly effaced : they might have seen Him in His works, or in the lives of holy men. There was always " a holy school of the knowledge of God and the conduct of the soul," but they heeded it not. God (13) had " to restore in us the grace of His Image " by the presence of His very Image, Christ." A portrait (14) once effaced must be restored from the original. So men's thoughts (15) were met half-way. If they worshipped men or creation or dæmons, they found He had conquered all these. He conquered even death. He came (16) to attract men's sense-bound affections to Himself as Man (Son of Man), and so to lead them on to know Him as God : for (17) all the time He was with the Father, and ruling the Universe. There was (18) the evidence of His Divinity in His miracles, especially the Virgin birth and the convulsion of nature at the crucifixion. Christ's death (20) was necessary ; necessary at the hands of others, that there might be a sacrifice : public (23) that it might attest the resurrection : not of His own choice, or they would have said He could conquer that sort of death, but perhaps not some other; on the cross (24) that His Body might not be divided, and because it was the worst death; if He was to bear our curse (25) He must bear the death appointed for the curse, and be hanged on a tree; (26) the Resurrection was not sooner than the third day that His death might be sure, and yet His incorruptibility proved; not later, that He might not disappoint His own or keep them too long in suspense; the certainty (27) of Christians that there is no death is witnessed by the martyrs; and (31) the tremendous living power of Christ in the world since His Resurrection. Then follows a controversy with the Jews about the fulfilment of prophecy, and with the Greeks upon the reasonableness of the alliance with the Word, in which they believed, with human nature, upon the decay of paganism and philosophic systems, and the influence of Christ over society and the individual. He came (43) as man and not in some nobler form, for He came not to make a display, but to heal and teach suffering humanity. Nothing in Nature was out of accord with the Divine Will except Man. All other things in Nature, knowing the Word as their Artificer and Sovereign, remained as they were originally made.[1]

This treatise gives in the clearest and most positive manner the theological position of Athanasius on what was to him the most important question. The main result of the Incarnation was the restoration of humanity from death to life. His theory of atonement certainly implies the idea of satisfaction, but it is the Godhead satisfying the Godhead.

His other works, with the exception of the Commentary on the Psalms, are not so much carefully thought out dissertations as protests by the man of action against the attacks of his opponents. The *Apology against the Arians* and the *History of the Arians* have chiefly an

---

[1] This analysis is founded on that in the Nicene Library.

historical value. The former is the best authority we have for the events up to 335, and the latter from 335–357. The *Discourses against the Arians* meet in detail all the theological difficulties raised by them. The forty-five *Festal Letters*, a few of which are only in fragments, also throw light on the history. They were his Easter addresses to his diocese, and he hardly ever failed to send them, wherever he was: consequently they are of great interest.

There is not much in Athanasius' writings bearing on Eucharistic controversy. In the *Letter to Serapion* (IV. 19) is a much-quoted statement, in which he draws a careful distinction between flesh and spirit. The actual Body, he says, would not suffice to be distributed to the whole world. He spoke of His Ascension to draw them away from the corporeal idea. " This (flesh) and the Blood from it shall be given to you spiritually at My hands as meat, so as to be imparted spiritually to each one, and to become for all a preservative to resurrection and life eternal." Yet as regards the Real Presence, he says definitely in the *Letter to Maximus* (61), " We are deified not by partaking of the body of some man, but by receiving the Body of the Word Himself."

Nor did Athanasius take any action either in assisting, or protesting against, the growth of Roman supremacy. He always showed great reverence for Rome as an apostolic throne, and recognized the close relations of Rome and Alexandria. He was also always, except for the unhappy lapse of Liberius, well treated by the Roman Church, especially by Pope Julius. But during the period embraced by his life, a great number of events took place bearing very closely on the Papal question.

At the Nicene Council, Sylvester, Bishop of Rome, was not present, but was represented by two priests. Hosius of Cordova presided. He signed first, and

Sylvester's representatives next. It seems, therefore, that the Roman Church was not considered to have any presidential authority in her own right at that time, and that the two Roman priests were not legates. But was Hosius acting as Papal legate? Roman Catholics hold that this must have been the case, but it is difficult to find any proof of it. He was well in the confidence of Constantine, and he also probably knew the mind of Sylvester. But Sylvester seems to have given no lead on the doctrinal question.

The sixth Nicene Canon gave Alexandria power over Egypt, Libya and Pentapolis, on the ground that Rome possessed a similar authority over outlying Churches in the West. How far this meant a merely metropolitan power over neighbouring Italian districts or a patriarchate over the whole West is disputed.

In 341, Pope Julius invited the Easterns to a Council at Rome. The reply was extremely disrespectful: that Christianity came to Rome from the East, implying that the Easterns knew better than Rome. Besides, all bishops, they said, were equal. And why had Julius addressed them in his own name, instead of that of his Church? And why did he ignore the decision of the Council of Tyre? Whether these arguments were right or wrong, it is hard to believe that the Easterns were familiar with the idea of a supreme authority vested in Rome. Julius had said " the custom was first to write to us and get a just judgment from this place." He had, however, previously said, " Word should have been sent to us all, so that a just sentence might have been given by us all " (that is, all the bishops).

At the Council of Sardica, 343, it was decreed that bishops might appeal from the decision of their metropolitan to Rome (as an Apostolic See), and that the Roman Bishop *might* order a fresh trial by bishops of the nearest province, and might send presbyters to advise them. This did not admit any claim on Rome's part, still less did it institute any court of appeal *at* Rome.

In 358 Pope Liberius disowned the Catholic position and became formally a heretic. Doubt in late years has been thrown on this by Roman Catholic writers, but it was never disputed till after Reformation times. Newman admits it. Fleury, writing in the eighteenth century, in a chapter headed " The Fall of Liberius," ends thus : " Thus did Liberius abandon St. Athanasius, whose cause was then inseparable from that of the Faith." And Athanasius himself says,[1] " Liberius, after he had been in banishment for two years gave way, and from fear of threatened death was induced to subscribe." It was at this time that Hosius of Cordova, who had been throughout a stalwart leader of the Catholics, but was now over a hundred years old, " was confined so straitly that at last broken by suffering he was brought though hardly to hold communion with the Arians." But he would not subscribe against Athanasius.

Among the literary works of Athanasius is a rather curious life of the hermit Anthony. Curious, because it is full of grotesque stories of temptation, by devils in various shapes, of a mediæval character. It is therefore unlike the usual practical style of Athanasius. Possibly they may have been interpolated, especially as regards a certain story of a dragon. But, apart from the dragon, the idea that dæmons or evil spirits, in whatever form they might appear, were always intervening in the affairs of men, had come down from the three previous centuries, and was generally accepted.

A more important thought, in connection with this work, is the growth of Monasticism, which was now a well-established institution in the East, Athanasius being the first of the Fathers with whose history it is connected. We hear of him hiding in the Egyptian

[1] *History of Arianism*, p. 41.

monasteries or lauras, and taking two monks with him
to Rome, the first probably who had appeared there.
It remained, however, for St. Jerome a little later to
familiarize the Roman mind with the monastic idea.
Lauras were a number of cells, near one another, in
which monks lived alone, but met for worship.

The first hermit had been Paul, in the time of the
Emperor Valerius. Anthony became one about 270.
At first it was an entirely solitary life; but gradually
the hermits drew together into settlements. In 325
Pachomius founded the first regularly organized settlement at Tabennæ in Egypt, and within quite a short
time a number of other settlements were formed on its
model; so that by the end of the fourth century the
Egyptian monasteries were numerous and celebrated,
and a century later Monasticism had become a power
throughout the Church.

It is difficult to avoid the reflection that the Church
in early days was very ready to accept the assistance
of the State in the management of her affairs. The only
serious protest that we find against State interference
came from the Donatists, who once resented the action
of the State in regard to charity. " What," they said,
" have Emperors to do with the Church? " But the
Arians became mere servants of the Emperor, and were
anxious to submit even their Creeds to him for his
approval. The Catholic party would never do this;
but even they used the State support for all that it was
worth, and allowed Constantine to be the presiding
genius at Nicæa. Indeed, during the bad years (350–360)
when the Catholic party in the West fell so low, the fall
was entirely due to Court influence. Anglicans may take
courage, when Henry VIII and Elizabeth are quoted
against them. Perhaps also they may point to the
French Church, whose submission to Rome depends
to a great extent on the policy of her kings.

CHAPTER XII

(Born 300–320. *Bishop of Poitiers* 353–368)

WHAT Athanasius did in the defence of orthodoxy for the whole Church, but especially the East, that Hilary did for the West, but more especially Gaul. In fact he was the great Catholic champion of the West against Arianism. Athanasius and Hilary never met, yet the former must have been well aware of the work of the latter, and Hilary recognized Athanasius as his chief. Hilary was both man of action and theologian, but he is best known to us in the latter capacity; for his episcopate, and indeed his whole Christian life, was short. He was converted in 350, consecrated, while still a layman, in 353, and died in 368. Five years of his episcopate were also passed in exile, although they were actively employed.

St. Hilary was born in or near Poitiers; but whether he was by origin a Gaul or a Roman, we do not know; nor the exact time of his birth. His parents were in a good position and he had an excellent education, and was trained for the profession of rhetoric, or, in modern words, for the bar. Here it must be observed, that the civilization of Gaul at this date was of a very high order. No sooner was Gaul finally conquered by Rome and brought within the Empire, than the Gauls at once rose to their position as Roman citizens. Their advance was very rapid, and by this time they were at least on a level in point of culture with the Romans themselves, the chief centre of that culture being Bordeaux. About the Christianity of Gaul we have heard nothing since the time of St. Irenæus; and it will be remembered that, when he was consecrated to the See of Lyons, he was the only bishop in the province. By this time there were of course many bishops, but even now they were much fewer and farther between than in the East. So that in the extreme West a bishop was generally a much more important personage than in the East, but at the same time, owing to distances, exercised less personal influence, except in his cathedral city. Thus when Hilary was exiled to Asia Minor, he continued to administer his diocese from afar; no one thought of intruding another bishop.

Hilary and Irenæus are to this extent alike, that both were imbued with the Greek spirit. Irenæus indeed *was* a Greek of Asia Minor, who migrated to Gaul: Hilary was a Gaul, who had deeply studied Greek literature, and especially Neo-Platonism. But he found its conception of God unsatisfactory, and it was only when he studied Moses, that he found what seemed to him the real definition, He that Is. " I am that I am " showed to him God as the source and sum of all existence; and in this thought he rested, till he was carried on by St. John to the realization of the Word made flesh.

He must have been anything from thirty to fifty at the time of his baptism, and within three years he was recognized as the one man for the episcopal throne. Two years later began his troubles. Constantius was now sole Emperor, and consequently West as well as East became submitted to Arian influence. Two bishops from Eastern Europe, Valens and Ursacius, who were acting as sort of ecclesiastical ministers to the Emperor for Western affairs, and Saturninus, Bishop of Arles, were denounced by Hilary as Arians; and he also wrote a letter to the Emperor, known as the First Book against Constantius, asking in the most loyal and respectful language for freedom of worship

for Catholics.   The result of this was a Council at Beziers
in 356, before which Hilary was cited, and by which
he was exiled to Phrygia, which meant in effect any
part of Asia Minor.   Hilary's alleged offence was one
not of faith, but conduct.   He was accused of making
trouble, and when he tried to raise doctrinal questions,
the Council refused him an audience.

But his exile was providential.   It brought him into
direct touch with the Eastern Arians, whose teaching
he was better able to examine and refute; and with
the Semi-Arians, for whom he had much sympathy,
believing them to be heretics only from a misunderstanding of terms, and not from any intellectual
depravity.   To his exile also we are indebted for his
two great works.   The first of these was the *De Synodis*,
or the Faith of the Easterns; which was not only an
excellent historical account and explanation of the
various Arian Councils, but also an attempt to draw
together East and West, by explaining the Homo-ousion
to the East, and the Semi-Arian position to the West.
No doubt this work, as well as the tolerant bearing of
Hilary towards the Semi-Arians, in whose churches
he at least prayed, though he could not communicate,
did much towards the ultimate fusion.

Towards the extreme party, however, he adopted
quite another attitude; for them no words were bad
enough.   He was summoned during his exile to the
Council of Seleucia (359) as a leading Western authority
who was in the neighbourhood, although it was supposed
to be an exclusively Eastern Council, and discovered
to his horror from a private conversation that the
Homoion (the likeness of Father and Son), which the
Homœan party were introducing as a watchword that
should bind all parties, meant no more than a likeness
of will.

The other great and indeed the greatest work of
Hilary, written during this period of exile, is the *De*

Trinitate,[1] which provided for the Latins what Athanasius' Discourses against the Arians did for the Greeks. It is the first systematic treatment of the subject by a Latin Father, and would be complete, if it had not stated somewhat inadequately the doctrine of the Holy Spirit.

The *De Trinitate* is divided into twelve books :—

1. Natural and first step towards Revealed Religion.
2. Explanation of the baptismal formula.
3. The two natures of Christ.
4. The One Person of Christ.
5. An Examination of Prophecy.
6. Refutation of the Sabellians and Manichees.
7. That the various heresies are mutually destructive.
8. That the Unity of God is not affected by the Sonship.
9–11. Replies to Arian perversions of texts.
12. General remarks against Arianism.

On the value of Hilary's work varying opinions have been expressed. Erasmus, for instance, considered that his speculations on the Trinity bordered on dangerous curiosity, and that his language against the Arians was too violent. But this was not the view of his patristic successors. St. Augustine called him an illustrious doctor, a man of no light authority in explaining the Scriptures and asserting the Faith; a keen defender of the Catholic Church against heretics. St. Jerome said that, like St. Cyprian, he was a lofty tree in the garden of the world, which helped to build up the Church of God. In another place he calls him "the Rhone of eloquence, whose writings I have traversed, and found no stumbling-block." In modern times, Dorner, in *The Person of Christ*, says that, "Hilary has not met with the appreciation he deserves. He is one of the most difficult Church teachers to understand, but also

[1] Hilary's own name for it was *De Fide*.

one of the most original and profound. His views of Christology is one of the most interesting in all Christian antiquity. He proved himself in a true sense a teacher of the Church."

In 360, after the Council of Seleucia, Hilary went to Constantinople with the view of personally addressing the Emperor; but as his influence was considered by the Court party to be mischievous in the East, he was sent back to his diocese, which he approached by very easy stages, only arriving about 362. In 364 we find him again in strong dispute with Auxentius of Milan, whom he accused of being an Arian in disguise, and therefore an exceptionally dangerous heretic. He was again sent to his diocese, where he lived for four quiet years, dying in 368. De Broglie says it is admitted on all sides that Gaul was freed from the guilt of heresy solely by the good work of Hilary (whom he calls the Athanasius of Gaul), and the Council of Paris which he called (361) had already made the first decided step towards the purification of the Western Church when it excommunicated Saturninus, and proclaimed the Homo-ousion. Other works of Hilary, not already mentioned, are two other books against Constantius, violent in their tone; a Commentary on St. Matthew (his first work as a bishop), in which he followed the lines of Origen, and was himself followed by Ambrose; and a Commentary on the Psalms, which is fragmentary, only Psalms 1, 2, 9–13, 51–69, and 91–150 remaining. But those that remain are full of deep theological reasoning.

Like others of the Fathers, Hilary, in his Pagan days, was first impressed by the beauty and order of creation, the very Greek word for the world, Cosmos, implying order; and from the contemplation of Nature, he was led to the God of Nature. If the Cosmos, he argued, is so beautiful, the Maker of it must be *most* beautiful, and the soul He has created must aspire to Him. And the essence of creation is surely life, not death; yet only

potential life. How to make it actual? Through union
with God. And later he found this through union
with the Word made Flesh. Already he had found
that " with the will to believe would come the power
to understand." [1] But also that " the work of the
Infinite and Eternal could only be grasped by the infinite
intelligence." [2] But then came from Moses the definition
of God as He that Is, the I am that I am. " I was
amazed," says Hilary,[3] " to find in these words an indica-
tion concerning God so exact that it expressed in the
terms best adapted to human understanding an un-
attainable insight into the mystery of the Divine Nature.
For no property of God which the mind can grasp is
more characteristic of Him than Existence, since Existence in the absolute sense cannot be predicated of that
which shall come to an end or had a beginning. . . .
Wherefore since God's Eternity is inseparable from
Himself, it was worthy of Him to reveal this one thing,
that He exists, as the assurance of His absolute Eternity."
But from Moses and the Prophets together he advanced
further than this; addressing God he says,[4] " From
Moses and the prophets I learnt Thy revelation that
Thou art not a lonely God. There is with Thee a God,
who is not another from Thee in nature, but one with
Thee in the mystery of Thy substance. God begotten
of Thee the Unbegotten, was born Man of the Virgin
to save *me*." And the existence of God being thus
grasped, as well as the Divinity of the Word, the edifice
is crowned by the teaching of St. John.

While Athanasius was brought up in the environment
of Alexandria, and so found himself to some extent a
follower of Origen, though in later life he withdrew
himself from his teaching, Hilary had studied the
Alexandrian school from afar. Traces of Origen appear
in his assertion of the dignity of man, and of free will,
and of the Incarnation as an obscuring of the Divine

---

[1] Tr. I. 12.   [2] *Ibid.*, 13.   [3] *Ibid.*, 5.   [4] *Ibid.*, VI. 19.

Glory : but especially in the importance assigned to knowledge, coupled with the toleration extended to those who conscientiously differed from him. Commenting on the text in Psalm 119, " I know, O Lord, that Thy judgments are right," Hilary says, " There is a certain greater effectiveness in knowledge than in faith. Thus the writer did not believe; he knew. For faith has the reward of obedience, but it has not the assurance of ascertained truth. The Apostle has indicated the breadth of the interval between the two by putting the latter into the lower place in his list of the gifts of grace. " To the first wisdom (see Origen), to the second knowledge (see Clement), to the third faith," is his message. For he who believes may be ignorant even while he believes, but he who has come to know is saved from the very possibility of unbelief."

But in spite of the importance of knowledge as a guide to conduct, Hilary showed, like Athanasius, a true Catholic reluctance to the multiplication of dogmas, or to scientific explanations of the traditional Faith. Such explanations were forced by heretic quibbles. " In simplicity is faith; God does not call us to the blessed life through the investigation of difficult questions." " The errors of heretics and blasphemers force us to deal with unlawful matters, to scale perilous heights, to speak unutterable words, to trespass on forbidden ground. Faith ought *in silence* to fulfil the commandments, worshipping the Father, reverencing with Him the Son, abounding in the Holy Ghost; but we strain the poor resources of our language to express thoughts too great for words. The error of others compels us to embody in human terms truths which ought to be hidden in the silent veneration of the heart." [1] And again, after writing of the Father, he says, " It is easier for me to feel this concerning the Father than to say it. I am well aware that no words are adequate to

[1] Tr. II. 2.

describe His attributes." [1]   Again, "Neither speech of
man nor analogy of human nature can give us a full
insight into the things of God.   The ineffable cannot
submit to the bounds and limits of definition." [2]   And,
"God cannot be known except by devotion." [3]

It is remarkable that just before Hilary was starting
for exile, when he had been a Christian for five years,
and two years a bishop, he first became acquainted with
the actual Nicene Creed, though it had been formulated
for thirty years.   But he found it exactly in accord
with what he had learnt and taught as the traditional
Faith, and he accepted it at once with the Homo-ousion.
Tradition to Hilary was simply Scripture; the day was
now passed when Christians made the oral tradition
the basis of the Faith.   Athanasius had authoritatively
pronounced on the Canon of the New Testament, which
was the same as ours, with one or two books added as
"read but not inspired."   And Scripture for Hilary (the
Alexandrian influence again) had a literal and spiritual
meaning, of which, however, only the spiritual was
important, though the words must be minutely studied.
Man, Hilary taught, must rely on Scripture for everything beyond his innate perception of God.

Hilary teaches that "it is to the Father that all creation owes its existence, and through Christ He is the
source of all.   In contrast to all else, He is self-existent.
He does not draw His Being from without, but possesses
it from Himself and within Himself.   He is Infinite,
for nothing contains Him, and He contains all things.
He is eternally unconditioned by space, for He is illimit-
able : eternally antecedent to time, for time is His
creation.   Let imagination range to what you may
suppose is God's utmost limit, and you will find Him
present there.   Strain as you will, there is always a
further horizon towards which to strain.   Infinity
is his property, just as the power of making such an

[1] Tr. II. 6.   [2] *Ibid.*, IV. 2.   [3] *Ibid.*, XI. 49.

effort is yours. Words will fail you, but His Being will not be circumscribed. Turn again the pages of history, and you will find Him ever present. Should numbers fail to express the antiquity to which you have penetrated, yet God's antiquity is not diminished. Gird up your intellect to comprehend Him as a whole; He eludes you. God as a whole has left something within your grasp, but this something is inextricably involved in His entirety. Thus you have missed the whole, since it is only a part which remains in your hands; nay, not even a part, for you are dealing with a whole which you have failed to divide." [1]

As God is Existence, so also involved in this Existence, or Ousia, is Christ, or rather the Son, for in Hilary's view the Son only became *Christ* at the creation, which was His work. Here Hilary, following the Alexandrians, differs somewhat from Athanasius, who rather attributed the creation to the Father. Between Father and Son there is a perfect indwelling, the one in the other. The generation of the Son is beyond all explanation. This is not strange, for we cannot explain even the mystery of our own birth. Christ was begotten, not so much of the will, as of the nature of the Father, both Father and Son being eternal; yet the will entirely co-operated in the generation, and the wills of both have always been in perfect correspondence. Christ is repeatedly called by Hilary, and the phrase is peculiar to him, the Only-begotten God. Though each corresponds with and completely comprehends the other and Himself in the other, yet the Persons are distinct, for the Son has free will, though it is never used contrary to the Father's. Though the two Persons are one in Being, they are not equal in dignity, because the Father is self-existent and the author of all Being.

So far, on the doctrines of the first and second Persons of the Trinity St. Hilary is clear and explicit. In regard

---

[1] Tr. II. 6.

to the third he is less so.   No controversy had yet arisen
on this subject, the Nicene Creed having been content
to close with the words, " And we believe in the Holy
Ghost." Although the controversy was imminent,
the writers of the time seemed anxious not to anticipate
it; feeling, perhaps, that one controversy was enough
at a time.   Neander says that Hilary never ventured
to call the Holy Spirit God, because this was never
directly stated in Scripture : yet he said that the Spirit
searches the deep things of God, and therefore He par-
takes of the Divine Essence.   It was really Athanasius
who first implied the Homo-ousion in connection with
the Spirit as well as the Son, by saying that if He were
created and not very God, then something created
would be admitted into the Trinity.[1]   Hilary says,[2]
" We are bound to confess Him, proceeding as He does
from the Father and the Son; and to know this is sufficient.   If any one asks what the Holy Spirit is, and is
not satisfied with the answer, that He is through Him
and from Him, through whom are all things; that He
is the Spirit of God, and God's gift to believers; even
Apostles and Prophets will not satisfy such a man, for
they only assert this of Him, that He is."

It is in his doctrine of the Incarnation that Hilary's
teaching is most important.   For he asserts that it
was not merely a necessity which arose out of the sins
of men.   If mankind had never sinned, still there would
have been an Incarnation of God; for the Incarnation
was part of the gradual revelation of God to man.   He
had been often revealed to men before in the Theophanies
of the Old Testament; now at last He was revealed
in the flesh, that He might be a witness *from among us*
to the things of God, and by means of weak flesh pro-
claim the Father to our weak and carnal selves.[3]   This
belief that the Divine appearances in the Old Testament

---

[1] *History of Christian Dogma*, Vol. I. p. 304.
[2] Tr. II. 29.   [3] *Ibid.*, III. 9.

were manifestations of the Logos was common to most of the early Fathers; but was subsequently discredited by St. Augustine, because it was used by Arians as an argument for the inferiority of the Son. He taught that they were appearances of angels.

The Divinity of our Lord is asserted everywhere in the strongest terms, as would be natural during the Arian controversy; so strongly, in fact, that, as will be seen presently, in dealing with His Humanity, he is led into dangerous ground. But when he is alluding to the Humanity, he continually uses expressions intended to assert all the while the Divinity, such as that Judas betrayed God; the death of the immortal God; and above all the often-recurring expression, which has been called his watchword, " the Only-begotten God." " Only God," writes Hilary, " could take an alien nature, could empty Himself of the attributes of Godhead." [1] " The glory of His Majesty is not forfeited, when He assumes the lowliness of flesh." [2] Christ, according to Hilary, created His own human soul : he does not refer to His birth as the operation of the Holy Ghost; He took a body not free from human infirmities, for otherwise it would have been hard for us to have believed in Him. " When God became Man [3] the purpose was, not that the Godhead should be lost, but that, the Godhead remaining, man should be born to be God. Thus, His name is Emmanuel, not that God might be lowered to the level of Man, but Man raised to that of God." In other words, it was the " taking of the manhood into God." And, as Christ was the Creator of all things, and created His own human soul, the Incarnation was not merely a submission, but also an omnipotent Divine Act which He performed Himself to manifest His glory, though in another sense it was a veiling of the Divine glory. God He always absolutely remained during His human life in all things outside the sphere of His

[1] Tr. II. 26.   [2] *Ibid.*, 27.   [3] *Ibid.*, X. 7.

work for men, both in form and nature. But within that sphere the form, though not the nature, was laid aside. He descended from God into man by an act of Divine power and will. The cost of the Incarnation lay not so much in Christ's sufferings as in the breach of the Godhead, the taking of the creature into the Creator, until at the Ascension the Manhood was finally elevated into the Godhead. On earth He was God *and* Man; but on His return to Heaven He became *totus Deus et totus homo*. At the end when all things are made subject, Christ will no longer be Man, but only God; yet the Humanity, transfigured in glory and translated into Godhead, will be eternal.

According to St. Hilary our Lord had several progressive births. The first birth was the Eternal Generation of the Son. Next came the second birth, when the Son passed into a new phase as the Creator. For this view he relied on the words of St. Peter,[1] " committing your souls as to a faithful Creator." Thirdly came the Incarnation, or, as he always called it, the Embodiment; although the word Incarnation was already known in Latin theology. The fourth was his baptism, at which he was consecrated to the final revelation to mankind. The fifth was the Resurrection, when Humanity was raised into the Divine life. Now all these were progressive revelations of God to Man, foreordained from all time, and did not depend upon man's fall. With the Crucifixion it was otherwise.

There must have been a death of some sort, even if there had been no Fall, to bring about a resurrection; but when man sinned, the Cross became a necessity. He offered Himself to the death of the accursed that He might break the curse of the Law,[2] offering Himself as a voluntary victim to the Father, in order that by means of a voluntary victim, the curse which attended the discontinuance of the regular victim might be

[1] Ep. I. 4, 19.   [2] Ps. liii. 13.

removed. Here, then, is a complete recognition of the
Latin doctrine of Satisfaction. The propitiation in
the atonement is fully expressed : yet Hilary always
preferred to dwell on the thought of the Cross rather
as the end of the earthly life and the transition to glory.

In his teaching about our Lord's Person, and the
relation of the Human to the Divine, St. Hilary took
up an original, a dangerous and an unsatisfactory
position, by affirming the impossibility that the Godhead could suffer. At least this is his general position,
for he is not always consistent : and in some places
he even emphasizes His sufferings. But there seems
to have been some confusion in his mind between the
two Latin words " pati " and " dolere," as applied to
theology. His main position, which he argued at great
length, was that Christ endured (pati) all things for
our sakes but did not feel pain (dolere). This idea
that God could not be humiliated to feel pain would
have brought him dangerously near to Docetism, had
not Hilary emphatically dwelt on the real and perfect
humanity of the Saviour. The explanation that he
gives of the various texts, such as " Take this cup from
Me," is too long to be given here, and will be found in
Tr. X. The doctrine of Hilary was that while Christ
was on earth, He was still always God, and that He
voluntarily submitted to suffering and to the necessities
of humanity by a series of dispensations, which were
detached acts of self-restraint and voluntary submissions.
But pain arises from the union of an imperfect soul
with an imperfect body.[1] How, then, could Christ, whose
body and soul were always perfect (and according to
Hilary, there was no difference between His Body before
and after the Resurrection), feel pain? St. Clement of
Alexandria had already said,[2] " He ate not for the sake
of the body, which was sustained by a holy power, but
in order that that false notion should not creep into the

[1] Tr. X. 46.   [2] Str. VI. 17.

minds of His companions, which in later days some have
in fact conceived, that He had been manifest only in
appearance." There are times, argued Hilary, when men
are in such a state of spiritual exaltation, that the body
cannot feel pain. The martyrs were in this state at
their martyrdom, but Christ was always in this state.

This teaching as to our Lord is certainly not that
generally accepted. But his view of spiritual exaltation
is very interesting, explaining, as it seems to do, acts
of bravery in history which seem almost physical impossi-
bilities, such as Cranmer steadily holding his hand in
the flame. In connection with this argument, Hilary
gives a remarkable passage as to the use of anæsthetics.
Deriding the idea that bodily pain cannot be numbed,
he says,[1] " When through some grave necessity some
part of the body must be cut away, the soul can be
lulled to sleep by drugs, which overcome the pain and
produce in the mind a death-like oblivion of the powers
of sense. Then limbs can be cut off without pain. The
flesh is dead to all feeling, and does not heed the deep
thrust of the knife, because the soul within it is asleep.
It is therefore because the body lives in admixture with
a weak soul that it is subject to pain." An interesting
argument for Christian Science !

St. Hilary is quoted by the *Catholic Dictionary* as
one of the chief patristic authorities for the Catholic
view of the Eucharist. There is not much allusion to
it in his works, but in Trin. viii. 13 he says, " For if
in truth the Word has been made flesh, and we in very
truth receive the Word made flesh as food from the Lord,
are we not bound to believe that He abides in us naturally, who, born as a man, has assumed the nature of
our flesh now inseparable from Himself, and has conjoined the nature of His own flesh to the nature of the
eternal Godhead in the Sacrament by which His Flesh
is communicated to us? . . . Whoever then denies

[1] Tr. X. 14.

that the Father is in Christ naturally must first deny
that either he is himself in Christ naturally or Christ is
in him. . . . The words in which we speak of the things
of God must be used in no mere human or worldly sense.
. . . As to the verity of the Flesh and Blood there is
no room left for doubt. For now both from the declaration of the Lord Himself and our own faith it is verily
flesh and verily blood. And these when eaten and drunk
bring it to pass that both we are in Christ and Christ
in us." These are very strong words; but without
disputing Hilary's Catholicism, it is necessary to point
out that in this, as in so many Eucharistic quotations
from the Fathers, the writer was not directly expounding
the doctrine of the Sacrament, but using it as an argument to prove something else : viz. that as our union
with Christ in the Sacrament was one not of will but
of nature, so was the union of the Father and the Son.
That Hilary had strong Catholic views on the subject
may, however, be elsewhere [1] inferred from the fact
that, when describing a riotous attack on a Catholic
Host at Toulouse, he said, " They even dared to lay
hands on Christ Himself."

St. Hilary seems to have held that the very good and
the very bad would be finally judged at death. But
that the former hardly exist, for even the Blessed Virgin
would need the purification of pain. And as to the
latter, nobody is certain to be condemned except for
the sin against the Holy Ghost, which is wilful and de-
liberate unbelief. Concerning such he held, literally as
it seems, that they would be " like the dust which the
wind driveth away from the face of the earth " (Ps. i. 19).

But there was no foreordaining of sin and destruction,
though sin was foreseen. Man has complete freedom of
will, but the human soul becomes contaminated by its
connection with the body. Yet all are capable of making
themselves worthy of election, and punishment is only

[1] Book *v.* Constantius.

reserved for sins actually committed. The soul meets sin half-way; but it can also meet grace half-way, which is freely offered. Thus man's security depends on his co-operation with God; and that is why right belief is so important, that man may know how most effectually to co-operate.

St. Hilary had some traditional reputation as a writer of hymns, but very few are extant. A Morning Hymn remains, and an Evening Hymn, though the authenticity of the latter is disputed; there remain also three doubtfully attributed to him: A Hymn on Christ's Life, a few verses on His Childhood, and an Epiphany Hymn (Jesus refulsit omnium). The *Hymnorum Liber*, mentioned in the seventh century by Isidore of Seville, is lost.

Having now dealt with the main facts in St. Hilary's life and the chief points of his teaching, it remains only to allude to those who were associated with him. He was a married man, and his wife and daughter Abra are supposed to have been converted with him. Several letters to Abra were till lately attributed to Hilary, but latest critics believe them to be spurious, and that there is no historical evidence even of Abra's existence. But St. Martin was a very prominent character of the time. We hardly call him a Father, since he was not a writer, but his fame as a missionary was great throughout France and even in Britain, where the number of churches dedicated to him and the season of Martinmas testify to his popularity. He was born in 316; was a catechumen from childhood, and baptized when eighteen and in the Army. The story of his giving his military cloak to a beggar is well known. When twenty years old he left the Army and joined Hilary, but on Hilary's exile went into Italy in retreat for many years. On Hilary's return in 360 he came back to Gaul and founded the first French monastery near Poitiers. Afterwards he was Bishop of Tours and founded the great Monastery of Marmontiers in that neighbourhood.   It was destroyed at the Revolution, but traces of the cells of Martin and his eighty-four monks in the rocks still remain.   From this Monastery he sent out a great many Bishops, and he is generally known as the Apostle of France.

CHAPTER XIII

(Born about 313. *Bishop of Jerusalem* 350. *Died* 386)

THE life and work of this Father present some points of great interest, although he was neither a great writer nor a great leader of his time. We know no theological work of any importance that emanated from him, except his *Catechetical Lectures*, a series of short addresses delivered in 347, before he became Bishop, to candidates for baptism. There are twenty-four in all; of which nineteen are on the Faith, and the last five, known as the Mystalogical, are explanations of the Mysteries, or Sacraments, of Baptism and the Eucharist, and were delivered to the same candidates *after* their baptism.

These Lectures, however, are extremely interesting, because they give us in a concise form the whole Catholic faith of that time, and have been pronounced by the best authorities to be exactly orthodox. On the doctrine of the Trinity, for instance, they are a sort of epitome of what Athanasius and Hilary had expressed in their much longer treatises. Yet they have no conscious reference to either of these Fathers; and this at once brings us to the second point of interest in connection with St. Cyril, that his early environment was distinctly Semi-Arian. He was but a child at the date of the Nicene Council, and soon after that date Palestine and Syria and Asia Minor, in fact the East generally, drifted into at least Semi-Arian tendencies. Cyril himself received consecration from Acacius,

178

among others, and the validity of his consecration was
accordingly at one time questioned. Also he always
in his teaching avoided the word Homo-ousion, though
towards the close of his life he formally accepted it.
This omission aroused hostile criticism from many
Church leaders of his time, although the *Catechetical
Lectures* are scrupulously Catholic, warn his pupils
against all the heresies, and entitle Cyril to be classed
among those whom Athanasius declared to be with him
in their beliefs, though they could not subscribe to his
formula. The third point of interest in Cyril is that we
get from him for the first time definite *ad hoc* instruction
on Sacramental Doctrine; and we get also the liturgy,
as well as the creed, of Jerusalem, which after all was
the Mother Church.

His parentage and the exact date of his birth are
uncertain, but it is most probable that he was born at
or near Jerusalem of Christian parents about 313. At
any rate his early life must have been spent in that
neighbourhood, for he recalls memories of what Jerusalem had been like before the building of the great
church by Constantine and the alleged finding of the
Cross by St. Helena. Besides this it was customary
at Jerusalem to elect a Bishop whose life was well
known to the people.

In the year 347 he was chosen for a task usually only
undertaken by the Bishop, the preparation of candidates
for baptism: two or three years afterwards he was
elected Bishop on the death of Maximus. The true
account of his election and consecration is difficult to
arrive at. He was accused by some of the Catholic
party, as for instance St. Jerome and Rufinus, of having,
as a condition of obtaining the See, renounced his
Catholic orders, and accepted reordination from Arians.
His life-work and teaching, however, seem to contradict
this, and the evidence in favour of it is, to say the least,
obscure. The strained relation between East and West

at that time over the affairs of Antioch, which will be related in the next chapter, may have warped the Western judgment. We know at any rate that he soon found himself in conflict with Acacius, the Semi-Arian successor of Eusebius, who had helped to consecrate him, and that the Second Œcumenical Council took pains to pronounce his consecration canonical, and to eulogize his defence of the Catholic Church on several occasions; and that since that time he has always been esteemed by the Church as a high authority and as a Saint.

One of the earliest events of his episcopal life was the appearance of some strange phenomenon in the atmosphere, which, whether really supernatural or not, took the form of a cross in the sky. Cyril embraced the opportunity to write to Constantius, describing this, and at the same time announcing his consecration. This letter, which is still extant, was used against him by his detractors, on the ground that he had addressed the heretic Emperor as " religious."

About 357 a dispute arose between Cyril and Acacius, who was Bishop of Cæsarea, over a matter of precedence. When the metropolis of Palestine had been assigned to Cæsarea instead of Jerusalem by the Roman Government, in course of time Cæsarea became the ecclesiastical metropolis as well; however, a canon of Nicæa had given a precedence of honour to Jerusalem, but without prejudice to the rights of the Bishop of Cæsarea. When, therefore, Cyril had repeatedly refused to appear before Acacius at Cæsarea, the latter accused him to Constantius of being " orthodox " and contumacious, and also of having sold a rich vestment which had been presented to his church by Constantine. This he had sold for the good of the poor. He was consequently deposed and exiled, and retired to Tarsus, where he was employed by the Semi-Arian Bishop Silvanus. With Semi-Arians he always, like Hilary, lived on the most friendly terms. In 361 the Council of Seleucia re-

instated him, but in the following year again a Council
at Constantinople confirmed his deposition.   When all
the Bishops returned to their Sees under Julian the
Apostate, Cyril was among the number.

Then followed the strange story of the attempt to
rebuild the Temple, in order to disprove once for all
the Christian interpretation of Jewish prophecy.   Cyril
calmly assured his flock that it would never be permitted.   The story goes that, when they were at work
on the foundations, great balls of fire came up out of
the ground, injuring and scaring the workmen.   This
occurrence is not only vouched for by several Christian
writers, but is confirmed by Ammianus Marcellinus,
a heathen, who was known as the philosophic soldier.
But whatever happened, one thing is certain :   the
enterprise had to be abandoned as Cyril had foretold.

Cyril was again deposed in 367 by Valens; but returned on that Emperor's death in 378, and remained
in peaceful possession of his See till his own death in
386.   In 381 he took an active part in the Second
General Council, where at last he confessed the Homo-
ousion.

The authenticity of his Lectures has been sometimes
questioned in modern times, but never had been previous to the seventeenth century.   There is the highest
authority from patristic times for believing them to be
the work of Cyril.   The internal evidence shows that
they were delivered in Jerusalem a little earlier than the
middle of the fourth century, and they were attributed
to Cyril by St. Jerome; by Theodoret; by Pope Gelasius
(492); by Theophanes (575).

The first nineteen (or eighteen, if the first, which is
only introductory, has no number) were delivered in
the great basilica of Constantine, built on the side of
the hill Golgotha.   At a little distance from one end of
this, and separated by a courtyard, was the little chapel
of the Anastasis (Resurrection), built, as it was believed,

on the very site of the Holy Sepulchre, the chapel being actually the inner of two caves, which were discovered by excavating the foundations of a temple of Venus. The outer cave was destroyed. In this chapel were delivered the five remaining Lectures on the Mysteries to the newly baptized.

The first Catechetical Lecture is introductory; the next two are on Repentance; the fourth on Baptism; the fifth on the ten points of doctrine; the sixth on Faith; the next thirteen on the clauses of the Creed; and it is thus that we are able to put together the ancient Creed of the Mother Church.

" We believe in one God the Father Almighty, Maker of heaven and earth, and all things visible and invisible. And in one Lord Jesus Christ, the Son of God, the only-Begotten, the Begotten of the Father, Very God before all the ages, by Whom all things were made; Who was Incarnate, made Man, crucified and buried, rose again from the grave on the third day, ascended into heaven, and is seated on the right hand of the Father, and will come again in glory to judge the quick and the dead, whose kingdom shall have no end. And in the Holy Ghost, the Paraclete, Who spake by the prophets; And in one baptism of repentance for the remission of sins; And in One Holy Catholic Church; And in the Resurrection of the flesh, and in life eternal."

This Creed should be compared carefully with the Cæsarean Creed suggested by Eusebius for adoption by the Nicene Council,[1] and also with the original Creed of Nicæa. It differs from the latter primarily in containing no clause in regard to Essence or Ousia; but it is also worth noticing that, instead of ending with a simple belief in the Holy Ghost, it adds attributes to the Holy Ghost, and further clauses about the Church, Baptism, and the future life. The third paragraph of the Creed

[1] See Chapter XI.

was now, in fact, expanding. It is probable that by this time the Eastern Churches generally had imported into the Creed the article of belief not only in the Church, but in One Church, and that the Catholic, in contrast to what Cyril called " other miserable gatherings." [1] Cyril himself emphasizes the authority of the one Church. " Learn," [2] he says, " from the Church what are the books of the Old and New Testaments." " Being a child of the Church, trench not on her statutes." Again,[3] he fully explains what the Church is, and enjoins them " not to ask where the Church is, but where the Catholic Church is," so entirely has the word Catholic come to mean the orthodox body. But there is no allusion whatever to Rome as the source of authority. " In this Holy Catholic Church receiving instruction and living virtuously we shall inherit the Kingdom of Heaven and eternal life." The difference between Cyril's creed and that of Eusebius lies chiefly in the words " Son of God " instead of " Word of God," and the omission of the words " first-born of every creature."

In the fourth Lecture (not counting the first which is introductory), Cyril states the ten points of doctrine, which he afterwards explains more in detail. These are—God, Christ, the Incarnation, Judgment, the Holy Spirit, the Soul, the Body, the Resurrection, Baptism, Scripture. In dealing with such a subject as the Trinity which is beyond human understanding, Cyril, like all the great Catholic leaders, seems to deprecate the importation of definitions. " Our [4] duty is to believe in Him, it is not necessary to know how the Son was begotten of the Father. Not even the Holy Ghost in the Scriptures has explained how the Son was begotten."

As St. Cyril does not raise any new theories, or teach any new doctrines, it will suffice to give extracts as

---

[1] XVIII. 26.　　[2] IV. 33 and 35.
[3] XVIII. 22–7.　　[4] XI. 12.

specimens of the concise form in which he presents the faith to his hearers.

Trinity.—" We neither separate the Trinity as some (the Arians), nor do we, like Sabellius, work confusion." [1] The unity of the First and Second Persons is shown in various places to lie in their nature, kingdom, will, and joint creation. The anathemas of the Nicene Council which followed the Creed are all expressed. " Neither let us say there was when the Son was not." [2] " The Son is eternally begotten by an inscrutable and incomprehensible generation." [3] " He did not bring forth the Son from non-existence into being." [4]

The Holy Ghost.—" Abhorred be they who dare to separate the operation of the Holy Ghost." " There is one God the Father, Lord of the Old and New Testament : and one Lord Jesus Christ, who was foretold in the Old Testament and came in the New : and one Holy Ghost, who through the prophets preached Christ, and when Christ was come, descended and manifested Him." " Living, subsisting, and always present together with the Father and the Son, not uttered or breathed with the lips of the Father and Son, nor dispersed into the air, but having a real substance, speaking Himself and working and dispensing and sanctifying." [5] And a little later the Spirit is spoken of as in union with the Father and the Son.

The Incarnation.—The Lecture dealing with this subject treats chiefly of the Virgin-birth, its actuality and its indispensability in the scheme, though the Creed of Jerusalem has no allusion to this doctrine, nor had the original Nicene Creed.

Original Sin and Redemption.[6]—" Wonder not that the whole world was ransomed, for it was no mere man, but the only-begotten Son of God Who died on its behalf. Moreover one man's sin, even Adam's, had power to

---

[1] XVI. 4. [2] XI. 17. [3] XI. 4.
[4] XI. 14. [5] XVII. 5. [6] XIII. 2.

bring death into the world—How shall not life much rather reign by the righteousness of One? . . . Shall not Jesus, Who gave Himself up for a ransom, put away the wrath that is against mankind?" Cyril does not seem to apply original sin to the individual quite as we should.

Free Will.[1]—"We come into such holy worship not of necessity but choice. . . . The adoption is in our power, for 'to as many as received Him gave He power.'"[2] "Sin is an evil of man's own choosing, and offspring of the will."[3] "Know also that thou hast a soul self-governed, the noblest work of God, made after the image of its Creater, immortal because of God that gives it immortality; a living being; rational and imperishable, because of Him that bestowed these gifts; having free power to do what it willeth." "Learn also[4] that the soul, before it came into this world had committed no sin, but having come in sinless, we sin of our own free will." In the last of these quotations it may seem that Cyril is denying original sin, but it is more probable that, while emphasizing the doctrine of Free Will, he is at the same time refuting Origen's idea that the Fall took place in a prior existence, and that this life was a discipline of the soul for sins committed in a previous existence.

Grace.—After describing the initial faith in believing the gospel, he says, "But[5] there is a second kind of faith which involves an assent of the soul on some particular point, which is bestowed by Christ as a gift of grace. . . . When enlightened by faith the soul has visions of God, and so far as is possible, beholds God, and ranges beyond the bounds of the universe, and before the end of this world already beholds the judgment and the promised rewards. Have, therefore, that faith in Him that comes from thine own self, that

[1] VII. 13. [2] II. 1. [3] IV. 18.
[4] IV. 19. [5] V. 6.

thou mayest also receive from Him that faith which worketh things above man." The higher faith, or assent of the soul, is therefore a gift of grace. Cyril says that grace is given through Christ at the new birth of baptism. In XVI. 1 that grace is necessary both to teach and to hear rightly. In I. 4, " As it is His part to plant and to water, so it is thine to bear fruit; it is God's to grant grace, but thine to receive and guard it. Despise not the grace because it is freely given, but receive and treasure it devoutly." And in I. 3, " If He finds a man worthy to learn, He readily gives the grace. He gives not holy things to dogs, but where He discerns the good conscience, there He gives the seal of salvation—Grace has need of believing minds."

Atonement.[1]—" God had appointed the sinner to die. There must needs, therefore, have happened one of two things : either that God in His truth should destroy all men, or that in His loving-kindness He should cancel the sentence. But behold the wisdom of God. He preserved both the truth of His sentence and the exercise of His loving-kindness. Christ took our sins in His Body on the tree, that we by His death might die to sin and live to righteousness."

Judgment.[2]—" We shall all be raised, all with our bodies eternal, but not all with bodies alike; for if a man is righteous, he will receive a heavenly body fit to hold converse with angels; but if he is a sinner he will receive an eternal body fitted to endure the pains of sins, that it may burn eternally in fire nor ever be consumed." .·

The antithesis of Eve and Mary, which was so frequent in the earlier Fathers, appears again in Cyril.[3] " Through Eve yet a virgin came death; through a virgin, or rather *from* a virgin must the life appear : that as the serpent beguiled the one, so to the other Gabriel might bring the good tidings." This is an excellent specimen

[1] XIII. 33.   [2] XIII. 19.   [3] XII. 15.

of the way Cyril provides an answer for an heretical objection, without stating the heresy. Similar instances occur throughout the Lectures. Christ took from the human body of Mary His own body, and did not, as some said, merely pass through her " as water through a pipe " without participating in her nature. Cyril therefore corrects himself, by saying " or rather *from* (not through) a virgin." At some point or other in his Lectures he manages to touch on every sort of heresy.

Scripture and the Canon.—No one has previously insisted on the paramount importance of Scripture so strongly as Cyril does. We from him hear nothing of the oral tradition.[1] " Concerning the holy and divine mysteries of the Faith, not even a casual statement must be delivered without the Holy Scriptures, nor must we be drawn aside by plausibility and subtleties of speech. Even to me, who tell you these things, give not absolute credence, unless you find the proof of the things which I announce in the divine Scriptures. For this salvation, which we believe, depends not on ingenious reasoning but on the demonstration of the Holy Scriptures."

The canon of both Testaments is the same as that given by Athanasius, except for a slight difference in the order of the books of the Old, the number of which he gives as twenty-two. This is, however, because certain books are grouped together, such as the two books of Kings, which count as one. The Minor Prophets all together also count as one. Also Ezra and Nehemiah are omitted; while two books of Esdras are included, and to Jeremiah and the Lamentations (as one book) is added the Book of Baruch. The New Testament is the same as our own, except that it lacks the Revelation.

It seems probable that in the Church of the third century, considerable importance was attached to

[1] IV. 17.

relics, and efficacy imputed to them; but however
that may have been, this idea was certainly strongly
developed in the fourth. The worship of relics and
faith in their healing powers was taught by Cyril, Basil,
Chrysostom, Ambrose and Augustine. Here is an argument of Cyril [1] for the truth of the story in 2 Kings, xiii.
of the dead man who was restored to life by touching
the bones of Elisha. " Though the soul is not present,
a virtue resides in the bodies of the Saints, because of
the righteous soul which has for so many years dwelt
in it, or used it as its minister. And let us not foolishly
disbelieve this, as though it had not happened; for if
handkerchiefs and aprons, which are from without,
touching the bodies of the diseased, raise up the sick,
how much more should the very body of the Prophet
(Elisha) raise the dead? " Here, then, is the whole case
for the possibility, as it is put by a modern scientist,
of virtue, emanating from mind or spirit, attaching
itself to matter !

A special instance of relic-worship also in this century
was connected with the finding, or supposed finding, of
the true Cross, fragments of which were distributed, as
Cyril says,[2] throughout the whole world " by means of
those who in faith take portions of it." Faith in what?
Surely in some power residing in the wood. Eusebius,
while recording the finding of the Sepulchre, ignores the
Cross altogether; but Chrysostom gives a full account
of the discovery; while Ambrose records that St.
Helena made a horse's bit from one nail and a diadem
from the other. Apparently, therefore, something like
a cross was found, but Eusebius probably thought the
evidence of its being the Cross of Christ insufficient.

Akin to the question of relics was that of the intercession of saints. Cyril does not contribute much to
this question, but a strong protest was made against
the prevalence of the belief by a Gallican priest,

[1] XVIII. 16.   [2] X 19.

Vigilantius, towards the end of the century. He disputed their powers of intercession, since they were not yet in heaven with Christ. To this, however, St. Jerome replied that they were wherever Christ was. The practical result was the careful distinction drawn by the Eastern Church between Latria, the worship of God, and the becoming reverence (τιμὴ σχετικὴ or δουλία) due to the saints.[1]

But by far the greatest interest connected with the study of St. Cyril lies in the last five or Mystalogical Lectures; for here we have something quite fresh, the unfolding of all the deep hidden meaning that underlay the symbolism and ritual of the Sacraments. Harnack claims [2] that from the fourth century interest was more and more transferred from the regulation of the whole life [3] by religion to its external consecration through the mysteries. Gregory of Nyssa indeed said that Christianity had its strength in the mystic symbols. The Sacramental idea was later expressed by Augustine as " aliud videtur, aliud intelligitur " ; one thing is seen, another thing is understood. With the early Christians the Sacramental idea was not limited to two or even seven definite mysteries. Whenever the passing event portrayed to them some deep meaning behind it, the idea of something sacramental was conveyed to them. In one place Christ's life and death are called a mystery or Sacrament. Still the mysteries of the two great rites which our Lord Himself had instituted would naturally be those which most needed careful and detailed explanation. We must picture to ourselves, then, the Catechetical Lectures as given during Lent to the catechumens from the pulpit that stood in the middle of the nave of the great church. Then at Easter they were baptized; and in Easter week the

---

[1] (We ask) that at their prayers and intercessions God would receive our petitions (XXIII. 9).

[2] *History of Dogma*, Vol. III. p. 162.

[3] Chapter on Clement of Alexandria.

baptized met in that most holy chapel of the Anastasis, the very site, as they believed, of the Resurrection, to learn what the great services of the Church were to mean to them. They were first reminded of what they had passed through in Baptism, which only the baptized might fully understand, and then told what the Eucharist would be.

The baptismal rite was replete with symbolism from beginning to end. First they had met in the outer chamber, faced to the West, and renounced Satan with the hands outstretched, and all his works, and all his pomp, and all his service. And these words were not redundant; each meant different temptations, which were carefully distinguished. Next they confessed their belief in Father, Son, and Holy Ghost and in the Baptism of repentance. Passing then to the inner chamber, they were led to the pool, because Christ was carried from the Cross to the tomb. They put off their garments, because they were putting off the old Adam. They were anointed all over with exorcised oil, the exorcised oil having received such virtue from the invocation of the Spirit and prayer that it not only cleansed away the traces of sin, but also dispelled the powers of evil. The Creed was then repeated, which they had learnt by heart, but had not been allowed to write down. The immersion, or actual baptism, was itself a symbol of Christ's burial; the triple immersion of the three days' burial. For baptism was not only the grace of the remission of sin, but also a counterpart of Christ's suffering. As St. Paul said, we are baptized into the likeness of His death. Naturally also the return from the water was a symbol of His Resurrection. Again the anointment was a symbol of Christ's anointment by the Holy Ghost. The application of the ointment or chrism to the different parts of the body had in each case a separate meaning. " Beware," [1] says

[1] Third Myst.

Cyril, "of supposing this to be plain ointment after the invocation, but the gift of Christ, and by the presence of His Godhead, it causes in us the Holy Ghost. It is symbolically applied to thy forehead and other senses, and while thy body is anointed with the visible ointment, thy soul is sanctified by the holy and life-giving Spirit."

It is strange to find that, although a century had passed since the days of Cyprian, the Church of Jerusalem still treated heretic baptism as invalid.

Still more interesting to us is the teaching of Cyril on the Eucharist and the early account we get from him of the Liturgy. Cardinal Newman, in his preface to *Cyril* in the Library of the Fathers, and writing therefore in his Anglican days, says he was remarkable, because, in spite of his training, when he came to explain himself, he expressed precisely the same doctrine as that of Athanasius, although avoiding the word Homo-ousion. He argues that though on this point his judgment was erroneous, it was his own; but his faith was not his own, but shared by him with the whole Christian world. Newman was not at the time thinking of his view of the Eucharist; but if his faith was generally that of the whole Christian world, is it not a possible inference that his view of the Eucharist was not unlike the general view? At any rate he is the first Father who states the doctrine definitely, and is not merely using Eucharistic doctrine as an analogy to prove something else; while his teaching, coming from the Mother Church of Jerusalem, must carry great weight. Harnack[1] brushes away the very forcible language of Cyril by saying that extravagancies of this sort still belonged at that time to the liturgical and catechetical element, but were not a part of theology. This may or may not be true; but this is what the Bishop of Jerusalem said: and we can hardly blame the Roman Catholic Church for quoting him as an authority.

[1] *History of Dogma*, Vol. IV. p. 293.

In Lecture XXII, after reciting the evidence of
St. Paul from which he takes his text, he says : " Since
then He Himself declared of the Bread ' This is My
Body,' who shall dare to doubt any longer?   And since
He has Himself affirmed ' This is My Blood,' who shall
ever hesitate, saying it is not His Blood?   He once in
Cana of Galilee turned the water into wine akin to
blood.; and is it incredible that He should turn wine
into blood?   When called to a bodily marriage, He
miraculously wrought that wonderful work, and on the
children of the bride-chamber shall He not much rather
be acknowledged to have bestowed the fruition of His
Body and His Blood?   Wherefore in the full assurance
let us partake as of the Body and Blood of Christ; for
in the figure (literally type) of bread is given to thee
His Body and in the figure of wine His Blood, that
thou, by partaking of the Body and Blood of Christ
mayest be made of the same body and blood with Him.
For thus we come to bear Christ in us (to be Christo-
pheri), because His Body and Blood are distributed
through our members.   Thus it is that, according to
the blessed Peter, we become partakers of the Divine
Nature.   Christ [1] on a certain occasion discoursing
with the Jews said ' Except ye eat my flesh,' etc.   They
not having heard His saying in a spiritual sense, were
offended and went back, supposing He was inviting
them to eat flesh."   After (5) alluding to the shew-
bread as a sort of type, he passes (6) to even stronger
language.   " Consider therefore the bread and wine
not as bare elements; for they are according to the
Lord's declaration, the Body and Blood of Christ; for
even though sense suggests this to thee, yet let Faith
establish thee.   Judge not the matter from the taste,
but from faith be fully assured without misgiving that
the Body and Blood of Christ have been vouchsafed
to thee."   Then (7 and 8) after allusions to the Old

[1] XXII. 4.

Testament, he ends (9): " Having learnt these things, and been fully assured that the seeming bread is *not bread, though sensible to taste,* but the Body of Christ, and the seeming wine is *not wine, though the taste will have it so,* but the Blood of Christ . . . mayest thou reflect as a mirror the glory of the Lord and proceed from glory to glory in Christ."

In the next Lecture (XXIII, on the Liturgy) he again says (20) : " Trust not the judgment of the bodily palate, no, but to faith unfaltering, for they who taste are bidden to taste *not bread and wine,* but the antitypical Body and Blood. In approaching therefore (21) come not with wrists' extended nor with fingers spread, but make thy left hand a throne for thy right as for that which is to receive a King, and having hallowed thy palm, receive the Body of Christ saying over It Amen. So then having carefully hallowed thine eyes by the touch of the holy Body, partake of It, giving heed lest thou lose any portion of It, for whatever thou losest is evidently a loss to thee, as it were, from one of thine own members." In 22, similar instruction is given as to the Chalice, for both elements were always received.

It would be clearly impossible to quote St. Cyril in defence of a belief, that the elements are nothing more than symbols or signs. There is certainly his reference to Christ's saying, " The flesh profiteth nothing "; but while Cyril taught a deep spiritual mystery as well, he does distinctly say that " the seeming bread is not bread." There is also the use of the words " type " and " antitypical," but " type " seems to mean the figure or shape presented to the senses; and if " type " is fairly used of the outward sign, " antitype " would with equal appropriateness be used of the inward grace. Dr. Pusey argued that Cyril intended to imply no substantial change, because in discussing the water and chrism of baptism, he had said they were no longer

o

mere water and oil after the invocation of the Holy
Ghost. Cyril's [1] words are, "Regard not the laver as
simply water, but rather regard the spiritual grace that
is given with the water. The simple water, having
received the invocation of the Holy Ghost and of Christ
and of the Father, acquires a new power of holiness."
Again in XXI. 3, "Beware of supposing this to be mere
ointment, for as the bread of the Eucharist after invocation of the Holy Ghost is mere bread no longer but
the Body, so also this holy ointment is no more simple
ointment, nor, so to say, common after the invocation of
the Holy Ghost, but it is Christ's gift of grace, and by
the advent of the Holy Ghost is made fit to impart the
Divine Nature." Dr. Pusey's argument, therefore, is
that if there is a change of substance after the invocation in the bread, there must be also in the water and
the chrism. But this nobody claims. Why then,
he adds, as the cases seem, according to Cyril, to be
analogous, claim it for the bread?

But another Anglican writer, Dr. Gifford, in his
preface to *Cyril* in the Nicene Library, considers this
argument fallacious. For Cyril never says that the
effect on the water and the chrism is the *same* as that
on the bread. Wherever there is an invocation of the
Holy Ghost, there is an objective change. With the
water is given spiritual grace; it acquires a power of
holiness; the chrism also is no longer common ointment
but Christ's gift of grace, and made fit to impart the
Divine Nature. But the bread, he says, is *no longer
bread*, but Christ's Body. Yet this writer still holds
that the Elements are only treated as types, but types
endued by the Word with life-giving properties analogous to the actual Body and Blood. If this was Cyril's
meaning, his actual words seem very misleading.

The twenty-third Lecture gives us clearly the order
of the liturgy of Jerusalem.

[1] III. 3.

1. Deacon brings water to the celebrant; he and the other priests wash their hands.

2. The kiss of peace.

3. The Sursum Corda and three following sentences; Preface; Sanctus.

4. The Invocation " We call on the merciful God to send forth His Holy Spirit on the gifts lying before Him, that He may make the bread the Body of Christ; and the wine the Blood of Christ; for whatever the Holy Ghost has touched is sanctified and changed." No mention is given of the words of institution, though doubtless they were used; but then, as still in the Eastern Church, it was the Invocation that effected the Consecration.

5. The long prayer of Intercession and Commendation both of living and dead, introduced at the most solemn moment. The prayers for the dead are specially defended (9) and explained by Cyril. " We, when we offer to Him our supplications for those who have fallen asleep, though they be sinners, offer up Christ sacrificed for our sins, propitiating our merciful God for them as well as for ourselves."

8. The Lord's Prayer. So important is this to the Liturgy that St. Cyril gives a detailed explanation of every clause.

7. The priest says, " Holy things to the holy," and the people reply, " One is Holy, one is the Lord, Jesus Christ."

8. The Communion. That of the celebrant was probably before the Lord's Prayer.

CHAPTER XIV

ST. BASIL THE GREAT

(*Born* 329. *Archbishop of Cæsarea in Cappadocia,* 370–379)

THREE years before the death of Athanasius, St. Basil became Archbishop of Cæsarea (the capital of Cappadocia) and Ex-arch of Pontus, Athanasius congratulating the Cæsareans on having found so glorious a Bishop. His episcopal work only extended over nine years; but during that time he was the most prominent figure in the Eastern, if not in the whole, Church. Some difficulty, however, in his relations with the West prevented his influence from being felt there as fully as it ought to have been, so that possibly in the West St. Ambrose was the recognized leader. But 'the cloak of Athanasius fell on Basil; and like Athanasius, Basil maintained the authority of the Church against the State, and with a like courage and pertinacity. Only after his death did the result of his work appear, in the pacification of the East; during his life he met with nothing but troubles and disappointments, which were aggravated by wretched health; and shortly before his death he cried, " For my sins I seem to succeed in nothing." His letters are full of his bodily troubles. " It is the scourge of the Lord that goes on increasing my pains according to my deserts; I have had illness upon illness, so that now even a child may see that this shell of mine must certainly fail, unless perhaps God's mercy vouchsafe me in his long-suffering time for repentance, and now, as often before, extricate me from

196

ST. BASIL. THE GREAT · 197

ills beyond all human cure." [1] And in the following letter, " For a whole month I have been treated by hot natural springs; but as the saying is, ' Warmth is no good to the dead.' " In the next he has had fever for fifty days, and his old plague, the liver, has held him on the confines of life and death. For nine years, in this deplorable state of health, with enemies besetting him on all sides both in Church and State, he defied success-fully the Imperial Government; carried out immense practical reforms; wrote theological treatises of great excellence; and paved the way for the reunion of the East. And only when he was gone was his true greatness discovered. After generations have known him as St. Basil the Great, while Theodoret called him " the light not only of Cappadocia, but of the world." And the Council of Chalcedon (450) called him " the greatest of the Fathers."

The map of Asia Minor shows that Cappadocia was its most Eastern Central Province; and Basil was to start with essentially an Eastern, grave, proud, ascetic. But his Orientalism was modified by an Athenian education. The gravity of the Eastern was tempered by the politeness of the Greek. [2] His Eastern pride in his bearing towards the world was also tempered by a true Christian humility, amounting to self-abasement. He cried out for love and affection; yet there was something austere about him, which seems to have wounded his friends, and made him difficult to get on with. He was profoundly sensitive, yet his practical disposition could not sympathize with the same quality in others. He had also, in spite of his gravity, a keen sense of humour. " Who," said his friend Gregory, " could tell a story with more wit ? Who could jest so playfully ? "

Fialon points out that in his Athenian education he had acquired the Greek love of his own city. The affairs of the Empire were of little importance to him,

[1] Letter 136.   [2] Fialon, *Étude littéraire sur S. Basile*, p. 78.

compared with the welfare and interests of Cæsarea.
Somewhat analogous to this was his attitude towards
the West. As an Eastern by birth, he was full of zeal
for the peace of the East. "Hitherto," he writes,[1] "I
have been unable to give any adequate practical proof
of my earnest desire to pacify the Churches of the Lord.
But from my heart I affirm that I have so great a longing,
that I would gladly give even my life, if thereby the
flame of hatred, kindled by the evil one, could be
assuaged."   And to this end, he always counsels patience
and toleration. "Not that I think it is our absolute
duty to cut ourselves off from those who do not accept
the Faith, but rather to regard them with the old law
of love, and to write to them with one consent, giving
them all exhortation with pity, and to propose to them
the Faith of the Fathers, and to invite them to union. . . .
If they obey you this will be best; if not, recognize the
real author of the war, and write me no more letters of
reconciliation." Yet when the West, and especially
Rome, would not do his bidding, notably in the question
of the schism of Antioch, he showed very little toleration.
His Athenian education gave him very little consideration for the Latins; for while the Latins looked on all
the world as barbarians, except the Greeks and themselves, the Greeks excepted only themselves. Basil
apparently knew no Latin; it is doubtful also whether
he knew Hebrew. But in Greek literature and philosophy he was thoroughly at home. His letters abound
with apt quotations, especially from Homer; he never,
however, alludes to Pagan deities in the conventional
literary fashion of later times—the Muses for instance;
he seemed to think it was too near Pagan days to do so
without danger.

Basil, Gregory of Nazianzus, his most intimate friend
and ardent admirer, and Gregory of Nyssa, his own
brother, are known as the three Cappadocians, forming

[1] Letter 128.

together the Cappadocian school, and their lives are much intertwined. The birthplace of Basil is a little uncertain. His father, also a Basil, a Christian and rhetorician, had property near Neo-Cæsarea, the capital of Pontus, the province with a seaboard due north of Cappadocia. But when Basil was ready to go out into the world, he was sent first to Cæsarea as being his birthplace. Probably, therefore, his father had property there as well. His early education he received from his grandmother, Macrina, who taught him the faith as she had received it from Gregory Thaumaturgus, at first the disciple of Origen, and afterwards Bishop of Neo-Cæsarea. As a young man he first studied at Cæsarea, then at Constantinople; and finally in 350, when he was twenty-one, he proceeded to the University of Athens. Basil remained there for seven years—till 357, when he returned to Cæsarea to practice at the Bar. At Cæsarea and Athens Gregory of Nazianzus was his constant companion, and at Athens Gregory protected him as a freshman. But another companion of both, and presumably friend, though Gregory from the first cordially distrusted him, was Julian, afterwards known as "the Apostate."

It is recorded of the two future Fathers that at Athens the only public places they frequented were the lecture-room and the Church. On Basil's return, however, to Cæsarea, he seems to have caused anxiety to his sister, who was called Macrina after her grandmother, on account of his worldliness and vanity. Becoming ashamed of himself, he carefully studied the Gospel, found an attraction in the monastic life, and in consequence retired to Pontus. "I awoke," he writes, ". as from deep sleep, and cast my eyes on that admirable light of the truth, the Gospel. Then I saw the vanity of the wisdom of the princes of this world, who toil without result. Long I wept over the misery of my life, and prayed that a hand should come and lead me, and teach me the lessons of piety. Then when I had read the Gospel, and learned that the best way of arriving at piety was to sell my goods and give them to the poor, and to be no longer anxious about this life, nor allow my soul to be distracted by any sympathy for earthly things, I wanted to find a brother who had chosen that path, that we might pass through the short agitations of life together." [1]

By this time monasticism had spread very widely through the East. In the district of Nitria in the deserts of Egypt alone, the monks numbered 5000; and in the whole of Egypt there were computed to be 76,000 monks and 27,700 nuns. In Asia Minor also communities were to be found in most provinces. Their influence was on the whole a good one, and their chief utility lay in keeping up a supply of clergy, and in acting as missionary centres in the outlying country districts. " They spread," says Milman, " a gradually increasing belt of Christian worship and were a quiet but successful aggression on the lurking Paganism." [2] For Paganism (as the word implies) lingered on in the country long after it had been formally ejected from the great cities. Besides this, the monastic system was constantly reorganizing itself by the establishment of off-shoots in which " the bond of aggregation was the common religious fervour," so that " the system was continually being remodelled, and reverting to its original purity." And again, from the earliest times, a certain influence was exercised by monks on literature. Basil and Gregory, for instance, during their retreat in Pontus, applied themselves to producing that selection from the works of Origen, which they called the Philocalia. At the root, however, of Monasticism lay a certain infection from Gnosticism; a feeling that there was inherent evil in matter, and that Christians must try to rid themselves of this, and elevate the soul into an

---

[1] Letter 223.   [2] *History of Christianity*, III. 195.

abstract state of close communion with God, and isolation from the world. The general celibacy of the clergy was probably a result of Monasticism, though neither Basil nor even Augustine insisted on it. The life of seclusion and contemplation practised by many communities had a tendency towards morbidity, ferocity sometimes, and strange heresies, such as Anthropomorphism. But Basil's conception of it was free from these tendencies, for with him prayer and work went hand in hand. When he fixed his retreat at Annesi, near the family property in Pontus, he described to Gregory his delight in the lovely scenery,[1] and begged him to come out and join him, while he conceived and carried out grand projects for improving the country. The monastic life for him consisted on one side of psalmodies, vigils, Bible-reading: on the other, stone-heaving, wood-drawing, planting and draining. Gregory, unable to join him at first through family ties, came later, and planted a tree to commemorate his visit. The attitude of Gregory towards Basil at this time is amusing. Awe and admiration of his friend, coupled with a mild protest against being expected to live up to his exalted standard. His letters after his return recall the labour of pushing carts uphill, and how he would have had no dinner, if Basil's mother had not fed him occasionally. Gregory was entirely human; Basil a little above the ordinary level of humanity. In 362 Basil returned to Cæsarea to attend the death-bed of the Bishop, Dianius, who had ordained him deacon and whom Basil loved; but from whom he had regretfully withdrawn, owing to his heresy; although Dianius confessed the Homo-ousion at the end.

Before leaving this subject, it must be noted that Basil was opposed to the solitary life, and though he founded many Monasteries in Pontus, he never encouraged it. "How can one be last," he said, "if he is

[1] Letter 14.

alone? Whose feet can he wash?" Also though he
is said to have sold all his goods to feed the poor, and
to have done so again, when he inherited property at
his mother's death, it is probable that he retained the
administration of the funds in his own hands. For he
was essentially practical. Indeed he was especially so
in regard to his Monasteries. Life vows, once entered
into, were binding, but they were not to be taken too
young, or without the most careful preparation. And
although he approved under certain circumstances of
education by monks, he encouraged secular learning and
the training of the Universities in most cases.[1] And so
did the Gregories.

Eusebius, at the time only a catechumen, was elected
to succeed Dianius at Cæsarea, and conscious of his
inexperience, asked Basil to help him. He in consequence remained some time at Cæsarea, and became
at once the leading personality of that Church. During
this period he wrote the *Hexameron;* and every day
he preached sermons suitable alike for the simple and
the wise, the workpeople crowding in the early morning
to church to hear him. The jealousy of Eusebius caused
him again to retire to Pontus, whereupon the Bishop's
troubles recommenced. After many years' interval
among his monks, during three of which Gregory was his
companion, the intervention of the latter brought about
a reconciliation with Eusebius, and again (in 368) Basil
resumed his work in Cæsarea, where he exercised an
immense influence over Christians, Jews and Pagans
alike, by all of whom he was beloved. During a famine
he displayed his great practical ability, by preventing a
corner in wheat, and by his skill in organizing the
distribution of provisions.

In 370, on the death of Eusebius, Basil was his obvious
successor. But he did not succeed without strong
opposition from the laxer among the clergy, the worldly

[1] See Homily 34.

among the laity, and from some who, on account of his
tolerant spirit, suspected his orthodoxy.　It was at this
time that the first cloud passed over the friendship of
Basil and Gregory.　Basil, knowing that he was essential
to the Catholic cause, desired Gregory's help in securing
the See; but wrote him a somewhat disingenuous letter,
asking him to visit him on account of his illness.　When
Gregory discovered the facts, he was annoyed, and
refused to come.　The election was, however, secured
through the organization of Eusebius of Samosata, who
always remained Basil's true friend, and of Gregory's
father, who was at that time Bishop of Nazianzus, and
was brought to Cæsarea in a litter to vote, though ninety
years of age.　The younger Gregory worked for the
election in the background.

　The constructive work of Basil during his episcopate,
and in spite of ill-health and opposition, was splendid.
The Church he found full of scandals; laxity in ordina-
tions [1] and simony were the worst.　Any one could be
a priest; in one case he found a slave bishop; in another
a bishop without a flock.　Yet before his death the
clergy of Cæsarea were of such a high standard, that
other bishops used to send for them to assist in the
work of their own dioceses.　In the State Basil was
confronted with all the evils resulting from extremes
of wealth and poverty; gambling and usury on one side,
distress on the other.　To relieve distress he founded
hospitals, even a leper hospital; and his Christian
humility is said to have shown itself in kissing the lepers.
But his great achievement was the Ptocho-tropheion,
called sometimes the New Town, and after his death
the Basileiad, which was a sort of combination of hospital
and workhouse, providing not only treatment for all
diseases, but work for the unemployed, with a church
and a clergy-house.

　In Basil's contest with the Arian Emperor, Valens, and

---

[1] Letters 53 and 54.

also with his emissary, the prefect Modestus, are the most vivid dramatic scenes in his life. Valens was determined to reduce Cappadocia to the Arian level, and demanded from Basil the admission of Arians to communion. To enforce this he sent Modestus, who summoned Basil before his tribunal, first tried to bribe him, and then proceeded to threaten him with confiscation, torture, death. As for confiscation, Basil replied that he owned nothing but a cloak and a few books; as for torture, Modestus had threatened to tear out his liver, and Basil said there was nothing gave him more trouble; as for death, he would gladly welcome it. When Modestus complained that he was not used to such replies, Basil retorted that perhaps he had never met a real Bishop before. So Modestus reported him to Valens as hopeless: " We have been worsted, sir, by the prelate of this Church. He is superior to threats, invincible in argument, uninfluenced by persuasion. We must make trial on some feebler character."[1] He conceived a great respect for him, and ultimately became his friend and correspondent.[2] Then Valens came himself, having first sent an advance guard of Arian Bishops; to whom Basil refused communion. On the Epiphany, Valens came to the church. The sea of worshippers, the weird chanting, " the unearthly majesty of the scene, Basil, erect as a column, celebrating (he would be behind the Altar and facing the people), the white-robed ministers in the sanctuary, overawed the Emperor." When he approached the Altar with his offering, and nobody came forward to receive it, Valens fainted. Basil himself stretched out his hand and accepted the offering, but of course communion was refused. Valens, however, like Modestus, conceived a great respect for Basil; was received by him to a theological discussion " behind the veil "; but under

[1] Gregory's *Oration on Basil*, p. 51.
[2] Letters 104, 110, 118, 279–81.

bad advice, decreed his exile. However, the Emperor's child fell ill; Basil prayed over it, and it recovered. Basil had made it a condition that he should baptize the child, but an Arian was allowed to do so instead, and the child died. Again Valens was on the point of exiling Basil; but the pen he was using to sign the warrant split, and Valens, taking it as an omen, reversed his decision, and decided to let Basil alone.

Already, previous to this, Basil had withstood another Emperor, Julian. Remembering their old acquaintanceship at Athens, this Emperor invited Basil to visit him. Upon his deferring his visit from time to time and finally declining it, Julian became incensed, and ordered him to contribute a thousand pounds of gold towards one of his expeditions. This is a specimen of the way Basil dared to address the Cæsar: [1] " Your Serene Highness did not find out for the first time yesterday that I do not live in the midst of superabundant wealth. My property amounts to so much, that I shall really not have enough to eat as much as I should like to-day. Under my roof the art of cookery is dead. My servant's knife never touches blood. Our most important viands are leaves of herbs, with very coarse bread and sour wine. . . . It is a serious thing for a private person like me to speak to an Emperor. It will be more serious for you to speak to God." The attitude of Basil to Julian, Modestus and Valens, shows the enormous progress that the Church had made in the sixty years since the Edict of Milan. Bishops could now say these things to the ruling powers with impunity.

Great annoyance was caused to Basil by the ill-will of many of the neighbouring bishops, especially during the first few years. Even his uncle, Gregory, was disloyal to him; and his brother Gregory, afterwards of Nyssa, aggravated matters by forging, with the best intentions, a letter from the uncle making peace. Gregory of

[1] Letter 41.

Nyssa, though Basil called him God-beloved, and recognized his fine intellect, was pronounced by his brother to be " really too silly for a Christian."

The people of Cæsarea, however, were from the first devoted to him, and when he resisted the Vicar of Pontus in an attempt to force an undesirable marriage on a Cæsarean lady, and the Vicar tried to arrest him, the whole population rose, and only by Basil's mediation was this imperial officer rescued from the mob.

Another sore trial to Basil was the partition of Cappadocia into two provinces. The result, whether intended by Valens or not, was that the bishop of the new capital claimed to be metropolitan of the new province, so that not only all the bishops on that side of the frontier were exempted from Basil's influence, but a bad influence was set up on ground which Basil had sown. To counteract this he founded new sees on the frontier, and to one of them, Sasima, he sent Gregory of Nazianzus, much to his indignation. It seems to have been a small town in a wild country, a sort of posting station in the wilderness, with nothing but a shifting population. It was dreary work, and work for which Gregory was quite unfitted, and it left a lasting estrangement between the friends. A rival bishop was soon appointed by the new metropolitan, and Gregory threw up the work and retired to Nazianzus.

The chief remaining feature of Basil's Episcopate was his appeal for help to Rome and the Western bishops; but his relation to the West will presently be treated separately. After nine years of most arduous and disheartening work, and thoroughly broken health, he died in 379 at the age of fifty, the whole population, Christians, Jews and Pagans alike, following him to the grave.

" No author's writings," says Dupin in his *Bibliothèque des auteurs ecclésiastiques*,[1] " makes a stronger impression

---

[1] II. 731.

than Basil's. He describes things so vividly, he explains his arguments with so much force, he pushes them so vigorously, he draws such horrible pictures of vice and exhorts so persuasively to virtue, his instruction is so ample and profitable, that it is impossible to read his works, without conceiving a love of virtue and a hatred of vice. . . . His expressions are sublime, his style is elegant, neat and convincing. His discourse seems always natural and unaffected. He persuades so pleasantly, he explains things so clearly, he seems to present things in so reasonable a light, that he may be considered as a model to approach Demosthenes and the best orators of antiquity." Yet it can hardly be said that his writings mark any new point of departure in Christian thought. It is true that his treatise on the Spirit deals in a masterly way with a subject which had not previously been brought into controversy; but many of his contemporaries dealt with it as well. His great advantages were his lucidity, his originality, and his scientific training. Fialon says [1] that " the originality of Basil's theology lies in a firm alliance between Greek philosophy and Christian theology. He invented nothing. He used all the philosophers and doctors who preceded him; yet he resembled none. His doctrine comes entirely from Plato, Aristotle, Plotinus, Origen, Athanasius; yet it is entirely personal. He belongs to no school : rather he founds a school of his own. He is in fact an eclectic, who knows how to combine a wise independence of thought with an intelligent respect for tradition. He is at once a philosopher and a theologian."

That Basil was much influenced by Plato may be seen from the similitude of argument and expressions used by both. A short American treatise, *The Influence of Plato on St. Basil*, by Theodore Leslie Shear (Baltimore, 1906), goes very minutely into this subject, but it

---

[1] *Étude littéraire sur S. Basile*, p. 478.

is rather a work for advanced scholars. We may cite,
however, a few points as examples. " Man," said
Basil, " was made upright, that he might look up to
Heaven." This is directly taken from *Timœus* 90.
Again his view of the relation of the soul to the body,
and his remarks on voluntary and involuntary wrong-
doing are quite Platonic : while the *Hexameron* shows
strong points of similarity with Plato's cosmogony in the
Timœus. But he draws equally on Aristotle, Homer,
and Plutarch : and on one occasion paraphrased most
of Plutarch's Essay on Debt.

His leading works are the *Against Eunomius*, which
deals with the main Arian points; the *Holy Spirit*, and
the *Hexameron*, or account of the Six Days of Creation.
These are all that St. Jerome thought worthy of mention.
In addition to these, however, there are 44 homilies;
some on the Psalms, some on the Monastic Life, including
the 55 Regulæ fusius tractatæ, and the 313 Regulæ
brevius tractatæ, and others on Christian duty and
discipline generally. But beyond all these are Basil's
wonderful letters, in all about 350, from which may be
gathered his life, his character, and his opinions.

These letters were evidently intended, according to
the fashion of the day, for publicity and general reading.
They are on all sorts of subjects. The following extracts
are from some of the most interesting :—

Letter VI. To a bereaved Mother. "To a soul
distressed by heavy sorrow words offered in the moment
of agony, even though they bring much comfort, seem
out of place. . . . I know what a mother's heart is. . . .
The Lord is now making trial of your love, . . . do not
measure your loss by itself; if you do, it will seem
intolerable. If you take all human affairs into account,
you will find some comfort is to be derived from
them."

Letter XIV contains the famous description of nature
which Basil wrote to Gregory from his retreat in Pontus.

Letter XVI protests against man's attempt to explain the ineffable, and employs an argument from nature.

"The man who glories in his knowledge about real existence ought meanwhile to describe to us the nature of the ant. After that he may give us a similar physiological account of the Power that transcends all human intelligence. But if his knowledge has not yet been able to apprehend the nature of the insignificant ant, how can he boast himself able to form a conception of the power of the incomprehensible God?"

Letter XXV gives an example of the gentle way in which Basil reasoned with his slanderers.

"They all agree that you, a man very dear to me, do not mention me in very pleasant terms, nor yet in such as your character would lead me to expect. . . . You would relieve me from my difficulty, if you would tell me plainly what has stirred you to be thus offended with me."

Letters XL and XLI are from the correspondence between Basil and Julian already referred to.

Letter XC is his appeal to the Western Bishops to come to the aid of the Catholic East, and gives a graphic picture of the distracted state of the Eastern Church.

" The doctrines of the Fathers are despised; apostolic traditions are set at nought; the devices of innovators are in vogue. Men are rather contrivers of cunning systems than theologians. The wisdom of this world wins the highest prizes, and has rejected the glory of the Cross. . . . Houses of prayer have none to assemble in them. Desert places are full of lamenting crowds."

When no help came from them, or even from Pope Damasus of Rome, whom he had reminded of the former charities of Rome to distant Christians, his wrath found expression in Letter CCXXXIX—

"What help can come to us from the frown [1] of the West? Men who don't know the truth, nor wish to

_____
[1] Or " superciliousness."

learn it, but are prejudiced by false impressions, are doing now as they did in the case of Marcellus, when they quarrelled with men who told them the truth, and by their own action strengthened the cause of heresy. I should like to have written to their Coryphæus, etc."

The Coryphæus is the Bishop of Rome! The word Coryphæus, however, is not apparently in itself contemptuous, as St. Chrysostom calls St. Peter the Coryphæus of the Apostles.[1]

Letter XCIII encourages frequent Communion, Basil's own habit being to communicate four times a week and on Saints' days. In case of need he allows the Communion to be taken by any one privately from the reserved elements.

In Letter CV, to two Deaconesses occurs a definition of the Trinity—

" Do not abandon this deposit; the Father, the origin of all, the Son only-begotten, begotten of Him; Very God; Perfect of Perfect; living image, showing the whole Father as Himself: the Holy Ghost having His subsistence of God, the Fount of Holiness, Power that gives Life, Grace that makes perfect, through whom man is adopted, and the mortal made immortal, conjoined with Father and Son in all things, in glory and eternity, in power and kingdom, in sovereignty and Godhead, as is testified by the tradition of the baptism of salvation. But all who maintain that either Son or Spirit is a creature, or absolutely reduce the Spirit to ministerial or servile rank, are far from the truth."

From Letter CXIII to CXXVII are graphic descriptions of the misery of the Church, and in the first he says it is " like an old coat, which is always being torn and can never be restored to its first strength."

Letter CLV shows his veneration of Relics. He understands there has been some persecution in Scythia and asks for some relics of the martyrs.

[1] Homily on St. Matthew.

Letter CLX is interesting at the present day, as dealing with the marriage of a deceased wife's sister. He quotes Lev. xviii. 6 : " None of you shall approach to any one that is near of kin to him, to uncover their nakedness;" and argues that the relation of a sister-in-law is equivalent to a blood-relationship.

Letter CLXIX gives an account of the extraordinary irregularity of a deacon, Glycerius, who placed himself at the head of a company of dancing virgins, and caused a notorious scandal.

Letters CLXXXVIII, CXCIX, CCXVII, are the so-called Canonical Letters. They were written to Amphilochius, his favourite pupil, whom he had made Bishop of Iconium, and contain close advice on the degrees of sin. They are probably the earliest examples of casuistry.

In Letter CCLXI he raises a question, which is taken as an argument against the Immaculate Conception.

" If the God-bearing flesh was not ordained to be assumed of the lump of Adam, what need was there of the Blessed Virgin ? "

Towards the close of the series will be found a characteristic correspondence with his old master at Constantinople, Libanius the sophist; which, if genuine, though this is questioned, reveals Basil as the cultivated man of the world on the most friendly terms with the pagan philosopher, to whom he introduced many pupils.

In spite of his familiarity with heathen philosophy and the free way in which he made use of it, attributing, for example, much of the wisdom of Moses and Daniel to their Egyptian and Chaldec learning, and advising young men not to be content with monkish teaching, but to attend also one of the Universities, Scripture was with him always paramount. If Science contradicted Scripture, then Science erred. Revelation came first; reason was given us to help us to understand revelation.

Yet apart from Scripture, he distinctly recognized

tradition. In the *De Spiritu* (27) he says : " Of the beliefs and practices, whether generally accepted or universally enjoined, which are preserved in the Church, some we possess derived from written teaching. Others we have received delivered to us " in a mystery " by the traditions of the Apostles : *and both of these in relation to true religion have equal force."* It is true that his illustrations of this deal chiefly with practice, yet he distinctly includes beliefs; and he adds (67) : " Of the rest I say nothing; but of the very confession of our faith in Father, Son and Holy Ghost, where is the written source ? "

When he comes to deal with the great mystery of the Trinity there is the usual reluctance to define, which is common to all the Fathers.

" If I laid down that all things were capable of being grasped by our knowledge, I might be ashamed to confess my ignorance. . . . The *peace* of God passes all understanding, yet Eunomius will not allow that the very substance of God is beyond all understanding and knowledge of men.[1]

" It is not in the invention of new names that our salvation lies, but in the sane confession of the Divinity in whom we believed." [2]

Theology with St. Basil, as Science had been with Plato, was an aspiration towards God, and the first thing requisite was the purification of the soul. The soul, when purified, will see God within itself in the conscience; the soul is, in fact, a miniature world ruled over, as the universe is, by God. But the soul will also see God in the visible world. No one better understood the beauties of both animal and inanimate nature than Basil, or delighted more in the works of creation. St. Gregory of Nazianzus said of the *Hexameron,* " Whenever I take his *Hexameron* in hand and quote its words, I am brought face to face with my Creator; I begin to

---

[1] Eunom. 3. 6.   [2] Letter 175.

understand the method of creation; I feel more awe than ever before, when I looked at God's work with my own eyes."[1]

The instruments of the soul's aspiration are Reason and Faith. Reason must be educated, yet by itself it can never find God. It is a great undertaking, according to Basil, to venture to speak of God, because the subject is far beyond our intelligence, and we have not even words in which to express our thoughts. But Revelation comes to the aid of Reason in the Scripture, which is in its entirety inspired by God and composed by the Holy Spirit. Revelation thus illuminates the reason.

The functions of the Three Persons of the Trinity are thus conceived by Basil;[2] the Father wills; the Son conceives and executes; the Holy Ghost vivifies.

In the books against Eunomius he argues the whole Arian question as regards the Son, and finally discusses separately the various texts on which his opponents relied. It may be useful to recall them.

"Then shall the Son also be made subject unto Him that put all things under Him; that God may be all in all" (1 Cor. xv. 28).

"My Father is greater than I" (St. John xiv. 28).

"Of that day and hour knoweth none, not even the Son" (St. Mark xiii. 32).

"Let this cup pass from Me" (St. Matt. xxvi. 39).

"I live by the Father" (St. John vi. 57).

"The Son can do nothing by Himself" (St. John v. 19).

"I am the true vine, my Father is the husbandman" (St. John xv. 1).

"Why callest thou me good? There is none good save One, that is God" (St. Mark x. 18).

"Father, glorify Thy Son" (St. John xvii. 1).

"The first-born of every *creature*" (Col. i. 15).

"The Lord *created* Me" (Prov. viii. 22. Septuagint translation).

[1] Or. 53. 67.   [2] Fialon, *Étude littéraire sur S. Basile*, p. 149.

" That they may know Thee, the only true God "
(St. John xviii. 8).

" Is not Mine to give " (St. Matt. xx. 23).

The subject of the Holy Spirit was one which Basil
wished to refrain from discussing. It was only now
becoming a prominent subject of controversy, though
it was the natural outcome of the Arian position. Basil
seemed to think it would be better, in the prominent
position which he held, to steer clear of this new polemic :
and he therefore made an arrangement with Gregory to
deal with it, while he concentrated his own energy on
teaching the Eternity of the Son.

Macedonius, a brutal persecutor of the Catholics, had
been deposed from the See of Constantinople by the
extreme party for his supposed moderate views (the
ostensible cause was his removal of Constantine's remains
from a church which was falling, without Constantius'
leave); yet he taught plainly that the Holy Ghost was
a creature. This heresy was therefore known as the
Macedonian, though the sect that sprang out of it was
generally known as the Marathonian, after Marathonius
of Nicomedia. They were a grave, pure and ascetic
body; but of course it was necessary to condemn their
view. Basil's reticence in public, though he defined
his view carefully in his correspondence, caused a sus-
picion of his orthodoxy; and besides, he had unusual
ways of saying the doxology, such as " Glory be to the
Father through the Son and in the Holy Ghost." His
protégé, Amphilochius, entreated him to clear up any
doubt, by publishing his views in a treatise, and he
accordingly did so in 374. It was his last work and
perhaps the most famous. The first eight chapters are
a defence of the prepositions he used in the Doxology,
and he afterwards treats the whole question very fully.
The leading argument is that all operations and relations
most exclusively divine are ascribed to the Spirit. If
God is good, the Spirit is good by His very Nature. If

the Son is a Paraclete, He sends the Spirit to be so too.
If Christ is our one Master, the Spirit comes to teach
us all things. If the Father and Son distribute their
gifts, so does the Spirit. The work of the Spirit is placed
side by side with that of the Father and Son by St.
Paul (1 Cor. xii.) when he speaks of " diversities of gifts,
but the same Spirit." And again, " He that raised
Christ from the dead shall also quicken your mortal
bodies by His Spirit that dwelleth in you " (Rom. viii. 11).
The Father quickens all things; the Son promises eternal
life; the Spirit quickens your bodies. Can He, by
whom God dwells in us, be Himself other than God?
How can the giver of renewal, who changes corruption
into incorruption, who makes of us a new creature that
abides for ever, be other than Very God?

The schism at Antioch was an important event in
Church History in Basil's time, owing to the unusual
features which it introduced, and also to the effect it
had of emphasizing the difference between the Eastern
and Western Churches. Some account of it falls naturally into a chapter on St. Basil, owing to the strong
support he gave to the side least popular at Rome, and
the independent attitude that he took up against the
Pope. Basil had apparently no knowledge of any
doctrinal claim on Rome's part to rule the Church at
large. " He desired," as Fialon puts it, " the same
independent union for spiritual matters between East
and West, which since Constantine had existed in politics.
The West and East were in his eyes two brothers, whose
rights were equal, neither owning supremacy nor the
rights of an elder. Basil recognized no necessity for a
great central power to hold the Church together, though
the Western Churches all did. The Greeks indeed have
never completely consented to this sacrifice or renounced
their autonomy. They recognized nothing as paramount
except a General Council. The decrees of Nicæa bound
Basil absolutely."

In 327 Eustathius, Catholic Bishop of Antioch, had been deposed on a charge of Sabellianism. Two Arians followed him; then Eudoxius, who was removed to Constantinople in 361, and succeeded by St. Meletius. The early associations of Meletius were distinctly Arian, and his consecrators were unorthodox. But from the first as Bishop, he taught the full Catholic faith, and was therefore almost immediately exiled. The bulk of the Church stood by him, but the extremists formed themselves into a separate party, and were known as Eustathians. At their head was Paulinus, a presbyter. In 362, a Council at Alexandria sent a commission to Antioch to conciliate the parties; but the hot-headed Lucifer of Cagliari anticipated it, and consecrated Paulinus; although he led a very small section of the community. In 375 Rome formally acknowledged Paulinus as the rightful Bishop: but all the great Eastern Bishops recognized Meletius. The Pope later even described Meletius and his party as Arians. Basil was the leading defender of Meletius against Rome, and Bossuet [1] says, " It is clear that the confirming of heresy was roundly and flatly, without any excuse, without any attempt to modify, imputed by Basil to decrees of two Roman pontiffs de fide." Meletius was elected president of the Second Œcumenical Council by both the Gregories, Cyril of Jerusalem, Amphilochius, and a crowd of Eastern Saints. His memory was held in the highest honour by the whole Church of the East, and in later days he found a place in the Roman Martyrology; yet it is most probable that he died out of communion with the Roman Church. The case is fully argued in Puller's *Primitive Saints and the See of Rome*, and replied to in Rivington's *Primitive Church and the See of Peter.* Whether Meletius really died out of communion with Rome or not, the fact must surely remain, that the whole Eastern Church, including some of her greatest Saints, were in violent

[1] *Gallia Orthodoxa*, ch. lxiii.

opposition to Rome in the matter, and that none of them recognized any right in Rome to overrule their own views.

Anglicans have sometimes claimed that Basil's views were in all points their own, except as regards the Invocation of Saints. The main grounds for this claim are apparently his independence of Rome, and a particular passage on the Sacrament: " On eating His Flesh and drinking His blood, being made through His Incarnate and Visible Life partakers of His word and wisdom. For all His mystic sojourn among us He called His Flesh and Blood, and set forth the teaching, consisting of practical science, of physics and theology, whereby our soul is nourished, and is meanwhile trained for the contemplation of actual realities. This is perhaps the intended meaning of what He says." [1]

The reader will judge whether this cursory remark may be taken as an authoritative exposition of sacramental doctrine; but at any rate the last sentence shows that teachers of that time looked on varieties of explanation as legitimate and admissible. It is in this last respect that Anglicans would claim him as an authority.

On the Invocation of Saints he is perfectly explicit. In Letter CCCLX he says, " I acknowledge also the holy Apostles, prophets and martyrs: and I invoke them to supplication to God; that through them, that is through their mediation, the Merciful God may be propitious to me, and that a ransom may be made and given me for my sins. Wherefore also I honour and kiss the features of their images, inasmuch as they have been handed down from the holy Apostles, and are not forbidden, but are in all our churches."

There still remain one or two minor points to notice about St. Basil.

It is probably that confession to a priest, instead of

---

[1] Letter 8.

public confession, may have been stimulated by Basil's rule for his monks, that every thought of the heart should be divulged in confession, but only to those who were properly appointed.

As regards Eternal Punishment, Basil held that it would certainly be eternal, but that the few and many stripes had relation not to duration but quality. To some, the punishment, though eternal, might be excessively mild.[1]

Re-baptism of those who had been baptized by heretics, Basil would have liked to enforce, but 'he conformed to the general rule; except in the case of the Marcionites, because they believed in the essential evil of matter.

In the Homily (6) on Fasting occurs rather an interesting passage : " It is not possible without fasting to dare to approach the sacred rites. Take care, however, that you do not suppose fasting to consist merely in. abstinence from food. For the true fasting is estrangement from evil." On the question of fasting, Basil was always practical, and avoided ostentation, though all his life he was ascetic. It is told of him that, to avoid ostentation, he only wore his hair-shirt at night.

The so-called Liturgy of St. Basil, " The Divine Liturgy of our Father among the Saints, Basil the Great," is still in occasional use in the Greek Church. But as a whole family of liturgies springs from St. Basil's, it is difficult to say how much of this is the original work of Basil himself, although in its general lines it probably is founded on his use.

[1] *Reg. fus. tract.,* p. 267.

CHAPTER XV

(About 326–391.   Patriarch of Constantinople 379–381)

NEITHER of the two Gregories, of Nazianzus or of Nyssa, were distinguished like Basil for practical ability or as ecclesiastical statesmen. The subject of this chapter was of a retiring disposition, and would have preferred to remain quietly at Nazianzus, of which his father was for many years Bishop : even the priesthood was forced upon him against his wish. Yet for two years of his life he occupied an exceedingly prominent position as Archbishop of Constantinople, presiding for a short time over the Second Œcumenical Council; and during that period he was mainly instrumental in reviving Catholicism in the Eastern capital. This he did, not by skill in organizing or administration, but by the flood of eloquence which he untiringly poured forth in defence of the doctrine of the Trinity. The Roman breviary calls him " the keenest champion of the Consubstantiality of the Son " (in other words, of the Homo-ousion); and adds that " while no one surpassed him in virtue (laude vitæ), so he easily surpassed all others in the solidity of his reasoning (gravitate orationis)." He acquired the title of *the* Theologian, which must be understood less in a general sense, than as " defender of the Godhead of the Word ": while De Broglie says of him,[1] " in a few hours and a few pages Gregory summed up and closed the controversy of a whole century." In fact, he fixed permanently the lines on which the defence of the

[1] *L'Eglise et l'Empire,* V. p. 385.

doctrine was hereafter to be made. Sometimes he has even shared with St. John the title " Divine."

In many respects he was the opposite of Basil, whom he so intensely admired. In his personal appearance he is described as " short, meagre, sickly, prematurely old (this was when he first appeared at Constantinople), with an aspect of habitual melancholy, with one eye gone, a scar on his face, stooping shoulders, downcast look, and shabby clothes." Again their literary style has been contrasted. In a work published anonymously at Lille in 1887, we read that both have eloquence, culture (*politesse*), fine and delicate thought; but Basil is more serious, Gregory more joyous and lively; the former tried to persuade, the latter to please. Basil was majestic and tranquil; Gregory had more movement and fire. Basil liked gravity, and shrank from raillery; Gregory made raillery innocent and subservient to virtue; Basil commanded more respect, Gregory more love.

The correspondence between Basil and Gregory in connection with the visit of the latter to Pontus shows something of the pleasant raillery of Gregory:[1] his chaff, for instance, of Basil, after his return, about the starvation that would have ensued, had not Basil's mother come to the rescue. But this letter was followed by a graver one, assuring his friend of the happiness he had derived from his monastic experience. For Gregory, from the time of his baptism, was always ascetic; only he practised his asceticism in the world and not in seclusion.

The chief features of his life must be rapidly sketched, as, except for those two grand years in Constantinople, it was not an eventful one, and something of it has already been seen in the last chapter. He was the son of Gregory, Bishop of Nazianzus, a small town in that part of Cappadocia which was cut off by Valens from Cappadocia proper, and Nonna. Nonna, to whom he owed much of

----

[1] See chapter on St. Basil.

his religious training, had converted her husband, and it is supposed that Gregory was born after his father became a bishop, or at any rate a priest. Roman Catholic writers have denied this, but it does not seem to us of very much consequence, as celibacy had not been enforced on the clergy at that date. The date of his birth is uncertain, but as it seems likely that he was a little older than Basil, we may fix it about 326. He was studying with Basil at Cæsarea; but when Basil left for Constantinople, Gregory went to the other Cæsarea (in Palestine); then to Alexandria; finally meeting Basil again at Athens. Thus Gregory had the great advantage of both Alexandria and Athens; of the philosophical and metaphysical environment of the former, as well as the literary and rhetorical environment of the latter. Although outwardly he was wanting in the grace and culture of Basil, for he always remained rather a country-man, his intellectual attainments were of the highest order, and as an orator he has been compared to Demosthenes. Dupin calls him the greatest orator of his age, and St. Jerome came from Syria to Constantinople to hear him.

He seems to have remained at Athens twelve years—till he was thirty, and not to have been baptized till his return; but at his baptism he vowed to devote his life to God's service, and at once assisted his father; as a layman, in administering the diocese. In 361 his father, with the support of his congregation, coerced him into taking orders, a not uncommon practice at that time, and he at once fled to Pontus. But after three months he returned and accepted the situation, preaching his famous *Oration* (2) *on the Priesthood*, which was the foundation of St. Chrysostom's subsequent work in six books. In 374 his father, after successfully resisting Julian's embassy, died, and Gregory administered the diocese for a year, refusing the bishopric; after which he retired to Seleucia.

The unfortunate incident of the appointment of
Gregory to Sasima, which caused an estrangement
between him and Basil, has already been described.[1]
In a poem on his own life, he describes it as " a frightful
and detestable little village. Everywhere you meet
nothing but dust, noises, waggons, groans, petty officers,
chains, instruments of torture. The whole population
consists of foreigners and travellers. Such was my
Church of Sasima." In an indignant letter to Basil (48)
he writes, " Why should I fight for sucking pigs and
chickens, which after all were not my own, as if it were
a question of souls and canons? And why should we
rob the (new) metropolis of the illustrious Sasima? "
However, he was not there long; for the Bishop of the
new metropolis appointed a rival, and Gregory escaped.

In 379 he reluctantly accepted a call to Constantinople,
with a view to reviving the Catholicism of the great
city. For a great change had now come in the state.
Gratian, who had been associated in the West with
Valens, was Catholic, and soon became sole Emperor.
He shortly afterwards handed over the East to Theodosius, a Spaniard and also a Catholic. There was,
therefore, revived hope for the orthodox Faith.

For many years Constantinople had been handed over
to Arians, and the Catholics were now a mere remnant.
The city " had passed through the death of infidelity;
there was left but one last breath of life. He had come
to the city to defend the faith. What they needed was
solid teaching to save them from the spiders' webs of
subtleties in which they had been caught." [2] " The
great mystery was in danger of becoming a matter of
mincing technicalities (τεχνύδριον)." Gregory established himself in a small private house, which he turned
into a church, and called the Anastasia (the place of
resurrection); and from this point he gradually, in the
short space of two years, restored the ascendancy of

---

[1] Chapter on St. Basil.   [2] Poem XI.

Catholicism. In 380 Theodosius handed over to him all the Churches of the Metropolis, and he accepted, although reluctantly, the archbishopric. In his wonderful sermons he dwelt continually on the doctrine of the Trinity, the chief being known as the five theological orations. There was not much novelty in the arguments : his strength lay in his condensed and lucid exposition of them. They were, however, the model of future theologians, and were quoted extensively much later in the *De Orthodoxa Fide* of St. John of Damascus.

In 381 came the Council at Constantinople, called at the express desire of Theodosius ; which, contrary to the original intention, became afterwards known as the Second Œcumenical Council. Meletius of Antioch at first presided ; but he shortly afterwards died, and Gregory, whom the Council had now confirmed in his see, succeeded him. However, all sorts of difficulties arose, which caused him at last to retire altogether both from his see and the city ; and after spending two years at Nazianzus, the remainder of his life, eight years, was passed in retirement at Arianzus, or in the neighbourhood, till his death in 391.

At the second Œcumenical Council of Constantinople one hundred and fifty Eastern bishops were summoned to the capital, to pronounce on certain points of faith ; to confirm the rights of certain bishops, whose jurisdiction was disputed ; and to settle the affairs of Antioch. As the East claimed the right to settle its own affairs, no invitations were sent to the West, even to Rome, and no Western sees were represented. It came afterwards to be treated as Œcumenical, although the whole Church was not summoned (for that was not considered essential), because its creed, and much later its canons, were accepted by the whole Church. It happened that a great number of Saints were present, especially the two Gregories, Meletius, Cyril and Amphilochius, and it is remarkable that the President, St. Meletius, was not

recognized by Rome at all. The canons of this Council
were not accepted by Rome for a thousand years.

The main work of the Council was to bring the Nicene
Creed practically into its present form. The words
"God of God," however, did not appear; only "Very
God of Very God," which of course included them; and
in some MSS. the word "Holy" appears before
"Catholic Church." The entire third paragraph now
appeared for the first time; the controversy about the
Holy Ghost being the prominent question of the day.
The Procession was, of course, from the Father only.
The words "And the Son" first appeared in Spain, in
the following century, and soon extended to France;
but they were firmly resisted in Rome. In fact, in the
ninth century, two silver shields were put up in St.
Peter's, showing the Creed in Greek and Latin without
the words; until at last in 1014 Benedict VIII admitted
them under strong pressure from the western West.

There is some doubt whether the Second Council did
make the additions to the Creed, as the members certainly professed to adhere strictly to the Creed of Nicæa.
The third paragraph had, however, already crept into
various local creeds, and may have been included without
prejudice to the original creed. The Fourth Council
(Chalcedon) attributed the Creed to the Second; it is
possible that the additions were made at a supplementary
local Council held at Constantinople in the following
year.

To show how thoroughly recognized at this date was
the Intercession of the Saints, it is worthy of notice that
the bishops, in their letter to Theodosius, write "May
God by the prayers of the Saints show favour to the
world, that you may be strong and eminent in all good
things."

The Heresies denounced were those of the Eunomians;
the Semi-Arians or Pneumatomachi; Sabellians; Marcel-
lians; Photinians; Apollinarians. Of these the Euno-

mians were practically the successors of the Arians. Eunomius, made Bishop of Cyzicus near Constantinople in 360, succeeded Aetius in the leadership of the Anomæan party, and became so identified with it, that the word Arian became merged in Eunomian. Thus Basil and the Gregories write not against the Arians, but the Eunomians. The Semi-Arians are now known as Fighters against the Holy Ghost; the Godhead of the Son had been practically conceded by them in all its fullness. The Sabellians have already been repeatedly referred to. Marcellus was the friend of Athanasius who was often accused of Sabellianism, and of whom Athanasius said that he had narrowly escaped heresy. The Photinians accepted the views of Marcellus in a somewhat modified form. There remains then the Apollinarian heresy, which was the beginning of a new series of controversies, viz. on the Person of our Lord; not on the question of his Divinity, so much as His Humanity. Apollinarius, in his zeal for the Divinity, underrated the Humanity, arguing from the triple division of St. Paul into body, soul and spirit; he conceded to Christ a human body and soul, but in place of the human spirit he placed the Logos. The Word, he said, was made Flesh, but not Spirit. If so, Christ was not Perfect Man, but something between God and man; and therefore, according to the Catholics, the act of Atonement would be incomplete.

This Council was first recognized as Œcumenical by the Fourth Council (Chalcedon, A.D. 450), though not by the bishops of the West. In 609 Gregory the Great recognized it for its creed only.

The Canons it passed were of considerable interest.

The First confirmed the Nicene Creed with extensions.

The Second enjoined in effect that each Church should mind its own business; Alexandria should not meddle outside her own sphere. Yet the principle involved was not limited to Alexandria. The East should settle the affairs of the East, and so on.

Q

The Third gave precedence to Constantinople next to Rome, *on the ground that Constantinople was new Rome.* Rome never allowed this until 1204, when a Latin patriarch was established there; but asserted the ancient precedence of Antioch and Alexandria. The sting of this Canon lies in the inference that Rome's position rested, not on being the See of Peter, but on being the capital of the Empire.

Benoit thinks this Third Canon spurious for several reasons; chiefly because the Western Council of Venice (Aquileia), held immediately afterwards, took no notice of it, although other proceedings at Constantinople were known at Venice. At any rate he says it was never confirmed by Rome, *and therefore null and void.* This is obviously begging the question.

The Fourth renounced Maximus, who had recently intruded himself into the See of Constantinople.

The Fifth referred to the schism at Antioch, and declared that all were to be considered Catholics who confessed the Trinity.

The Sixth forbade appeals against Bishops to the Emperor or civil courts.

The Seventh, which is of doubtful authenticity, enjoined the re-baptism of all who had been baptized by Eunomians, Sabellians or Montanists.

As the work of the Council proceeded, a contingent of Egyptian Bishops arrived on the scene, and brought trouble. They complained that as translations were forbidden by a Canon of Nicæa, Gregory, being Bishop of Sasima, could not be translated to Constantinople: a view which was also held by Rome. Further, they supported an intruder, Maximus, as having been canonically consecrated. This Maximus, known as the Cynic, was a wretched person who imposed on Gregory and even on Peter of Alexandria; but the Alexandrians afterwards found him out and disowned him. Then also came the question of Antioch. An arrangement had been made between the followers of Meletius and Paulinus, that when one died, the other should rule alone. Now Meletius was dead, and Gregory felt that the compact should be observed. The Council, however, under the influence chiefly of the younger members, insisted on appointing Flavian, and continuing the schism. So Gregory withdrew; acquiesced cordially in the appointment of Nectarius as his successor; delivered a celebrated oration, known as the Last Farewell; and retired first for two years to Nazianzus, where he got a new bishop appointed, and then to Arianzus. For another eight years he lived there in great simplicity, his only luxury a garden and a fountain, and even that he was obliged to give up. He appears to have held some property and kept several slaves, though probably their slavery was really a voluntary service. From his will we learn that he left a farm at Arianzus, with a brood-mare and sheep to two kinsmen : to a virgin, Rufiana, an annuity and two female virgin slaves, who had the option of freedom; to three servants, apparently slaves, as they also had the option of freedom, a little money. Apart from a few other legacies, the residue to the poor at Nazianzus, after the death of the Deacon Gregory, who had a life interest. Nazianzus seemed always to be his real home. This Will is an interesting document, because it throws light on the attitude of the Church at that time towards slavery, and of slaves towards the Church; for it seems quite an open question whether the slaves would exercise their options.

In the *Five Theological Orations* we have condensed the whole teaching of Gregory on his favourite subject, the Trinity, in which his whole heart and soul were bound up. With him, as with all the Catholic teachers, there is reluctance to express the mystery of the Godhead in human language, to discuss eternal things in the language of time. As with God, so with Eternity. " The Æon, that interval which is co-extensive with

eternal things, is not divided or measured by any motion,
or by the revolution of the sun, as time is measured."
" The Æon is neither time nor part of time; it cannot be
measured." [1] So also we know nothing of the Nature
of God, nor of the generation of the Son; or what means
the Procession of the Holy Ghost. But, as Charles
Kingsley puts it in the Preface to *Hypatia*, " the wonderful metaphysical subtlety of the Græco-Eastern mind
saw in phrases and definitions, too often unmeaning to
our grosser intellect, the symbols of the most important
spiritual realities." The Church, therefore, had to see
that they were rightly expressed; that God, according
to modern times, was both Transcendant and Immanent,
and also Incarnate, and each of them equally.

The *First Theological Oration* combats generally the
Eunomian views. The Second shows that the Nature
of God is beyond human ken. The Third deals with the
Trinity and especially the Son. The Fourth answers all
the Arian or Eunomian objections *in detail*, meeting
dilemma with dilemma, or disproving the major premises.
The Fifth is on the Holy Ghost.

The Godhead [2] is, according to Gregory, a Monarchy
that is not limited to one Person. Now it is possible
for Unity that is at variance with itself to come into a
condition of Plurality, but one which is made of equality
of nature and unity of mind and identity of motion has,
in consequence of these elements, Unity. Such an
unity would be impossible to created natures; but in the
Godhead, though the Persons are numerically distinct,
yet there is no severance of essence. Therefore Unity,
having from all eternity arrived by motion at Duality,
found its rest in Trinity. The Father is Begetter and
Emitter; the Son is the Begotten; the Holy Ghost is
the Emission. We can only know Them as the Unbegotten, the Begotten, and That which proceedeth from
the Father. When did the Second and Third Persons

[1] Or. 38. 8.   [2] Third Theol., Or.

come into being? They are beyond all " When "; it is outside the sphere of time or the grasp of reason. Though Eternal, they are not Unoriginate. The Cause is not necessarily prior to the Effect, for the sun is not prior to light. The generation of the Son is passionless, because incorporeal. His generation in the flesh differed from that of all other men; so, too, His divine birth. It is useless for men to discuss the generation of God, seeing that they cannot explain or understand their own, or their growth, or the union of soul with body, or mind with soul, or mind with reason. But even if they could, they could not explain God, for God is harder to trace than man. The Begetting of God must be honoured by silence. It is a great thing for us to learn that He was begotten; but the manner of His generation we will not admit that even angels can conceive. Shall I tell you, asks Gregory, how it was? It was in a manner known to the Father who begot and the Son who was begotten. Anything beyond this is hidden by a cloud and escapes our dim vision. Did the Son exist before He was begotten? This is a foolish question, for it expresses eternal things in the language of time. Foolish also is the statement that the Begotten and the Unbegotten cannot be the same. Father and Son are always of the same nature. Wisdom and Unwisdom are not the same in themselves, yet both are attributes of man who is the same, only they are not essential attributes. If they were, God, being innocent and immortal and immutable, would have several essences. What, then, is the essence of God? For us it will be a great thing, if ever, even in the far future, we learn this, when this darkness and dullness has passed away from us, as He has promised it will, Who cannot lie. The Arians say that if the First and Second Persons are of the same essence, then the Father being Unbegotten, the Son must be so also. This is false, because Unbegottenness is not of the essence. Again they say that if God has never ceased to beget, the Generation is incomplete: if He has ceased, He must have begun. Gregory replies that if everything that has an end had a beginning, then what has no end has no beginning. What, then, about the human soul and the angels? Again they say that the fact of the Father being the cause necessitates His being greater than the Son. But here the premiss is wrong; because they assume He is the cause by nature, and therefore that He is greater by nature. Gregory next passes to the Scriptural proofs and also to the Arian objections from Scriptural texts.[1] He gives a flood of quotations from St. John and St. Paul on the Divinity, and then clearly distinguishes between both the acts which Christ did and the words which He spoke, either as God or as Man. " Learn," he says, " to be more sublime, and to ascend with His Godhead, and then you will not remain permanently among the things of sight, but will rise with Him to the world of thought, and come to know which passages refer to His Nature, and which to His assumption of human nature." [2] Not, however, satisfied with this, he takes in the Fourth Oration all the texts claimed by the Arians, and explains them in detail. He also investigates the meaning of the various titles of the Son.

In the *Fifth Theological Oration* he treats of the Spirit. The Spirit is either a substance or an attribute; yet not the latter, because He separates (Acts xiii. 2), and is grieved (Eph. iv. 30). He is therefore a substance, and consequently either creature or God. How could we believe in, or be perfected by, a creature? He must, they say, be either begotten or unbegotten. If the latter, then there are two First Causes. If the former, of Whom? If the Son, then He is a sort of grandson; if of the Father, then there are two brothers. No, He proceeds, as Christ tells us (S. John xv. 26). It is useless to try to explain this. " We, who cannot

---

[1] See Basil.   [2] Or 29. 18.

even see what lies at our feet, or count the sand, or the raindrops or the days of eternity, much less can we enter into the depth of God, and supply an account of that nature, which is so unspeakable, transcending all words. The word Proceeding implies no inferiority; it is only a difference of relation. The Spirit is Homoousion: and that again is a mystery, though not without some faint analogies in nature. If we are Tritheists for believing in the Spirit, then those who accept the Son are Ditheists. But all this difficulty is solved by the Homo-ousion. It is true that Scripture said but little about the Spirit, but that was because Revelation is progressive and the Spirit was not revealed till Pentecost. The Old Testament proclaimed the Father openly, the Son more obscurely. The New Testament manifested the Son, and suggested the Divinity of the Spirit; now the Spirit Himself dwells among us, and supplies us with a clearer demonstration of Himself. Mankind could not absorb the truth more quickly. Christ, indeed, only manifested Himself gradually to His disciples. But during His life light was gradually breaking upon them as to the Spirit also." At the close Gregory tries to find some safe type of the Trinity in nature, as was done by several of the Ante-Nicene Fathers, but he finds them all dangerous in use.

At Constantinople more than anywhere else we see how purely intellectual, and consequently worldly, was the position of the real Arians. Among the Semi-Arians it was often quite otherwise. But from Arius with his Thalia to Eunomius with his constant disputations in and out of season, reverence among the Arians was dead. The position of Eunomius was that there was one God unbegotten and incapable of begetting; therefore Eternal Generation was inconceivable; therefore the generation of the Son must have had a beginning. The Son was the first creation of the Divine Energy; and, as the organ of creative power, was the express image and

likeness of the Father's Energy but not of His Essence.
Similarly the Spirit was the noblest production of the
Son. Eunomius baptized into the name of the Creator
and the death of Christ, without mention of the Trinity;
therefore his baptism was invalid. Under his influence,
the highest questions of the faith became matters of
everyday gossip; the Churches were like theatres;
" every market-place," [1] says Gregory, " must buzz
with their talking; every dinner-party be worried to
death with silly talk; all the women's apartments,
accustomed to simplicity, be thrown into confusion,
robbed of their modesty by the torrent of words."
This intellectual religion became a mere stepping-stone
to ambition. The very first cry of Gregory, therefore,
was, Be reverent : God must not be discussed but at
suitable times and in a suitable spirit. At best we can
know little of Him; it is impossible to detach ourselves
sufficiently from our environment and habits of thought.
We shall never realize God till that in us which is God-
like, our mind and reason, shall have mingled with its
like, and the Image shall have ascended to the Arche-
type, which is now only its desire, and we shall know as
we are known. But we can see something of Him in
His works, and recognize Him as the efficient First
Cause of all created things.

" Whatever," says Canon Bright, " Gregory taught
his people as the fundamental mystery was pervaded
and illuminated not only by the reverent caution which
discouraged all attempts to comprehend the Infinite, to
grasp the supreme essence in a formula; but by the
adoring spirit of one whose spirit lived on the truths
he was defending, and by the profound conviction of
their practical bearing on life." [2]

The Three Christmas Orations, viz. the Theophany,
the Holy Lights and Baptism, [3] were preached at Con-

[1] First Theol., Or. 2.
[2] *Age of the Fathers*, Vol. I. p. 411.   [3] Or. 38–40.

stantinople on Christmas Day, the Epiphany, and the day after the latter feast. There is a little uncertainty about how these feasts were observed in the Early Eastern Church. The Epiphany seems to have been the most important, but it celebrated the manifestation of Christ—in His baptism, and not to the Magi. It was, therefore, the great day for baptizing, and the baptized carried about the holy lights. The sermon on the Theophany, however, delivered a week before that on the Lights, is evidently a Christmas sermon.

It commences with a cosmogony: it describes first the creation of the spiritual spheres; then the physical; then man; then finally as the crowning work of God comes the Incarnation. In this sermon is some curious allegorizing on the Garden of Eden. Adam was to till the plants, by which may have been meant the Divine Conceptions. The Tree of Knowledge was perhaps Contemplation, which Adam was not mature enough to indulge in. The coats of skins represented the coarser flesh, mortal and contradictory. Man's sins grew deeper and deeper, and the usual remedies of defects, such as wars, fires and the like became insufficient. Then the Word had to descend. Then Uncontained became Contained through the intervention of an intellectual soul between God and the flesh.

In the sermon on the Holy Lights we get an account of the various baptisms: of Israel in the cloud and the sea; of John; of Christ; of martyrdom; and of penance. The Third Oration (Baptism) teaches first that Baptism is not to be deferred, and enjoins distinctly the baptism of infants; also that the unworthiness of the Minister is no prejudice to the efficacy of the rite; it teaches the baptized their obligations, expounds the Creed, and explains the ceremony of the lights.

The Oration on (his) *Flight to Pontus* (after his forcible ordination) gives a full account of the priesthood, and was the foundation of St. Chrysostom's subsequent work on this subject: of that by Gregory the Great; and of Bossuet's work on St. Paul. Four chapters of it are devoted to St. Paul as the ideal priest. According to Gregory apparently the sacrificial aspect of the priesthood is not the most prominent; it is mentioned only incidentally. The main duty of the priest is the distribution of the Word. That is why accurate theology is so essential. On the other hand, the care of the priests for each individual soul has great prominence, and the advantage of some sort of direction seems implied. The Incarnation is the medicine of the soul, the priests are the dispensers. Every soul is to be watched and studied even more carefully than a physician studies the body.

Oration 37, the only sermon with a text, treats of the indissolubility of marriage, and pleads for the equality of the woman with the man. Gregory complains that " they who made the law were men."

In Oration 30, occurs a remark which shows that Fasting Communion was general: " We celebrate in houses of prayer and before food."

From Oration 31, it seems that the Communion was received in both kinds separately, not in a mixture: " the Bread of which you have partaken; the Cup in which you have communicated."

There is not much teaching on the Eucharist in this Father: but he speaks of the antitypes [1] of the Blessed Body and Blood; and says, " How could I dare to offer the external sacrifice, the antitypes of the great mysteries? " In his Letter 171 to Amphilochius, he says, " Cease not to pray and plead for me, when by your word you draw down the Word, when with a bloodless cutting you sever the Body and Blood of the Lord." The Real Presence could hardly be more definitely stated.

As regards the Last Things,[2] he speaks of the unquench-

---

[1] Or. 8 and 2.   [2] Ibid., 40.

able fire, which is eternal; but adds, " though some may prefer even in this place to take a more merciful view of the fire, worthily of Him that chastiseth." Such people, he apparently thought, were not to be condemned.

Prayer to the Blessed Virgin is alluded to in Oration 24, *On Cyprian,* where a maiden in danger is said to have implored the Virgin Mary to fortify her against temptation. This seems, however, to be an ordinary instance of the Invocation of Saints, not to place St. Mary in any special position above the rest. The Virgin was the natural saint to apply to in this case.

Gregory's letters do not compare in interest with those of Basil; with the exception of a few on theological points, and the celebrated correspondence with Basil when the latter was at Pontus, they are for the most part only private and personal.

As a poet criticisms on Gregory vary considerably. By some he has been thought a poet of quite a high order: by others his poems are treated as merely versified prose. Ullmann, who is a great authority on Gregory, calls them the work of his old age, and says that they were cramped by the subject, and too didactic for poetry. A certain mystic melancholy runs through them, contrasting the peace and beauty of God's works in nature with the restlessness of the human heart. Unlike Basil, Gregory had no objection to introducing Pagan deities into his poems. We find such lines as these :—

> " He whom the Graces to the Muses gave : "

and

> " What shall we do ? the weeping Graces said,
> Ye kindred Muses, speak."

Lastly must be mentioned his Eulogies of the dead; which were sometimes delivered as funeral sermons, and sometimes on the anniversaries of the Saints. Of these the most famous is his oration on Basil. It is from this that we gather many of the incidents of Basil's life, and notably the scenes with Modestus and Valens. Whatever coldness may have sprung up between the two saints in Basil's life, after his death Gregory's love for him was stronger than ever, and he ends the Eulogy with this touching peroration :—

" This is my offering to thee, Basil, uttered by the tongue that was once the sweetest of all to thee, of him who was thy fellow in age and rank. If it has come up to thy desire, thanks are due to thee, for it was from confidence that I undertook it. But if it falls far short of thy expectations, what must be our feelings who are worn out with age and disease and regret for thee? Yet God is pleased when we do what we can. Still mayst thou gaze on us from above, thou divine and sacred person. Either stay by thy entreaties the thorn in the flesh which God has given us for our discipline, or teach us to bear it boldly : guide all our life to that which is of most profit to us, and if we are translated, receive us there also in thine own tabernacle : that as we dwell together and gaze together more clearly and perfectly on the holy and blessed Trinity, of which here we have in some degree beheld the image, our longing may at last be satisfied, by gaining this reward for all the battles we have fought and all the assaults we have endured."

CHAPTER XVI

(Born about 331. Bishop of Nyssa 372. Died about 395.)

THE life of St. Gregory of Nyssa, like Nazianzen's, was uneventful, and did not even contain anything to compare with the brilliant two years of the other Gregory at Constantinople. The interest lies entirely in his writings; and here again, although he wrote at great length on questions of orthodoxy, the main interest is rather on the philosophical and speculative side of his work, than in his conflict with heresy. " His orthodoxy," says Eucken,[1] " is less the animating spirit than the framework of his religious life."

The " Star of Nyssa," the younger brother of Basil, was born in 331, or perhaps a little later, and was educated at home; chiefly by Basil himself, whom he called his master, and partly by his sister Macrina. Yet, in spite of his lack of a university education, he was deeply imbued with Greek philosophy; with Platonism especially; Neo-Platonism; and the work of Origen, of whom he is the natural successor. There is a story that in his youth he fell asleep during a long service on the Festival of the Forty Martyrs and, in consequence of a vivid dream, resolved to devote himself to the Church; but that afterwards he drifted back to Rhetoric. Finally, however, Macrina converted him, and he then joined Basil in Pontus. When Basil became bishop, he recognized the great intellectual acquirements of Gregory, but distrusted his

[1] *Problem of Human Life,* p. 200.

practical ability: he therefore appointed him to the
obscure bishopric of Nyssa, saying that he should give
lustre to the See, instead of receiving lustre from it.
On several occasions Basil curbed his practical efforts:
he checked, for instance, his desire to summon synods,
and restrained him from joining a deputation to Damasus of Rome.   A synod at Antioch, however,
entrusted to him an important mission to reform the
churches of Arabia and Babylon.   On this occasion,
passing through Jerusalem, he was struck by the corruption of that city; and consequently wrote his
treatise on *Pilgrimages*, strongly deprecating them, and
pointing out not only their uselessness and waste of
time, but also the temptations to which the pilgrims,
and especially women, were exposed on the way.

Gregory's tenure of the see of Nyssa was by no means
a peaceful one, for he was accused by the Arians of
misappropriating funds; and though Basil cleared him
at first, further charges were advanced; and at last,
on his refusal to attend a synod appointed to try him,
he was deposed by Valens as contumacious in 374, and
retired till 378 to Seleucia.   At the Council of Constantinople there is no doubt that he took a prominent
part, preaching the funeral sermon on St. Meletius,
and reading to the Council a part of his work against
Eunomius.   It has also been sometimes supposed,
though without much evidence, that he suggested the
additional clauses which were added to the Creed.

Gregory's chief works are:—*Thirteen Books Against
Eunomius; The Great Catechism; Treatises on The
Trinity; The Holy Spirit; That there are not Three
Gods; Faith; Virginity; The Deaths of Infants;
Pilgrimages; The Making of Man, and The Soul and
the Resurrection;* Orations on St. Meletius and Bap-
tism; besides a great number of miscellaneous sermons
or treatises and his extant letters.

Before considering the philosophical position of St.

Gregory, it is desirable to see something of that last school of Greek thought, which was at once the climax and the ruin of Hellenic Philosophy, and was known as Neo-Platonism. The chief representative of this school was Plotinus, whose life extended over most part of the third century. Neo-Platonism was the supreme effort of the Greek mind, because it aimed at forming a religious system, which was to gather together the best of all other religions under its own ægis; it exalted the ideal as the only thing worth looking for, but at the same time so despised the material, that all science and knowledge were put out of court. Metaphysic was to rule alone, and metaphysic was only for trained intellects; for the masses, therefore, there was nothing left open but a return to barbarism. The metaphysic of Plato was generally adopted, but the Neo-Platonists went a step further by finding a new principle, the supra-rational. Man, in fact, had a spirit as well as a soul. Thought was not the highest thing; it was only an intermediate stage between the senses and that higher state of rapture, ecstasy or spiritual intuition—a sort of communion with the Divine—to which man could under certain conditions, such as trance, and after long preparation sometimes attain. Plotinus only professed to have reached it on a very few occasions during his life. But while in that state it was presumed that truth was revealed. So that they aimed in two ways at arriving at certainty, i. e. revelation; one was by the use of the supra-rational principle; the other by the study of all the old religions.

The Neo-Platonic system was undoubtedly very beautiful, high-minded and spiritual. The ideas that man could not live by knowledge alone, that there was a higher principle in him than his intellect, that his highest good was the rapt contemplation of God as pure Being (which last idea specially influenced Gregory of Nyssa) came very near to Christianity. But the system broke down, as St. Augustine pointed out, because it lacked a founder, had no word for the masses, and failed to show how one could permanently maintain the mood of blessedness and peace.[1]

The metaphysic of Plotinus taught that God was One, that everything was in Him and derived from Him. Yet the derived had a separate existence. The wider became the circle of derivations or emanations, the less was their share of the one original essence, till at last they became mere phenomena. The metaphor is of course taken from the result of throwing a stone into the water. The first emanation is the Nous, or Mind, which is a complete image of the One; as an Image quite equal, but as derived, quite different. Next comes the Soul, which is to the Nous as the Nous to the One. It will at once be seen how near he approached to the doctrine of the Trinity. This World-soul embraces all individual souls, and they may at their will turn to the Nous or drift away towards the world of mere phenomena. The human soul that is sunk in the material must be converted and gradually work up through virtue and asceticism (this word meaning " exercise " or " training ") to the power of contemplating God. The highest thing that we can contemplate is still the Beautiful, but the Beautiful and the Good are one; and that One is Pure Being, or God.

Now it is in the treatise On Virginity that Gregory comes nearest to this mode of thought. A quotation will be found in the Chapter on St. Clement of Alexandria from Plato's Symposium, in which he says that the contemplation of the Ideal Beauty, if it could only be found, would claim all a man's energy, and lead him to the life eternal. And this thought comes down, through the Neo-Platonists, to Gregory. The Vir-

---

[1] Eucken, *Problem of Human Life* (section on Gregory of Nyssa).

ginity that Gregory was discussing had nothing to do necessarily with conventual systems; it was rather the absolute detachment from the things of this world. " The man who longs for union with God must detach himself from all worldly business." " It is impossible for the mind which is poured into many channels to win its way to the knowledge and love of God." Marriage, by the way, is one of these channels. He does not, however, condemn marriage, which he looks on as indispensable for the many : it is only a hindrance to complete detachment. " Let no one think we depreciate marriage. We are well aware that it is not a stranger to God's blessing. But as the common instincts of man can plead sufficiently on its behalf, it is superfluous to formally compose an exhortation to marriage." And then he says : " No one is so mentally blind as not to understand this without telling; that the God of the Universe is the only absolute and primal and unrivalled Beauty and Goodness." And again : " Take a character that is strong enough to turn from all that is human, from persons, from wealth, from the pursuit of Art and Science, even from whatever is deemed right in moral practice and legislation (for in all things error creeps in through making sense the criterion of the Beautiful); such a character will feel as a passionate lover only towards that Beauty which has no source but itself, which is not such at one time and relatively only, but which is Beautiful from and through and in Itself, which is above all increase or addition, incapable of change or alteration. I venture to say that to one who has cleansed all the powers of his being from every form of vice, the Beauty which is essential, the source of all beauty and good, will become visible. To the innocent soul there comes the power of seeing the light; and the real virginity, the real chastity, ends at no other goal than this, the power thereby of seeing God."

R

But this "seeing God" is, as Eucken points out, less the nearness of person to person than the mystical union with underived Being: it is less communion or fellowship than the striving for complete absorption into the Eternal Unity, out of which the soul had originally come. The name Father implies rather a metaphysical than an ethical relation. It is in this respect that Gregory of Nyssa is not only Platonic, but also accentuates the general attitude of the Eastern, as opposed to the Western Church. The moral aspect of Christianity was subordinated in the East to the metaphysical. "What he longs for is not more love or justice, but more of the essential and eternal, as opposed to the ever-changing and vanishing (Eucken)." "God being unlimited transcends all limits of thought and reason; so we want wings to soar above the visible and changeable, the phenomena, to abiding nature, unchangeable, self-dependent power." The ideal Beauty is the victory of the higher over the lower everywhere; and the lower must eventually be everywhere subdued and brought back again into the higher.

The love of Nature appears strongly in all three of the Cappadocian Fathers; for what is beautiful in Nature is a reflex of God. The idea of the beautiful, which in Nature is order (Cosmos), is in human nature the good. "We ought not to wonder at the beauty of the vaulted sky, nor at the rays of light, nor any other form of visible beauty, but be led by the beauty discerned in these to a longing for the beauty whose glory the heavens declare." "When I see every rocky ridge, every valley, every plain, covered with new-grown grass, the variegated beauty of the trees, and at my feet the lilies doubly enriched by nature with sweet odours and gorgeous colours; when I view in the distance the sea, to which the changing cloud leads out, my soul is seized with sadness, which is not without delight. . . . He who looks at these things with the thoughtful eye of the soul feels the littleness of man in the greatness of the universe." Nature, in its quietest forms, the murmuring wood, the lonely desert, affects him most; for here the soul can withdraw within itself and contemplate the eternal.

A still further application of the Ideal by Gregory is that of the Ideal Man, the Perfect, as opposed to the Fallen or Actual Man. For he thought there was an ideal humanity, a Prototype, in the mind of God; but it was essential to that ideal, which was made in God's image, that it should possess free will. Now only the Uncreated is changeless : the Created must change. Therefore it was inevitable that man would sin, and this was always foreseen and provided for. So curiously Gregory argues that first God created man (the ideal) in His own image, which was sexless; and then male and female (the actual) created He them. " The first man on earth, or rather he who generated evil in man, had for choice the good and the beautiful lying all round him in the very nature of things; yet he wilfully cut out for himself a new way against this nature, and in the act of turning away from virtue, which was his own free act, he created the usage of evil. . . . The habit of sinning entered with fatal quickness into the life of man, and from that small beginning spread into this infinitude of evil." [1] Thus the fall is not something accidental in history. " In the form of narrative Moses taught the doctrine." [2] With the capacity for, and indeed necessity of change, Man sinned : yet still the ideal man turns towards God and finds blessing. The actual or fallen man has always been as he is now; for after, as Moses taught, the primæval man was brought into contact with what was forbidden, and was thereby stripped naked of his primal blessed condition, the Lord clothed him with coats of skins, which Gregory distinctly says are not to be taken in their literal

---

[1] Virg. 12.　　　　　[2] Great Catechism, VIII.

meaning.[1] They were the liability to death taken
from the brute creation, and the necessity of sex.
Every human being is sinful, because imperfect, and
liable to change; but at the general Resurrection,
when every soul has been purged by the Fire, the Ideal
humanity will be restored.

Hitherto no great Christian philosophers had appeared
except Clement and Origen. The rest were more
strictly theologians. Gregory therefore, when he
launched out into speculation, naturally took his cue to
a great extent from Origen, although the controversies
of a century enabled him to discriminate. The main
points in which he followed Origen were : the absolute
freedom of the will; the fact that evil was caused by
the free choice of man; that matter was not evil;
that evil was a negative (the absence of good); and
that there would eventually be a complete end to evil.
" When the evil passions have been purged and utterly
removed by the healing process of the fire, then every
one of the things which make up our conception of the
good will take their place : incorruption, life, honour,
grace, glory and everything else that we conjecture is
to be seen in God's own image, Man, as he was
originally made." [2]

While Origen tried to make use of Hellenic methods
in constructing a scheme of Christian philosophy,
Gregory tried still further to reconcile the best results
of Greek thought with the formularies of the Church :
but he also made a much stronger point than Origen of
Redemption as an all-controlling event that took place
in history.[3] Each of them used Plato's terminology
when it suited their purpose. Gregory, while often
disowning him, adopted his division of man into body,
soul and spirit, as an analogy of the Trinity, on the
ground that it was proved by consciousness. We can-

[1] Great Catechism, VIII.   [2] *Soul and Resurrection.*
[3] Harnack, *Outlines of Dogma*, p. 318.

not do better than learn from the things within us to
know the secret of God; to recognize the Triad from
the triad within ourselves. Although Gregory dwells
on the act of Redemption as something that took place
in history, his arguments are generally based on
metaphysics rather than on history; facts, types,
prophecies, and the regularly approved weapons of the
Church.

Gregory differs from Origen by discarding his theory
of Pre-existence, and the idea that this life is a discipline for the sins of a past existence. The soul, he
thought with Tertullian, was transmitted from father to
child in generation, a theory which is known as the
Traducian. Also he did not think, as Origen did, that
there would be no resurrection of the original bodily
elements : although he did think that matter was so
unimportant that the resurrection of the soul was all
that was essential. That of the flesh was only necessary, because Creation was to be saved by men carrying
their created bodies to a higher sphere.

Matter was something unreal; it was shifting,
becoming, imperfect; a mere concourse of attributes
or qualities. He went so far as to draw a subtle distinction (using the words οὐδέν and μῆδεν) by saying that
matter was not nothing, but no thing. Matter is
therefore in this respect like evil, something negative;
yet matter and evil are by no means, as the Gnostics
said, synonymous. The great distinction is not, as
with Plato and Origen, into the Intelligible and the
Sensible, but into the Uncreated, and the Created
which is Changeable, Passionate, and therefore sinful.
And all the Created, even the angels, have fallen or
can fall. The greatest spiritual fall was that of the
angel who had the supervision of the world.

The Psychology and Eschatology of Gregory will be
found chiefly in the treatises on the *Making of Man*
and on the *Soul and the Resurrection;* also in the

Great Catechism. To some extent alsó in the treatise on *Infants' Early Deaths.*

The soul is created, living, and an intellectual being, with the gift, by means of the bodily organs, of sensuous perception; but the whole relation between the soul and the body is as ineffable as are all the great mysteries of religion. "The speculative and critical faculty is the soul's most God-like attribute.[1] If any one asks where the soul is, the same question might be asked about God. The soul indeed resembles God as a copy does the original. Being simple and uncompounded, it survives the composite body, and after death it watches the scattered bodily elements, in order to gather them together again at the Resurrection. "You will behold this bodily envelope, which is now dissolved in death, woven again out of the same atoms, not indeed into this organization with its coarse and heavy texture, but with its threads worked up into something more subtle and ethereal: so that you will not only have near you that which you love, but it will be restored to you with a brighter and more entrancing beauty." [2]

The statement of St. Gregory as to his belief in the final restitution of all things, and that God shall be all in all is repeatedly expressed; and in the Soul and Resurrection he says definitely: "It appears to me that Scripture teaches the annihilation of all evil." The question is most fully stated in the same treatise thus: "God's end is one and one only; it is this: when the complete whole of our race is perfected from the first man to the last (some have at once in this life been cleared of evil; others have afterwards in the necessary periods been cleansed in the Fire; others have in their life been equally unconscious of good or evil); to offer to every one of us participation in the blessings that are in Him, which scripture says ' eye

---

[1] *Soul and Resurrection.*   [2] *Ibid.*

hath not seen, nor ear heard,' nor thought ever reached. But this is nothing else as I understand it but to be in God Himself." Of course this is not a dogmatic statement, but a speculative opinion. It is claimed by some critics that this was not Gregory's view, because after the purifying of every soul by the Fire, and the first Resurrection, there was still to be a judgment. The author of the article on Gregory in the *Dictionary of Christian Biography* (Canon Venables), however, claims that this is no contradiction of his generally expressed view elsewhere.

The great work which the Cappadocian Fathers did for the Trinitarian controversy was to distinguish in proper theological terms the meanings of Ousia and Hypostasis, which had hitherto been confused. Athanasius at the synod of Alexandria found that the words were used with different meanings by different persons, who were quarrelling over words, while their views really coincided. He therefore agreed to let each party use what terms they liked, so long as they agreed in the meanings. And this was the first step in the recovery of the Semi-Arians. But this looseness of expressions was a danger to permanent theology. The original Latin position was one Hypostasis or Substance, three Prosopa, or Forms; and Substance still remains in our Western creed where a Greek would say Essence. The Greek, after substituting Essence or Ousia for Substance, used Substance to mean Person; and especially hated the word Prosopon, or Mask, as being Sabellian. The final expression of the Greek mind by Basil was one Ousia in three complete Hypostases. The Greeks and Latins therefore used and still use the word Hypostasis or Substantia in exactly opposite meanings. Basil and Gregory of Nyssa were at any rate determined, however the words might be used, that the difference between the Essence and the Personality should be fully understood. Basil explains it to Gregory in his letter 38 (although this letter is sometimes thought to have been written by Gregory himself): and also in letter 214 to Terentius, where he says, " The term Ousia is common, like Godhead, or goodness, or any similar attribute; while Hypostasis is contemplated in the special property of Fatherhood, Sonhood, or the power to sanctify. If, then, the Persons are described as without Hypostasis, the statement is *per se* absurd; but if they concede that the Persons exist in real hypostasis, as they acknowledge, let them so reckon them that the principle of the Homoousion may be preserved in the Unity of the Godhead, and the doctrine preached may be the recognition of true religion of Father, Son and Holy Ghost in the perfect and complete Hypostasis of each of the Persons named."

Gregory explains that the difference between Ousia and Hypostasis is that between a common noun and a particular noun. It is like the difference between Man generally, and men. James, Peter and John are each of them essentially Man, but their personality is that of James, Peter and John. The objection of course then comes, that James, Peter and John were three different men; why then are there not three Gods? To this Gregory replies, first, that the numerical idea is not one that is applicable to Deity at all, being only a conception of the human mind.[1]

But feeling that this argument is somewhat insufficient, he argues further: that we know nothing of the real nature or essence of God; the Godhead is only realized by us in Its operation; and we find that every operation of each Person of the Trinity is the operation of all jointly, one movement of the Divine Will. Therefore they are essentially one. In the case of the Divine Nature we do not learn that the Father does anything by Himself in which the Son does not work conjointly;

[1] See Treatise *That there are not Three Gods*.

or, again, that the Son has any special operation apart from the Holy Ghost. But every operation that extends from God to creation, and is named according to our varying conception of it, has its origin from the Father, proceeds through the Son, and is perfect in the Holy Spirit."

Gregory has been always referred to as a high authority for the doctrine of the Real Presence; and he also uses words which seem like an approach to Transubstantiation, if indeed they do not fully imply it. The best known quotation [1] is this: "Rightly do we believe that the bread which is consecrated by the Word of God is *changed* into the Body of God the Word." But in the same connection the subject is argued very fully, in reply to a question which he puts himself: How can the one Body be so multiplied as to incorporate Itself into myriads of men? " Since then that God-containing flesh partook for its substance and support of this particular nourishment (bread and wine), and since the God who was manifested diffused Himself into perishable humanity for this purpose, viz. that by this communion with Deity man might also be deified; for this end it is that by dispensation of His grace He disseminates Himself in every believer through the flesh whose substance comes from bread and wine, blending Himself with the bodies of believers, to secure that by this union with the immortal, man too may be a sharer in incorruption. He gives those gifts by virtue of the benediction, through which He *transelements* the natural quality of the visible things to that immortal thing." It is true that in the Oration on Baptism he compares, like St. Cyril, the heightened efficacy of the elements to the heightened efficacy of the baptismal water and the anointing oil; but he shows clearly that the change is not the same in each case. After stating that a change takes place

[1] Great Catechism XXXVII.

after benediction in the baptismal water, he says, " The bread again is at first common bread; but when the sacramental act consecrates it, it is called *and becomes* the Body of Christ.   So with the wine; so with the oil; though before the benediction they are of little value, each of them, after the sanctification bestowed by the Spirit, has *its several operation.*"   And later, " *Water, though it is nothing else than water,* renews the man to spiritual regeneration, when the grace from above hallows it."

The Great Catechism, a somewhat lengthy treatise, deals fully with the doctrines of the Trinity, the Incarnation and the Sacraments; and it is on the subject of the Incarnation, including the whole scheme of men's salvation, that it is chiefly interesting.   It shows that Redemption could not so well have been carried out by a mere proclamation of the Almighty. To heal suffering humanity it was necessary to touch it: humanity was on earth; God therefore must descend to earth.   Gregory vindicates the justice and wisdom of the Incarnation as well as the time at which, and also the manner in which, it took place, and also the manner of Christ's death, the Crucifixion.   Like Origen, he looks on redemption as a ransom paid to Satan, and as a just deception of the deceiver of mankind, who did not know that the Divine was clothed in the human.[1]   " He who first deceived man by the bait of sensual pleasures is himself deceived by the presentment of human form.   But, as regards the aim and purpose of what took place, a change in the direction of the nobler is involved; for whereas he, the enemy, effected his deception for the ruin of our nature, He, who is at once the Just, the Good and the Wise One, used His device in which was deception, for the salvation of him who had perished, and thus not only conferred benefit on the lost one, but on him also who had

[1] Chapter xxvi.

wrought our ruin." The conclusion therefore follows that not only humanity but the devil himself will eventually be saved. Which was the view of Origen, and one of his opinions which specially laid him open to the charge of heresy.

We see then in Gregory of Nyssa the true spirit and mind of the Eastern Church. With him the story of the Arian controversy is closed. Gregory of Nazianzus summed up the Catholic faith in five sermons: Gregory of Nyssa disposed of Arianism in detail in his thirteen books against Eunomius; the second Council put an end to it officially. All the Fathers had taught the same thing, as the groundwork of the truth, viz. that the nature of God could not be known; all we could deal with was the way He impressed Himself on the human mind. A living writer has said half humorously: "The true result of all experience and the true foundation of all religion is this; that the four or five things that it is most practically essential that a man should know are all of them what people call paradoxes. That is, that although we all find them in life to be mere plain truths, yet we cannot easily state them in words without being guilty of seeming verbal contradictions." [1]

Gregory, like Origen, preferred the spiritual to the moral; like him, he indulged in speculation and allegory, seeking always the spirit behind the letter. Like all true Easterns he sought the ideal, while the Westerns were seeking the practical. For the Eastern, when the world troubled him, sought consolation in self-communion, meditation, detachment; while the Western opposed to the world's influence the splendour and majesty of the visible Church.

[1] G. K. Chesterton, *Tremendous Trifles*, p. 66.

CHAPTER XVII

(Born 347. Archbishop of Constantinople 397. Died in exile 407)

THE active life of St. Chrysostom was spent during a truce in what Canon Bright called " the wars of the Lord." The great *theo*-logical controversy with the Arians was practically over, when he was ordained priest in 384 and became a great preacher at Antioch; the great *Christo*-logical controversy, as to the relation of the Divine and human natures in Christ, had hardly begun. The interest of his life lies, therefore, partly in his conflict with the State, in which he was by no means successful; but chiefly in his edification of the Christian life by means of that eloquence which won him the title of the Golden-Mouthed, and also in his learned and practical commentaries on the Bible.

John, surnamed Chrysostom, was born at Antioch in 347 of Christian parents; but his father dying when he was an infant, his education was carried out by his pious mother Anthusa. He was baptized when already an adult, after three years' careful preparation by St. Meletius; and was only prevented by his mother's earnest entreaty to stay with her from at once becoming a monk. When shortly afterwards Meletius was exiled, Chrysostom continued his studies under that bishop's deputy, Diodorus, afterwards a famous bishop of Tarsus, and in the company of two friends named Basil and Theodore. The latter was afterwards bishop of Mopsuestia; a great writer who would probably have been considered a Father, had not his works been held in some degree responsible for two heresies, Pelagianism and Nestorianism. At his mother's death he did retire for some time into a monastery; but the ascetic life so injured his health, that he was obliged to return to Antioch, where he was ordained deacon by Meletius just before his departure to the Council of Constantinople, and priest by his successor, Flavian, in 384. From 384 then till 397 Chrysostom was constantly preaching at Antioch, and it was during this period that his best exegetical sermons were delivered.

Either when a layman or a deacon (it is not certain which) he wrote his celebrated work in six books on the Priesthood. It was founded on Gregory of Nazianzus' apology for his flight into Pontus; and, like Gregory, Chrysostom continually points to St. Paul as the ideal priest. The occasion which produced this work is remarkable, as it is an instance of that curious "economy" of the truth, which some of the Fathers did not scruple to apply to what they considered a worthy end. His friend Basil and himself both shrank from ordination and agreed to act together. Basil was subsequently ordained, owing to Chrysostom's eulogy of his merits, and believed that the latter had been also. When he protested on finding that Chrysostom was still a layman, or possibly a deacon, Chrysostom explained the circumstances in the first book of the Priesthood, and apologized in the second for his own reluctance to assume that sacred office on account of its temptations, dangers and responsibilities; which he describes in detail in the third book.

This third book is in the highest degree sacerdotal, and more in the tone of Cyprian than of the Greek Fathers. The offering of the Holy Sacrifice and the power of absolution are discussed in definite language. "What priests do here below," he says of absolution, "God ratifies above; the Master confirms the sentences of His servants." On the other hand he seems rather to have suggested that members of a family could better help one another than the priest could direct them. " You know one another better than we priests can ever know you."

In the fourth book he deals with a priest's qualifications, especially oratory and controversial ability; in the fifth with preaching, pointing out the importance of learning; the necessity of indifference both to praise and slander; how the skilful preacher needs to study even more closely than the unlearned on account of the danger of being carried away; how the verdict of the masses must neither be overrated nor underrated, but taken for exactly what it is worth, etc. This book and the sixth, which deals with various other duties, are full of wisdom for all time. In the last he contrasts the life of a recluse with that of a priest. " If any one admires the solitary life, I should say such a life betokened patience, but not a sufficient proof of entire fortitude of soul." The difference is like that between a man who steers his boat in harbour, and one who guides his vessel in the open sea.

It is rather strange that, in spite of the complete understanding that he claimed of St. Paul, which arose, as he said, not from any cleverness of his own, but because he was always studying him and loving him, he under-estimated his social and intellectual standing, and seems to have looked on him as a poor tent-maker in a lowly position of life, who without intellectual qualifications of his own, received everything from inspiration like the fishermen of Galilee. He also dwells on Paul's " poverty of speech." " He had a far greater power than that of speech, a power which brought about greater results; for his bare presence, even though he was silent, was terrible to the evil spirits. Men of to-day, if all collected in one place, could not with infinite prayers and tears do the wonders that were done by the handkerchief of St. Paul." [1] As regards Miracles, it is worth noting here that Chrysostom believed that they had ceased, or at any rate were very few and far between in his day; though Augustine took quite a different view. The miracles of the Gospel had with Chrysostom an educational intent, and the world was now educated to Christianity; therefore they were no longer necessary.

The personal appearance of Chrysostom was dignified, but not imposing; he was short in stature, but his limbs were long; and so thin had his early austerities made him (probably from the ruin of his digestion) that he compared himself to a spider. His forehead was lofty and wrinkled; his head was bald; his eyes deeply set, but keen and piercing; his cheeks were pale and withered; he had a pointed chin and a short beard.

According to Milman, he was " the model of a preacher for a great capital; clear rather than profound, his dogmatic is essentially moulded up with his moral teaching. His doctrine flows naturally from his subject or from the passage of Scripture under discussion; his illustrations are copious and happy; his style free and fluent; while he is an unrivalled master of that rapid and forcible application of incidental occurrences, which gives such life and reality to eloquence. He is at times in the highest sense dramatic in manner." [2] The forcible application of incidental occurrences was probably carried further than we have evidence of, as it was his custom first to preach his written sermon, and then from the basis of it to launch out extempore into the incidents of the day.

Perthes, in a life of Chrysostom founded mainly on Neander's, says, " He delays in simple exposition no longer than seems indispensable for the general understanding of the passages. He then proceeds directly to make use of his explanation for impressing the minds

[1] *Priesthood*, IV. 6.   [2] *History of Christianity*, III. 9.

and hearts of his audience, and on it he expends the whole strength of his intellect, the exhaustless power of his invention, and the full compass of his abundant knowledge." [1]

His knowledge was not only of the sacred books, but also of human nature. In early days he was very fond of the theatre; but he used to say that, after—as a Christian—he gave it up, Antioch became his theatre; and in her streets he studied men, instead of on the stage. Yet his knowledge of men did not give him much tact in dealing with them; and his want of tact was aggravated by an irritable temper. To set against this, however, he had immense bravery; attacking the highest personages, even the Empress herself, in the pulpit without the slightest compunction. And this was more remarkable in the servile Orient than it would have been at Rome: one may remark in this connection the contrast between the respective attitudes towards Theodosius of Ambrose of Milan and Flavian of Antioch on occasions which will be recounted in their place. But, if he lacked tact, he was at any rate full of the broadest sympathy for humanity; for it is said of him that he had no pity for sin, but an infinite pity for the sinner.

What was the state of the world and the Church when St. Chrysostom set himself to reform them? During his earlier days at Antioch, Theodosius was still on the throne; a great emperor, indeed the last great one, and a strong supporter of the Church, whose main fault was a violent temper. From this temper Antioch, which had broken out into revolt on a question of taxation, and destroyed the statues of the Imperial family, nearly suffered destruction. Flavian the bishop went to Constantinople to implore forgiveness, and ultimately obtained it; and Chrysostom meanwhile preached every day to the people his famous Homilies on the Statues. But

[1] See also Gibbon, ch. xxxii.

Theodosius died, and the Empire passed into an entirely new phase under his two sons, Honorius in the West and Arcadius in the East; two poor creatures, who no longer ruled jointly, as formerly, but as rulers of two distinct Empires. The Roman Empire was fated to be extinguished altogether within a century; the Byzantine Empire passed at once into that " Premature and perpetual decay (as Gibbon calls it [1]), which was to be prolonged for a thousand years." It was on this visit to Constantinople that Flavian's humble bearing was contrasted so forcibly with the attitude of the Western Ambrose.

The condition of Antioch at this time was very much the same as that of Constantinople, and what applies to one city applies generally to the other. At least half the populations were nominally Christians; among the other half were Jews, Pagans and members of semi-Christian bodies. Really, however, large masses of the population were hovering between Christianity and Paganism. Morality was at the lowest ebb. The Pagan Emperor Julian said of the nominally Christian Antioch, " I escape from a city full of all vices : violence, drunkenness, incontinence, impiety, avarice and impudence." As regards the Christians Chrysostom himself said, " The duties of religion have become mere formalities, only fulfilled to satisfy the conscience; there is nothing, but routine." [2] Ignorance of the Bible was universal; though it was treated with such superstitious reverence that people washed their hands before touching it. Yet the whole Bible was read aloud in the churches in the course of a year.

There were, of course, great extremes of wealth and poverty. Statistics on this head do not seem very formidable; 10 per cent. of very rich, 10 per cent. of very poor, and 80 per cent. with enough to live upon. But poverty was aggravated by the hardship of slavery

---

[1] *Decline and Fall*, ch. xxxii.   [2] Acts, Hom. 29.

8

and consequent discouragement of free labour; and wealth was made ugly by boundless extravagance, dissipation, ostentatious display, idleness and effeminacy. Chrysostom continually denounces the gorgeous equipages, brocades and silks, and the gluttonous feasts. It was not uncommon for a great man to possess from 1000 to 2000 slaves. Add to this oppressive taxation, venality of administration, excessive usury, insecurity of life, depression of agriculture, and the perpetual danger to peace from a great standing army. As a sign of effeminacy, it was about this time that the soldiers of the West refused any longer to be burdened with armour; and whatever was true of the West was worse in the East, owing to the enervating influence of the climate.

The laxity of the marriage-tie was another feature of the age. This had been gradually increasing since the time of Cicero, when divorce had already become common. But divorce was now so easy that marriage was a mere temporary arrangement. Some one said that as the State counted the years by the consuls, so a fashionable woman might remember them by her husbands. It was partly to counteract this that the Church so strongly upheld Virginity, and woman's dignity and equality with man. Virginity displayed the highest standard of purity; and when it was objected to Chrysostom that it militated against the upkeep of the population, he replied that wherever high standards of purity were maintained as an example, the population would increase.

The Theatre was another institution with which the Church was constantly at war. In earlier times one great objection to the stage plays and games had been their association with Pagan festivals. But now there was nothing left of the old Greek drama; nothing but pantomimes and ballets, usually founded on adultery, and produced amidst the most indecent surroundings

and with sumptuous mounting. There were also contests of wild beasts, and captives, though gladiatorial
fights were strictly illegal. The depraving influence of
the theatre was not confined to the immorality of the
plays or the cruelty of the shows; it apparently absorbed
in a mischievous way the whole minds and lives of the
people. Chrysostom complained that his congregation brought the customs and manners of the theatre
into church, and rushed away from his sermons, even on
Good Friday, to the theatre. Perhaps to some extent
the splendid ritual of the Church was intended to serve
as · a counter-attraction to the theatre. Again the
actresses and actors were almost worshipped by the
people. At Antioch, Pelagia, surnamed the Pearl, was
led in triumph through the city, bedecked in jewels like
a queen. This woman, by the way, was afterwards
converted to Christianity and ended her days as an
ascetic in the desert, so that she was no doubt the original
of Kingsley's character in *Hypatia*. A further objection
was that the actors collected round them a body of
parasites, a *claque*, composed of the worst characters of
the province, who figured prominently in every rising
of the people.

Two other degrading features of the time remain to
be mentioned. The public baths, to which all classes
could resort on payment of a small entrance fee, and
which were constructed and decorated with the utmost
magnificence, had, to say the least, an enervating and
probably an immoral effect; while the back-stair influence of the eunuchs, a horrible importation from the
still further East, of whom Eutropius was perhaps the
worst example, brought the Imperial family into hatred
and contempt.[1]

Charles Kingsley summed up the political system thus :
" The Empire (was) a great tyranny, enslaving the

---

[1] Africa was at this time exporting 20,000 eunuchs per annum.

masses, crippling national life, and fattening itself and
its officials on world-wide robbery." [1]

But there was at hand a *corpus sanum* (we again quote
Kingsley) which the *mens sana* of, at any rate, the Western
Church was destined to inhabit : and that was supplied
by the great southward march of the Goths. Unfortunately, they never obtained any firm foothold in Asia,
though at this time there was a fair sprinkling of Goths
in Constantinople.

In the latter part of the third century the Goths had
come down South from the Baltic to the Black Sea and
established themselves in the South-Eastern provinces.
Temporarily they spread into Cappadocia and Galatia,
carrying away from these countries many captives, and
among them the ancestors of Ulfilas, their chief missionary bishop, who translated the Bible into Gothic,
except the Books of Samuel and Kings, which he thought
would encourage their already too warlike tendencies !
Readily they accepted Christianity; but as the Emperor
(Valens), who admitted them to settle within the Empire
and protected them from the savage Huns who were
pressing on their footsteps, was Arian, they accepted
only the Arian modification. These Goths were a
fruitful soil for Christian influence; their previous
religion was awful and mysterious; they had a priesthood
which was judicial as well as religious; they had also
the highest reverence for women and the family life.
On the whole, too, they were frank, honest and truthful.
But Arians they remained till Reccared their King made
them Catholics, partly by persuasion and partly by
force, in 587.

In 397 Nectarius, the indolent successor of Gregory,
died, and Chrysostom was chosen, by the advice of the
Eunuch Eutropius, for the See of Constantinople; to
prevent opposition from the people of Antioch, he was
carried away by stealth. At first all went well, for a

[1] Preface to *Hypatia*

famous preacher was just what the capital wanted. On
the occasion of a great festival and the translation of
some relics, Eudoxia the Empress walked seven miles
in the procession, and even Arcadius visited the shrine
in his carriage. But except with the poor, who always
adored him, Chrysostom soon made plenty of enemies.
His outspoken criticism alienated the rich; his simple
life was imputed to him for pride; his determination to
raise church standards estranged many of the clergy.
Eutropius attacked him by disputing the right of
sanctuary; but falling soon afterwards into disgrace
through grossly insulting the Empress, fled himself to
the altar, and was protected by the Archbishop; who,
as Eutropius crouched underneath the altar, " more
frightened than a hare or a frog," preached a celebrated
sermon on the vanity of human life and inveighed against
his crimes. It was not long also before Eudoxia became
his bitter enemy.

In 400 Chrysostom, who had already effected great
reforms in various parts of Asia Minor, which were really
outside his jurisdiction, composed certain difficulties
by request at Ephesus; and while he was away for three
months in this business a strong party was formed
against him. Theophilus of Alexandria also, who had
always hated him, coveting the patriarchate of Constantinople for himself, and had only under compulsion
consecrated him, was always watching for his opportunity, which soon came.

At this time the Egyptian monks were divided into
two parties, the followers and the opponents of the
teaching of Origen. Theophilus, being an anti-Origenite,
had ejected wholesale the Origenite monks of Nitria
from their monasteries, and they accordingly fled for
refuge to Constantinople. Chrysostom received them
with the utmost kindness, and housed them; only refusing them communion, till an explanation arrived from
their own bishop. Theophilus was then summoned to

the capital by the Emperor to give an account of what he had done, and Chrysostom was to try him; which Chrysostom at once disclaimed the right to do. For Constantinople, being comparatively a new see, had a very limited jurisdiction outside the city, although it had been granted an honorary precedence next to Rome : whereas Alexandria had formerly been, and still claimed to be, the second see of the Church.

Theophilus [1] arrived with a great retinue of Egyptian bishops, and turned the tables on his appointed judge. To make matters worse, he had invited Epiphanius of Salamis to precede him. This man was the great hammerer of Origenites of his day. He is usually accounted a Saint and even a Father; really he was an honest but bigoted zealot who interfered too much in the business of other bishops, notably that of the Bishop of Jerusalem. He wrote many books which are not thought to be of much value; the most noted was the *Pannadium*, which dealt with eighty heresies. On arriving at Constantinople, he began by ordaining a deacon, which he had no right to do, and then denounced the fugitive monks. However, they were a match for him : for when they had argued their case, he admitted his mistake, and soon after left Constantinople in disgust at the whole business and died on the way home.

The Egyptian bishops, having convinced the Court, held a synod at a suburb called the Oak, and summoned Chrysostom on thirty most frivolous charges; finally, on his refusing to appear, they condemned him for contumacy, and he was removed from the city with a view to his exile: So soon as he had been taken across the Hellespont, not only did the people rise and revolt, but a terrible earthquake shook the foundations of the palace, to the great terror of both Emperor and Empress, who at once recalled him. The re-entry of the Arch-

[1] This man was responsible for the burning of the Serapæum at Alexandria with its famous library.

bishop amid the acclamations of the people resembled the
return of Athanasius to Alexandria. But his enemies
were too strong for him. Soon after this Eudoxia
caused a great silver statue of herself to be erected just
outside the cathedral, and the noise of the ceremony
interrupted the service in the church. It was then that
Chrysostom is supposed to have said in the pulpit,
though the story lacks confirmation, "Herodias is again
furious; again she dances; again she demands the head
of John." The outcome, at any rate, was that another
synod of hostile bishops was summoned, which cited a
canon of the council at Antioch in 341, that a deposed
bishop cannot be reinstated by the secular arm; and
by this means Chrysostom was finally overwhelmed.
In 404 he was again exiled under cruel conditions, and
three years afterwards he died. The last tragic scene
in his bishopric was a forcible entry of soldiers into the
cathedral during the baptisms of Easter eve, when a
scene of sacrilege occurred, which reduced Chrysostom
to despair.

It has been aptly said of St. Chrysostom that his whole
heart was inflamed with the love of God, and that his
works are a practical exposition of how best to attain
to it. The Bible, he said himself, was the curer of all
ills; and of the Bible he had a profound knowledge,
though he was sometimes hampered in explaining it by
his ignorance of Hebrew, and also of the Jewish customs
and modes of thought in New Testament times. There
was also a tendency in his sermons to exaggerate the
relative importance of the subject which he was treating
at the moment. His chief merits were his sound common
sense, the vigour and lucidity of his exposition, and the
sympathy with fallen humanity which always shone
through it.

The common-sense element was attributable partly to
his training at Antioch; for it was characteristic
throughout of the Antiochene school, as contrasted with

the allegorical interpretations of Alexandria. The Arians, by their appeal to Scriptural texts in order to enforce their views, had encouraged a closer study of the Bible by the Church, and it was from Antioch that the soundest system of interpretation came. The Antiochene method was to extract from Scripture all that it was capable of, but not as the Alexandrians did, to put all they could into it in the shape of allegory. To see type and metaphor was allowable; but Chrysostom disclaimed allegory, except where allegorical intention was obvious, as in Isaiah v. the allegory of the Vineyard; where the mind of Scripture was allegorical, allegory was permissible, but the allegorizing tendency must be restrained. Again, Scripture was the word of God, but it was delivered through human channels; the writer's own natural powers were illuminated and quickened, but not superseded, by the spirit. The Old Testament revelation was one with that of the New; Christianity had always existed; the prophets knew Christ, or how could they have written of him? God's gift of the Bible to men (Chrysostom is the first to speak of the Books, the Biblia, the Bible) was akin to the gift of the Incarnation. In each case there was the same " Condensation " ($\sigma\upsilon\gamma\varkappa\alpha\tau\acute{\alpha}\beta\alpha\sigma\iota\varsigma$). As in the Incarnation, so in the Bible, God's glory was revealed, but veiled; in the latter it was veiled in human thought and language. The revelation was also conditioned not only by the instruments through which it came, but also by the moral and intellectual developments of those who received it. Revelation was gradual; and thus the Antiochene school recognized the gradual education of the human race. The historical books were real history; only the historical element was subservient to the spiritual.

In St. Chrysostom's homilies will be found valuable hints as to the order and date of the gospels; he believed St. John's Gospel was clearly written within a generation of the events described, and he pointed out that its intention was entirely theological. The parables, on the other hand, he held, were always intended to encourage a holy life, rather than orthodoxy. Throughout his sermons is the closest attention to words; for instance, in the parable of the Sower he points out that the seed *fell,* by the wayside; the Divine sower did not *cast* it there.

In dealing with St. Paul's epistles, he shows the same attention to their order, and to the place where they were written, as throwing much light on their purpose. He examines minutely St. Paul's metaphors, military, agricultural, building, etc., and not only appreciates but adopts his irony, and his habits of paradox, reductio ad absurdum and " going off at a tangent.",[1] St. Paul was always his chief master.

The theology of Chrysostom [2] was more Western than Eastern; one may almost say it was more Western than the West. Not only did he care very little for metaphysical speculations, and therefore we find but few philosophical terms; but his teaching is simpler than that of most of the Westerns; because, although they cared little for metaphysics, they also had a science of their own, jurisprudence; consequently their theology was influenced by the analogy of the forum. Chrysostom, although he occasionally borrowed metaphors and illustrations from Plato, altogether repudiated him as a teacher. He says once, " Plato, who talked a great deal of nonsense in his day : "[3] yet he admitted that Plato was the first of Pagan teachers, and that St. Paul's greatest victory was to have overcome him.

Chrysostom divided man into Soul and Body, and avoided the triple distinction of Body, Soul and Spirit. The " image of God " meant with him that man shared with God the domination over the rest of Creation.

---

[1] See Chace, *St. Chrysostom : A Study of Bible Interpretation.*
[2] See Stephen's *Life of Chrysostom.*   [3] Acts iv.

The cause of sin was with all men, as with Eve, moral negligence; for man, if he chose to use it, had absolute freedom of will. This apparent denial of original sin made him suspected of at least *semi*-Pelagianism; from which charge Augustine took pains to clear him. He believed, not in hereditary sin, but in an hereditary tendency to sin. The tendency to sin was universal; yet the freedom of the will was essential. His saving position, however, was that man could do no good without grace; only grace was assistant, not prevenient; it was always there ready, but it must be sought. " God," he said, " foreordained all men to holiness and salvation, and Christ died for all and is able and willing to save all, but not against their will, and without their free consent. When we have begun, when we have sent our will before, then God gives us abundant opportunity of salvation." [1] Faith and works are necessary conditions of justification and salvation, though Christ's merits alone are the efficient cause. We can do no good thing unless we are aided from above.[2] Chrysostom's witness against the Arians is to be found in a few homilies delivered at Antioch, and is not important. As to the new controversy about Christ's nature, he taught that, while man is soul and body, Christ was God, Soul and Body; that is, the Human soul, as well as the human body, was there; but the body and soul were united with, not fused in, the Godhead.[3]

On Redemption he was not precise, and there is some trace of the theory of ransom from, coupled with deception of, the Devil.[4]

Infant Baptism he seems not to have pressed, though he strongly deprecated deferring adult baptism.

Damnation he believed to be eternal; but that it was mitigated by God's mercy, and that prayers of the living for the dead were efficacious.

[1] John i. 38.　　　[2] *Ibid.*, vi. 44.　　　[3] Phil., Hom. VII.
[4] Matt., Hom. III.; 1 Cor., Hom. XXIV.

. And as the living could help the dead, so surely the dead could hear and help the living. "Let us constantly visit them, touch their shrines, and with faith embrace their relics, that we may derive some blessing therefrom; for like soldiers who converse freely with their sovereign, when they display their wounds, so these (beheaded by Julian) bearing their heads in their hands, are easily able to effect what they desire at the court of the King of heaven." [1]

Three points were evidently clear in Chrysostom's view of the Eucharist, a Sacrifice, a Real Presence and a Real Reception; but the words in which he generally expressed himself, carried away as he was by his enthusiasm, are easily interpreted differently by different schools.

As to the Sacrifice, he says,[2] "Christ is our High Priest, who offered the sacrifice that cleanseth us. That sacrifice we offer now also, which was then offered, and cannot be exhausted. This is done in remembrance of what was then done : for He said, "Do this," etc. It is not another sacrifice that we make, as the high priest did of old, but always the same; or, rather, we perform a remembrance of the sacrifice."

As to an objective Presence he uses the strongest possible words : for instance, "When you see the Lord laid there and the priest standing over the sacrifice and praying and all stained with that precious Blood." [3] In another place he speaks of the communicant's lips being empurpled by the Blood. But these words are so vivid that they seem to overreach the mark; since no one has yet claimed that the accidents (e. g. the colour) of the wine are changed. It is therefore questioned whether the whole language is not figurative or mystical.

There is also a letter to Cæsarius, which has been

---

[1] Hom. in Juvent and Max.   [2] Hebr., Hom. XVII. 3.
[3] *Priesthood*, III. 4.

sometimes attributed to Chrysostom, in which he says :
" It is liberated from the appellation of bread, and
thought worthy of the appellation of the Lord's Body,
although the nature of bread remains in it." But the
best authorities consider this letter spurious.

When the English Reformers discouraged those, who
were not then communicating, from remaining in
Church (as they certainly did, though it was never
actually forbidden), they appealed to the example of the
Primitive Church, and the words of St. Chrysostom.
The same words have continually been quoted since;
notably in Hook's *Church Dictionary.* He asked his
people how, if they were not fit to communicate, were
they fit to join in the prayer? Had they not better stay
at home? The author of *Notitia Eucharistica* also gives
this as the Patristic authority for the English Reformers;
but he quaintly adds that the result of the rebuke was
not to bring them to Communion; they took him rather
at his word and stayed at home.

In the very primitive Church certainly there was no
such thing as hearing Mass, for the simple reason that
the communions of all Christians were very frequent.
The question of going to Church between times hardly
arose. In Cyprian's time Christians communicated
daily, and often took home consecrated breads for
private consumption; so that communions were even
more frequent than celebrations. Even in Augustine's
church weekly communions were almost universal.
St. Basil speaks of the custom as daily at Rome. But
in the fourth-century in the East, things began to be
different, as the idea of the "tremendous mystery"
developed. In 340 the Council of Sardica issued a canon
excommunicating those who thoughtlessly or irreverently
left the Church before the Eucharist proper had begun.
And throughout the Church generally, as frequent communions dropped out, the tendency was always to dis-
courage any baptized person from going away. In the

fifth century, not so long after Chrysostom's time, an Alexandrian writer said : " If thy conscience condemn thee, decline the communion, but stay during the prayer, and do not leave till dismissed." About 500 a bishop of Arles ordered his people to stay till after the Lord's Prayer, which immediately followed the celebrant's communion; and this injunction was soon afterwards confirmed at a Council of Orleans. If, therefore, Chrysostom's view was what Protestants claim, it was not in accordance with the mind of the Church of the following century.

In 404 Chrysostom was exiled. After a fortnight's stay at Nicæa, he was deported to Cucusus in Lower Armenia. From there he wrote most of his 242 letters that are extant, and from these we gather that he still exercised a considerable influence even at Constantinople. He also evangelized the Lebanon district, a last stronghold of Paganism, and at that time in a condition almost of savagery. But by a cruel order of the Court he was dragged away to a more desert spot by forced marches which caused his death, before he had arrived at Pityus, his destination. Thirty years afterwards Theodosius II and his sister ordered his remains to be brought back to Constantinople; and the Emperor, laying his face on the reliquary, implored the forgiveness of God for the cruelty of his parents.

The relations of Pope Innocent and Chrysostom are interesting. The Pope defended him bravely; but was too much occupied with troubles at home to do much good, for Alaric and his Goths were threatening Rome.

What was really Chrysostom's liturgy, or how much he added to the existing one, is entirely unknown. What is known as his liturgy is used always in the Greek Church, except on the eves of Christmas, Epiphany and Easter, when Basil's is substituted. Quite early in it occurs the prayer so familiar to the English Church.

In his work on St. Chrysostom, the Abbé Martin says,

" Chrysostom was the supreme effort and last splendour of the Christian genius in the East.   After him, its fall was rapid, dragging everything with it into the tombs, the future as well as the past.   There are still a few champions of orthodoxy to come, like Proclus, Cyril of Alexandria and John of Damascus.   But the grandeur, the strength, the fecundity, the genius disappeared from the worn-out and degenerate East with Chrysostom."·

That he was so greatly hated by some is hardly to be wondered at, when we remember the scorn with which he spoke of the Empress; or of Eutropius, as he lay at his feet; or when we remember that he deposed thirteen Asia Minor bishops, over whom he had no legitimate jurisdiction, and on one occasion told his hearers that he thought very few of the bishops would be saved : that most of them were eternally lost.   But ·the poor and the good alike adored him.   In every poor man he saw Christ.   " Gain a victory," he says, " overi the Church; put us to shame; surpass us in liberality; keep a room in which Christ may come : say this is Christ's cell : this is set apart for Him.   Be it but an underground chamber; He disdains it not : naked and a stranger ·Christ goes about; it is only a shelter He wants : give it Him, though only this; you ought, indeed, to receive Him in an upper chamber : but if you cannot do this, then though it be below, and where thy servants and mules are housed, at least there receive Him.   Perhaps you shudder at this; but you do not even do this." [1]   " Better at least receive Christ in the stable than outside the gate."

Cardinal Newman says he was " a bright and cheerful and gentle soul, whose unrivalled charm lay in his singleness of purpose, his fixed grasp of aim, his noble earnestness; he had a sensitive heart, a temperament open to emotion and impulse, and all was elevated, refined and transformed by the touch of heaven. He

[1] Acts xlv.

was indeed a man to make both friends and enemies, to inspire affection and kindle resentment; but his friends loved him with a love that was stronger than death, and his enemies hated him with a hatred more burning than hell, and it was well to be so hated, to be so beloved." [1]

Although Chrysostom's works include a number of minor treatises, and panegyrics, and the famous Homilies on the Statues, which last contain some of the best examples of his eloquence, his most valuable works are the homilies expounding Scripture. He is believed at one time or another to have expounded the whole Bible; but all that have come down to us are Genesis, Psalms, St. Matthew, St. John, St. Paul's Epistles and the Acts. The first four, and Romans and Corinthians were given at Antioch, and are his best work : it seems that at Antioch he had more leisure to do himself justice. There are also five Homilies on Hannah; three on David and Saul; and a few on the first eight chapters of Isaiah.

[1] *Historical Sketches,* pp. 234, 237.

CHAPTER XVIII

ST. JEROME

(Born-probably about 346. Ordained priest 379. Died 420)

St. Jerome was not a great theologian, and could hardly be called an original thinker; even his commentaries contain rather a collection of the views of the best authorities than any new ideas of his own. Nor was he mixed up with any of the great historical events of his time. Nor was he apparently of a very lovable disposition. Yet he did more than any other man, more perhaps than even the great St. Augustine himself, to shape the tendency and direct the current of the Western Church; so that he is said to have "lived and reigned a thousand years." He was one of the four great doctors of the West, his claim to the title being fully justified by his Latin translation of the Bible. The other three were Ambrose, Augustine and Gregory the Great, of whom the last does not come within the date limit of this book.

It will be useful to first summarize the natural divisions of his life, and then to deal with the subjects that arise out of them.

Eusebius Hieronymus Sophronius, known as Jerome in France and England, Girolamo in Italy, and Hieronymus for literary purposes, was born according to the best authorities in 346 at Strido, near Aquileia, the capital of Venetia. By some the date is given as early as 336; but this is improbable. From 363 to 366 he was educated at Rome; where after a short period of dissipation, he became serious and was baptized,.

probably by Pope Liberius. From 366 to 370 he travelled in Gaul for purposes of research, and produced his earliest work, *On Obadiah*. From 370 to 373 he was at Aquileia, where he had his first experience of a sort of monastic life; and in connection with it, established a friendship with Rufinus, with whom in later life he engaged in bitter controversy. The few young men, who joined him here in what turned out rather an unsuccessful experiment, were discouraged by the bishop; whom Jerome consequently described as " the ignorant, brutal, wicked, unskilful pilot of a crazy bark." Evagrius, a priest of Antioch, who came to Aquileia on the business of Paulinus, persuaded them to return with him to the East and learn about monasticism in its own home : and in 374 Jerome travelled through the East; made his first visit to Jerusalem; and then retired into the desert of Chalcis for about five years, practising the most intense asceticism, but perpetually haunted by reminiscences of the world and the flesh. He took, however, his classical library with him, and comforted himself with Greek and Latin; till one night he dreamed that a judge, before whom he was brought, punished him for being a Ciceronian and not a Christian; whereupon (in his dream apparently) he vowed to devote his intellect entirely to the Scriptures, and on waking proceeded to learn Hebrew. But his health broke down, and we find him in 379 at Antioch, where Paulinus ordained him priest; but so much against his will, that he is believed to have never exercised priestly functions. In the following year, 380, he gratified his great wish to hear Gregory of Nazianzus by going to Constantinople; and in 382 returned to Rome, having been present at the Second Council. From 382 to 385 in Rome he is conspicuous for two things : for his close friendship with Pope Damasus, to whom he acted as literary adviser, and perhaps Papal Secretary; and for his friendship with several noble ladies, who had devoted themselves to the ascetic life. He became, however, so unpopular in Rome, owing to his encouragement of asceticism, that he declared he was " singing the Lord's song in a strange land," and so resolved to finish his life in the East. In 886 therefore, after spending some time in Alexandria, and listening to the lectures of Didymus, the blind head of the Catechetical School, he went to Jerusalem, and established himself at Bethlehem till 420, when he died. Almost all the best work of St. Jerome was done during these thirty-four years at Bethlehem. Such is a brief epitome of his life.

Jerome was not only a Western, but an Italian; and in spite of the great importance at that date of Milan, no doubt the supremacy of Rome had by this time more firmly established itself in Italy than elsewhere. This must be taken into consideration when judging how far a celebrated letter of Jerome to the Pope is an evidence of any general recognition of the authority of the see of Peter. It is a very strong letter. Jerome finds at Antioch three rival bishops : Meletius, representing the great body of orthodox Christians; Paulinus, representing the extreme Catholics and supported by Rome; and Vitalis, representing the Semi-Arians. He is puzzled by their conflicting views, and especially by the Catholic use of the word Hypostasis in the East; and he writes to Damasus, the head of the Church in his own country, in despair, using such words as these : " Although your greatness awes me, your humanity encourages me. It is to the successor of the fisherman and the disciple of the Cross that I speak. I, who have no other guide by Christ, unite myself in communion with the chair of Peter; I know that on that rock the Church is built. Whoever shall eat the lamb outside that house is profane. If any one finds himself outside the ark of Noah, he will perish in the deluge." [1]

[1] Letter 15.

He had previously said, " I consult the chair of Peter and the Church that was praised by Paul. I appeal for spiritual food to the Church whence I received the robe of Christ (*i. e.* baptism)." The latter quotation somewhat modifies the former.

When Jerome returned to Rome in 382, he was appointed secretary to the Council, which Damasus had summoned, intending it to be Œcumenical and to override the Council at Constantinople of the previous year, which was purely Eastern. But the latter was recognized as Œcumenical by subsequent ages, and the Roman Council was not. The Eastern bishops refused to attend; except Paulinus of Antioch, who depended on Roman support, and Epiphanius of Cyprus. There was also an official deputation of minor bishops. The main object of the Council was to decide between rival claimants to the sees of Constantinople, Antioch, Alexandria and Jerusalem. With the exception of Alexandria, the Council seems to have judged unwisely : contrary, that is, to the judgment of the East and of posterity. It confirmed the intruder Maximus at Constantinople, and supported Paulinus against Meletius at Antioch, Hilarius against Cyril at Jerusalem. But one good result came of it : Epiphanius worsted the Apollinarians in argument, and effected their reconciliation. It is also to be noted that Damasus summoned the Council in very moderate words : " Although we do not claim the prerogative of judgment in this matter, we do claim a part in a decision which affects the whole Church." Reasonable, surely, since the Western bishops had not even been invited to Constantinople.

By this time Jerome was already recognized at Rome as the great authority on biblical interpretation, especially by Damasus; who consulted him frequently, and at whose request he made a fresh translation into Latin of the New Testament. The

fame, in fact, of Jerome and his influence on the Western
Church may be traced to two causes; his translation
into Latin of the whole Bible, which, under the name
of the Vulgate, is in use to the present day; and the
great impetus that he gave to monasticism.

It is not true that Jerome *founded* Western monasticism, though he did so much to encourage it. Even
before the time of Constantine some of the Roman
ladies had withdrawn into ascetic retirement. The
visit of Athanasius, however, to Rome in 341 with two
monks first awakened public interest in the ascetic
movement of the East. Similarly his long stay at
Trèves introduced the idea into Gaul. In the latter
country it was rapidly developed under the influence
of St. Martin and others, and the convent of Marmon-
tier, till the time of the Revolution one of the most
important in France, dates back from the middle of
the fourth century.

But in Rome, when Jerome came, the formation of
actual communities had hardly commenced; although
several prominent ladies had devoted themselves to an
ascetic and charitable life. However, Marcella, who
had been the beauty of her time, gave up her palace on
the Aventine as a meeting-place for others like herself,
and with them formed something like a community.[1]
Jerome was called in as a sort of Director, and used to
speak of her house as the " domestic church." About
this time also Melania, losing her husband and two of
her three children, resolved to sacrifice all her wealth,
and spend the rest of her life in the Holy Land; leaving
her remaining child to be provided for by God. This
was the beginning of the great " Roman Emigration
to the Holy Land," [2] in which Jerome and Paula presently played the chief part. The desertion of her child

---

[1] Letter 127.
[2] Amédée Thierry, *St. Jerome, la Société Chrétienne à Rome,
et l'émigration Romaine en Terre Sainte.*

by Melania provoked an outburst of indignation in
Rome, especially against Jerome, who took her part;
it was, in fact, the moment at which his popularity
began to wane. The current began to set strongly
against all this asceticism: the more strongly because
among the old families of senatorial rank there still
lingered a strong remnant of Paganism,[1] resting not so
much on religious conviction as a conservative support
of the religion of ancient Rome. Many of the senators,
in fact, held priestly offices, and it must have been a
great mortification to them to see their women-folk not
only Christians, but sacrificing both their wealth and
their social position. As for Melania, she met in Egypt
Rufinus, the former companion of Jerome, went with
him to Palestine, and on the Mount of Olives they
jointly founded a monastery and a nunnery. Up to
this time the learned Jerome, the friend of the Pope,
had been marked out as his successor[2]; but in 384
(December) Damasus died, and Siricius was elected by
popular acclamation. Jerome's popularity was then
dead. The new Pope discouraged asceticism. Blesilla,
the widowed daughter of Paula, Jerome's especial ally,
died from the effects of much fasting, and popular
indignation knew no bounds. Jerome was, they said,
"too free with his tongue, uncharitable, sly, a hypo-
crite, the arch-monk. To the Tiber with all the monks."
So he decided to spend the rest of his days in the Holy
Places of Palestine, and the saintly Paula and her
daughter Eustochium agreed to meet him there.

The life of Paula is so interwoven with that of Jerome
that it is necessary to pay some separate attention to
her. She was the widow of Julius Toxotius, who belonged to one of the oldest families in Rome, as she
also did herself. Widowed when only twenty years
old, she brought up four daughters and a son, who all
more or less come into her story. The eldest, Blesilla,

---

[1] Gibbon, ch. xxviii.   [2] Letter 45.

was also left a widow in her youth, at once surrendered all her luxuries, became ascetic, and shortly afterwards died. Her death, as has been already mentioned, was attributed to her austerities, and made St. Jerome unpopular. Paulina, the second daughter, married Jerome's friend, Pammachius, a cousin of Marcella, and died young; her husband then devoted his life to good works, and founded a hospital. The third, Eustochium, definitely " took the veil " and is said to have been the first patrician who did so; she accompanied her mother to Bethlehem, and carried on her work at her death. Rufina, the fourth, married and remained at Rome. The son, Toxotius, married Læta, and had a daughter Paula; who was devoted to virginity from her birth; went out to Bethlehem; and after the deaths of Paula and Eustochium became the third head of the convent of Paula.[1]

Jerome, Paula and Eustochium all met at Antioch. They made first a preliminary visit to the Holy Land, and then passed on to Egypt, with the view partly of studying under Didymus at Alexandria, and partly of observing the life of the Egyptian monks at Nitria. When these ends had been accomplished, they finally settled at Bethlehem, and proceeded to found a monastery and a nunnery. In this work Paula's share seems to have been the most important. Paula is, in fact, the organizer and administrator: Jerome devotes himself in his cell, close to the site of the Nativity (his " Paradise " he called it), to reading and writing. When he came out it was generally to teach; either to comment on the Bible to his fellow-monks, or to give general instruction to the young. For the last purpose, in spite of his dream vow, he resumed the classics. But even in his literary work, Paula and Eustochium helped him considerably; for they also had learnt Hebrew. Paula seems to have been a most remarkable woman

---

[1] Letter 108 (*Life of Paula*).

on both her practical and intellectual side, while Jerome
laid no claim to administrative ability. His monastery
was rather a hostelry, to which the world might come
and rest; and it is here probably that Jerome's influence
on Western monasticism is to be found. He created
an object lesson on monasticism at the most sacred spot
in the world, and he invited the world to come and
learn. And the world came, for his hostelry was continually filled with travellers from the West. In consequence three great features of the Catholic West
appear now, which have continued ever since: the
reverence for the monastic life; the reverence for
sacred places and sacred things; and the habit of pilgrimages. But there is no Rule of St. Jerome, as there
is of St. Pachomius, St. Basil or St. Benedict, and no
monastic order was named after him. Paula, on the
contrary, though she followed mainly the Rule of
Pachomius, was practically the founder of nunneries,
and her convent served as a model for all time.[1] The
Psalter was repeated every day; five offices were held
during the day, and one in the night: portions of
Scripture had to be regularly learnt; the costume was
woollen and uniform; mortification was enjoined:
work was essential, consisting chiefly of the copying of
MSS. and the making of clothes for the poor. Lastly,
all communication with the outside world was strictly
forbidden.

What Jerome did for the religious life was to press
it on his followers, to advise on it, to display it, but not
to organize it. Still less did he do, like St. Martin,
missionary work in connection with it. Yet the
Western Church looks back to him as being mainly
responsible for it.

There are other ways also in which the great learning
and influence of Jerome seems to have directed the
current of Western Catholicism, especially as regards

[1] Letter 108.

the respect for authority, of the Pope in the first place,
but also of the priesthood generally; though it seems
that he considered the offices of priest and bishop to
be essentially the same, except as to the power of
ordaining.[1] The volume on Jerome in the Lille edition
quotes at great length a devotional passage to the
Blessed Virgin, which is quite like mediæval or modern
devotion; making her not only Mother of God, but
also Queen of Heaven, pattern and protectress of
mankind; whose aid is to be directly invoked; and
even calling her the living image of God. No reference is given; but according to Migne the letter is
spurious.[2]

As regards the need of the monks in the Church,
Montalambert says, " The Roman Empire without the
barbarians was an abyss of servitude and corruption;
the barbarians without the monks were chaos.[3] The
barbarians and the monks united recreated a world
which was to be called Christendom." We are apt to
suppose that in the monasteries great masses of men
were hidden away in seclusion, who might have been
more actively employed in fighting for the cause of the
Church; but besides holding up a high standard, they
were always at work; and when the occasion justified
it, they emerged, sometimes individually, sometimes
collectively, from their retreats to join in the fight.
Thus St. Antony came to Alexandria on the invitation
of Athanasius, to preach against the Arians: when
Antioch was under the sentence of Theodosius, the
monks came *en masse* out of the desert and caused
the suspension of the sentence. Sometimes less wisely
they came into the cities and joined in a religious riot.
Telemachus, when Honorius revived the gladiatorial
contests at Rome, came all the way from the East,

---

[1] Letter 14. Priests "have the keys of heaven, and judge
men to some extent before the judgment."

[2] Migne, *Jerome, Litt. supposititia,* X.

[3] *Monks of the West,* end of Book I.

and threw himself between the gladiators. He was stoned to death by the populace, but the contests were never again revived. Many of the great bishops of the age also had served their time in retreats; and Jerome with his controversies and commentaries was a living power all through the Bethlehem period.

In 383, Jerome replied to a pamphlet by one, Helvidius, claiming that the brethren of Jesus were really his brothers, and that the Virgin did not always remain so; arguing that the state of virginity was therefore less blessed than that of marriage. Jerome replied at great length that the brethren were cousins or kinsfolk, and that virginity was the highest state. He called Helvidius an ignorant boor, besides using many other offensive expressions; for he never seemed to consider it unworthy of his profession to be scurrilous. With this exception most of his controversial work came from his retreat at Bethlehem.

Jovinian (393) also attacked virginity, saying that it was no better in God's sight than marriage; but he extended his attack much further, denouncing fasting as well; declaring also that no sin was possible after a true baptism of the spirit, and that there would only be one class of rewards and punishments hereafter. Jerome said he was one of those " seducing mockers " who, St. Peter prophesied, would come; " walking after their own lusts," and heaped a great deal more infamy on him. But his reply, which runs into two books, displays a great mass of learning; for he cites in endless detail the Old and New Testament, Greek and Roman history, philosophy, mythology, poetry, and even Buddhism.

The treatise against Vigilantius is the most violent of all his controversial works. This man, whom Milman calls a " premature Protestant," attacked prevalent Catholic customs—veneration of relics, prayers to the dead, vigils at martyrs' tombs, lighting of candles in church, alleged miracles, and also the ascetic life. Jerome's reply contains some interesting side-lights. One is that many bishops refused to ordain an un-married man, which refusal became subsequently the general Greek custom. Also we read that it was uni-versal in the Eastern churches, to light candles as a sign of joy at the Gospel. Jerome also speaks of " an apocryphal book, which under the name of Esdras, is read by you and others of your feather. I have never read the book; for what need is there to take up a book which the Church does not receive ? " [1]

These treatises in favour of Virginity were considered by St. Augustine as so extravagant that he toned things down by writing one in praise of marriage.

Origenism also brought Jerome into a good deal of controversy. He was always an immense admirer of Origen, but in later years found that many of his doc-trines were unsound, and he then restricted his admira-tion to Origen's literary side. In 399 Epiphanius came to Jerusalem, and denounced the Origenism of the bishop John. This naturally involved the Convents at Bethlehem and on the Mount of Olives. Rufinus and John were ranged against Epiphanius and Jerome, and the latter wrote a treatise to Pammachius against John of Jerusalem. Rufinus continued openly for the time his friendship with Jerome, but shortly afterwards went to Rome. There he published a free translation of Origen's *Periarchon* and alluded in the preface to Jerome as his predecessor, thus adopting Jerome as an Origenite.[2] Jerome published a literal translation of the book, and never forgave Rufinus; not even, for he survived him,[3] his memory.

Augustine on one occasion reproached Jerome by letter for treating the dispute between Paul and Peter

[1] See Church of England, Art. 6, and Jerome's Preface to Books of Solomon, and elsewhere.
[2] See Letters 82 and 84 for refutation of Origen.
[3] Letter 125.

(Gal. ii.) as a feigned dispute arranged in order to make the truth clear, and for thus casting doubt on their sincerity. Unfortunately the letter got opened at Rome and never reached Jerome. A second letter similarly went astray. Jerome, with his naturally angry temper, accused Augustine of attacking him behind his back. At last a most courteous and dignified letter from Augustine put everything straight, and they were afterwards fast friends in frequent correspondence. Jerome accepted Augustine's explanation, asking him when he wrote to him in future, to take care that he got the letter unopened. There is a story, but it altogether lacks confirmation, that Augustine administered to Jerome the last rites.

St. Jerome was a voracious reader, gifted apparently with a wonderful memory; he was also a most industrious writer, and a patient scholar; for he acquired a complete knowledge of both Hebrew and Aramaic: but he had no talent for historical criticism, nor did he care much for theology. His historical work is an excellent résumé of what others had done; in theology he followed along the lines enjoined by authority; was very nervous about getting off them: but had no interest in examining them. But in his translations he had absolute confidence in his own judgment and maintained strictly his independence. Thierry says that he was the last great man of the early Church; Augustine certainly survived him for a few years, but was practically his contemporary: and when both had died, " darkness fell on the West."

The main interest lies in his 150 Letters and his translation of the Bible into Latin, known ever since as the Vulgate. The letters, with the exception of those that were controversial or exegetic, form really an autobiography, and practically everything we know of the personal incidents of his life comes from them, especially his relation to his various friends and enemies.

At the request of Damasus, he revised the current translation of the New Testament, and also the Psalms by reference to the Septuagint, and his translation of the Psalms was at once adopted as the Roman Psalter. During his first few years at Bethlehem he made a further collation of the Bible, with the help of Origen's *Hexapla*, and by reference to the Hebrew. Probably he dealt with the whole Bible, but this is uncertain, as only Job, the Psalms, and a Preface to the books of Solomon have come down to us. But this translation of the Psalms was soon adopted in Gaul for general use and was therefore known as the Gallican Psalter. In Rome it was not brought into Church use till 1566, but it found its place early in the Vulgate to the exclusion of Jerome's direct translation from the Hebrew.

The final work, the Vulgate itself, came from his recognition of the insufficiency of all translations from the Greek; and in order to carry it out he perfected his previous moderate knowledge of Hebrew. He also learnt Aramaic, and translated from that language Tobit and Judith in spite of his repudiation of the Apocrypha from the Canon.

The following are the order and dates of the books of the Vulgate, all of the Bethlehem period :—

> 391–2. Samuel and Kings, and the Psalms about the same time which were not taken into the Vulgate.
>
> 393. The Prophets and Job.
>
> 394. Ezra, Nehemiah and Chronicles.
>
> 398. The books of Solomon.
>
> 400 and later. The Pentateuch.
>
> 404. Joshua, Judges, Ruth, Esther.

Jerome's commentaries are sometimes his own and sometimes direct translations from Origen. He also produced certain works illustrating Scripture, such as a book of Hebrew names, and questions on Genesis. He also translated from Eusebius a work, on the sites and names of Hebrew places and his *Chronicle* : also Didymus' book on the Holy Spirit. He began the last at Rome when Damasus chaffed him, for not working hard enough, and finished it at Bethlehem. Also he translated the Rule of Pachomius. As to biography, he wrote a catalogue of ecclesiastical writers and *Lives of the Hermits*. Finally came his controversial works, which, with the exception of a treatise against the Pelagians and the followers of Lucifer of Cagliari, have already been noticed.

But by far the greatest work that Jerome accomplished was to give to the Western Church the Bible correctly translated into the vulgar tongue (the Vulgate). For not only was Latin at that time the general language of the West, but right through the Middle Ages it was the language of the educated, so that any one who could read at all could probably read Latin. He had the advantage not only of the environment of the sacred places, of his own profound learning and constant study, but also the aid of the Rabbinical College at Tiberias.

The earliest Latin translation seems to have come, like all other beginnings of Latin Christianity, in the middle of the second century from Africa; but owing to its provincialism, a new version of at any rate the Gospels was issued by authority in North Italy in the fourth century, and known as the Itala. Many minor revisions were also made without authority, so that in the time of Jerome there was great confusion in the MSS. And now that East and West were drifting apart both in Church and State, it was of the utmost importance that a correct Bible should be secured for the West in time. Jerome was the one man best suited for this work and devoted fourteen years of his life to doing it. Finally the East profited also, as Sophronius translated the Vulgate into Greek.

The New Testament of Jerome was not a new translation, but a correction of the old Latin by recourse to the Greek. The Apocrypha Jerome repudiated; consequently this remained in the language of the Old Version, except Judith and Tobit, which he rather cursorily revised from the Aramaic. But the canonical Old Testament was entirely re-edited from the Hebrew. Naturally it met with a great deal of opposition, and he was accused of innovating, and of upsetting the very foundations of the Faith. Even St. Augustine preferred to go on expounding the Old Version, to which his hearers were accustomed, and wrote to Jerome (another letter which failed to arrive, and caused mischief) advising him to revise the Septuagint translations rather than translate afresh. Jerome's Bible gradually made its way, tolerated at first rather than adopted; yet even in the eighth century it had hardly come into general use. And, further, corruptions crept into it, as into the old versions. In 802 Alcuin was ordered by Charlemagne, who is thought to have personally assisted in the work, to restore the Vulgate itself to its original state; which he did with fair accuracy. In 1546 the Council of Trent decreed that all MSS., but especially the Vulgate, or old and common edition, should be printed as correctly as possible. In 1590 Sixtus V brought out a new revision, which he ordered to be the only authorized edition for all time; but this again was revised two years later under Clement VIII, and that revision is still the authorized version of the Roman Catholic Church. As has already been said, till the sixteenth century (1566) Jerome's translation of the Psalms, known as the Gallican Psalter, was not taken over by the Roman Church, so that up to that time the old Roman Psalter (his revision from the Septuagint) remained in Church use although the Gallican Psalter had got into the Vulgate. The version of the Psalms in the English Prayer Book is taken from the " Great English Bible " of 1540, which was a translation of

the Vulgate, and therefore differs from the Authorized
Version. In either case (Rome of the fourth and England of the sixteenth century) there was a reluctance
to give up familiar versions, in everyday use and
learnt by heart, in favour of later direct translations.

Jerome's view of the Bible was this: "All that we
read in the Scripture is light; even when we do not go
below the surface. But it is in its marrow that its
great treasures are hidden. You must break the shell
in order to reach the kernel." [1] This may be compared
with the more beautiful words of Augustine: " I
referred to the depth of the mysteries, and its authority
appeared to me the more venerable, and more worthy
of religious credence, in that, while it lay open for all
to read, it reserved the majesty of its mysteries within
its profounder meaning, stooping to all in the great
plainness of its words and lowliness of its style, yet
calling forth the intensest application of such as are
not light of heart; that so it might receive all in its
open bosom, and through narrow passages waft over
towards Thee some few, yet many more than if it stood
not aloft on such a height of authority, nor drew
multitudes within its bosom by its holy lowliness." [2]

In 404 the Vulgate was finished, and Paula was dead.
During the remaining sixteen years of his life, Jerome
saw much trouble, although his influence on the Church
deepened, and the range of his correspondence widened:
The private means of both Paula and himself were
exhausted, and it became difficult to make both ends
meet, especially to maintain the hospitality that was
expected of him. When the terrible sack of Rome by
Alaric and his Goths came in 410, and numbers of
Romans fled to Palestine, the burden became still more
serious. It seems strange that Romans should have
fled for refuge to a place so difficult of access to us as the
Holy Land: but Roman rule was very different from

[1] Letter 58.   [2] *Confessions,* VI. 5.

Turkish. It was then merely necessary to cross the Mediterranean in order to find a province enjoying the best Roman civilization, and one of the most interesting parts of the Empire.

But Palestine had its own troubles as well as Italy. The Isaurians, who annoyed Chrysostom in his last journeys, were hovering over the North; at one time also there was a fearful scare from the Huns. When the Pelagian controversy broke out, which is more connected with Augustine's career than Jerome's, these heretics made Jerusalem their headquarters, and Pelagian monks attacked and partially destroyed the monasteries at Bethlehem. Then Jerome's health and eyesight failed him, and in 418 Eustochium died. He seemed to have outlived all his early friends and associates; for Pammachius had disappeared in the sack of Rome, and Marcella had died from injuries and indignities received at the same time. At last, in 420, after an illness of twelve months, Jerome died too; and even if Augustine was not present at the end, his friendship must have cheered and encouraged his last years. Up to the end he continued his Commentaries with unabated vigour, and when he died he left that on Jeremiah unfinished.

Many people shrink from criticizing Jerome's life and views, because the general feeling of the Christian world has been to regard him as a great Saint. If untiring industry makes a Saint, he certainly was one, and the work that he did for the Church in translating the Bible correctly can never be forgotten. The rest of his life was absorbed by the monastic idea; he even read it on every possible occasion into his Bible commentaries. The ideal that he had before him was celibacy *per se,* quite apart from meditation, devotion and work. But it was not permissible to disagree with him, for his vanity was sensitive. And nothing can be coarser than the rancour with which he attacked his opponents.

Something of the same coarseness even appears in his letter on Virginity, in which he contrasts the bride of Heaven with the brides of earth. His contempt for cleanliness is another sign of coarseness, anticipating the Middle Ages. " I wholly disapprove of baths for virgins of full age. Such a one should blush at the idea of seeing herself undressed." [1] Yet he was capable at times of great and unexpected gentleness; sometimes too he tempers his austerity with much commonsense; as when in a letter to a young virgin he says: " I do not lay on you as an obligation any extreme fasting or abnormal abstinence from food. Such practices soon break down weak constitutions and cause bodily sickness before they lay the foundations of a holy life." [2] He was always kind to the poor, and respectful to women.

Tillemont, one of the fairest of French Catholics, was, as Robertson points out, continually distracted between his own impressions of Jerome, and the authoritative judgment of his Church; and Newman, writing in his Anglican days, says reluctantly that there are things in his writings and views from which he shrinks: " I cannot force myself to approve or like contrary to my judgment or feeling; but I am willing to take certain characteristics of this learned and highly-gifted man on faith "; faith, that is, in the judgment of the Catholic world.[3] At any rate posterity has been more lenient to his weak points than he was to the faults of his contemporaries. It is curious to contemplate that, living into the fifth century, Jerome was the first Latin Father and after Origen the second Father of the whole Church that knew Hebrew.

[1] Letter 107.   [2] *Ibid.*, 130.
[3] *Church of the Fathers*, p. 263.

CHAPTER XIX

(Born 340. · *Archbishop of Milan* 874.   *Died* 397)

In St. Ambrose we have a man of action and also a man of letters. Gibbon says of him, " Ambrose could act better than he could write. His compositions are destitute of taste and genius; without the spirit of Tertullian, the copious elegance of Lactantius, the lively wit of Jerome, or the grave energy of Augustine." [1] But in spite of this sarcasm of Gibbon, Ambrose has always been accounted one of the four doctors of the Latin Church, although certainly his influence as an ecclesiastical statesman on the Church was greater than the influence of his writings. He brought the Church up to her proudest position in relation to the State, setting Church and State side by side as equals, one supreme in spiritual matters, the other in temporal. In this he was warmly supported by the Catholic loyalty of the Emperors Gratian and Theodosius; especially the latter, whose reign extended through almost the entire period of his Episcopate.

Theodosius was the last great Emperor of the West. In 410, only a few years after his death, Alaric and his Goths entered Rome and sacked the sacred city; and from that time there only lingered on in the marshes of Ravenna a shadow of the Imperial dignity, till in 476 even that disappeared. Theoretically the Western Empire was absorbed into the Eastern at that date; practically, however, the East ceased to trouble itself

---

[1] Gibbon, III. p. 175.

with the affairs of Italy, and the Popes planted themselves on the Imperial throne, till Charlemagne restored the Imperial dignity and created or recreated the Holy Roman Empire.

The ideal of that mediæval Empire is graphically described by Freeman [1] in a review of Bryce's *Holy Roman Empire*, and his description is interesting in the present connection. " The theory of the Mediæval Empire is that of an universal Christian monarchy. The Roman Empire and the Catholic Church are two aspects of one society, a society ordained by the Divine Will to spread itself over the whole world; of this society Rome is marked out by Divine Decree as the predestined capital, the chief seat alike of spiritual and temporal rule. At the head of this society, in its temporal character as an Empire, stands the temporal chief of Christendom, the Roman Cæsar. At its head, in its spiritual character as a Church, stands the spiritual chief of Christendom, the Roman Pontiff. Cæsar and Pontiff rule alike by Divine right, each as God's immediate Vicar within his own sphere. Each ruler is bound to the other by the closest ties. Cæsar is the advocate of the Roman Church, bound to defend her by the temporal arm against all temporal enemies. The Pontiff, on the other hand, though the Cæsar holds his rank not of him but by an independent divine commission, has the lofty privilege of personally admitting the lord of the world to his high office, of hallowing the Lord's Anointed, and of making him in some sort a partaker in the mysterious privilege of the priesthood."

Now, although this is descriptive of a relation between Church and State existing some five hundred years later, it is a fair account of what was probably the ideal of both Ambrose and Theodosius, except that neither of them yet realized a *monarchy* over spiritual things, as represented later by the Roman Pontiffs.

[1] *Historical Essays*, VI.

Still, if there was to be one spiritual head, Ambrose would no doubt have conceded the position to Rome. Nor did the Church consecrate the Emperor; yet by invitation, not by right, the Emperor was admitted into the sanctuary. But the absolute mutual dependence of Church and State was fully established by Ambrose and Theodosius, and the supreme authority of each in her own sphere.

Theodosius was a Spaniard, the son of a General who had done good service to the State and had then been executed out of jealousy. He was born in 346 and called by the good sense of Gratian in 379 from the retreat he had prudently sought after his father's death, to assume the purple in the East. By conviction a Catholic he was then baptized, and immediately took strong measures against heresy and paganism. In 380 the edict of Thessalonica, addressed to Constantinople in order to strengthen the position of Gregory, stated that the religion which St. Peter taught the Romans and which Damasus of Rome and Peter of Alexandria professed, was alone true: only the adherents of the doctrine that Father, Son and Holy Ghost should be equally adored were to be called Catholics; all others were heretics, whose places of assembly were not to be called churches, and whose souls were threatened with divine punishment. In 381 heretics were forbidden to meet for religion, and in 383 they were forbidden to build churches or ordain. In 389 the Emperor forbade Arians to bequeath property or to receive bequests.

As regards Paganism, in 382 Theodosius abolished the Altar of Victory in the Senate house, and confiscated the property of the Vestal virgins. In 389 the Christians of Alexandria destroyed the Serapæum, with the magnificent library it contained, when Pagans had taken refuge there during a riot. In 392 an edict of the Emperor made all Pagan worship illegal. In the Abolition of the Altar of Victory, which was a symbol to the conservative Roman of the whole history of the city, Ambrose took a prominent part; in the suppression of heresy by force he seems to have passively acquiesced. On two notable occasions, however, he went beyond the Emperor, when a Bishop destroyed a synagogue, and some riotous monks burnt a Gnostic chapel. As these were acts of insubordination, Theodosius would have punished the offenders, had not Ambrose condoned their acts. However, when the Emperor Maximus put to death the leaders of an obscure sect, known as the Priscillianites, Ambrose and Martin of Tours expressed their strong disapproval on the ground of persecution.

It is clear that Theodosius wielded a temporal arm which was of great value to the Church; but further he submitted himself humbly to a public penance imposed on a memorable occasion by the Archbishop. Theodosius was a great ruler, brave, just and generous; his chief fault was a violent temper, and this temper twice brought him into antagonism with the Church; first in the matter of Antioch described in the chapter on Chrysostom, and secondly after the massacre of Thessalonica, when he was humbled by Ambrose.

St. Ambrose in many respects resembles St. Cyprian, though they were separated by an interval of more than a century. Both of them were laymen till middle life, Cyprian not even a Christian. Both held influential positions, Cyprian at the Bar, Ambrose as the Governor of a Province. Ambrose while still a layman was called by popular acclamation to a bishopric; Cyprian also by popular acclamation only two years after his baptism. Of each of them action was the chief characteristic; but each of them was also a writer, whose skill lay less in originality than in a clear, lucid and graceful style, a definite aim and a practical effect. But above all they were alike in advancing the sacerdotal theory of Church government, which

was always so much more characteristic of the West
than the East. Cyprian, in whose days the Church
could not have contained at most a fifth of the population, consolidated the sacerdotal principle within the
boundaries of the Church; Ambrose used it to control
the State. Milman [1] calls Ambrose " the founder of
sacerdotal authority in the Latin Church "; but he
seems to have gone even further than this, and to have
aimed at making Church and State one and the same
thing.

It is remarkable also that Ambrose was a far more
important figure than Pope Damasus in the State
affairs of the West, probably because Milan was the
seat of the Emperor rather than Rome; indeed whenever there were two Western Emperors, such as Gratian
and Valentinian, or Maximus and Valentinian, Trèves
and Milan were generally the seats of their respective
courts. Ambrose does not seem to have consulted
Damasus in his relation to the Emperor. On the other
hand the Eastern Church heard little of Ambrose: it
was Rome alone that interfered in the policy of distant
Churches.

Ambrose was born about 340, his parents being Christians and in a high position. It is uncertain whether
his birthplace was Trèves, Arles, or Lyons, but Bright
gives it definitely as Trèves. In 374 we find him
Governor of Liguria, and a wise, clement and just
Governor. On the death of Auxentius he presided
over an assembly called to nominate the new Archbishop of Milan, when some voice, apparently that of a
child, cried " Ambrose Bishop," and the cue was taken
at once by the people, who insisted on his election.
He tried to evade the post by curious subterfuges,
such as ordering a prisoner to the torture, causing
improper characters to be brought into his house, and
finally by flight. But it was of no avail: the idea

[1] *Latin Christianity*, Vol. II. ch. iv.

appealed to the popular imagination; he was obviously the right man, and he was forced on to the throne. He then found himself teaching before he had time to learn; but he rectified this by the closest study. His first literary work was *On the Faith*, which he sent to Gratian at his request, that he might be fully instructed in the Catholic doctrine.

During the first nine years of his episcopate things went smoothly at Milan, where Justina acted as Regent for Gratian's half-brother Valentinian, her child. Meanwhile in 379 Gratian associated Theodosius with himself as Emperor of the East. In 383 Gratian was murdered, and Maximus usurped the rule of Gaul and Britain, and was of necessity recognized for a time by Theodosius; and at this time Ambrose appears as envoy from Justina to Maximus, the first time in which we find an ecclesiastic engaged in active State diplomacy. But from 385 to 387 a severe struggle took place between Ambrose and Justina, the latter being an Arian. Ambrose refused to comply with her request to surrender one of the churches to the court for Arian services. "Churches," said Ambrose, "cannot be alienated or surrendered." "Yes," was the reply, "to the Emperor: his rights are absolute." "No," said Ambrose, "the Emperor is not above, he is within the Church."[1] This great principle was successfully combated by Ambrose, who had the people behind him. Justina appointed a Court Bishop Auxentius and summoned Ambrose to plead his cause at Court. This he of course refused to do. Then she tried to exile him; but he took refuge in the basilica, which the populace guarded, while he taught the congregation to sing antiphonally; possibly also he composed some of his hymns for the occasion. Then it was that Augustine was so much moved by the beauty of the music of the Church. It was not long, however, before Maximus,

---

[1] Sermon V.

who was himself Catholic and claimed that all Italy, Africa, Gaul, Spain, and Aquitania were also, took hostile measures against Justina and Valentinian, bringing Theodosius on to the Western field in their defence. They were given a residence at Thessalonica: and Theodosius, after a year's conflict, put an end to Maximus, and assumed personal control in the West.

Another important incident must be noticed in the career of Ambrose, the consecration of the church at Milan, on the site of which was built in the thirteenth century the Church of San Ambrogio, and the finding of the relics of two martyrs, Gervasius and Protasius. Ambrose, on being asked to consecrate the new church, said he must first find some relics, the first impression recorded of the necessity that a church should contain relics. He found them, in accordance apparently with a dream, under the altar of another church; and the relics, when found, are said to have worked wonderful miracles, especially in giving sight to a blind man. Not only did Ambrose evidently sincerely believe this, but also Augustine, who carefully recorded it as an undoubted, well-attested fact in his *Confessions;* although Augustine was by no means credulous on matters of this kind.

In 390 occurred the dramatic scene between Ambrose and Theodosius, in which Ambrose raised the authority of the Church to the point of refusing Communion, or even admission to the church, to the Emperor, until he had done penance for a wholesale massacre at Thessalonica, ordered in revenge for the murder by the mob of an unpopular Governor. Ambrose met Theodosius at the door of the church, and is said to have actually laid hands on him to prevent his entrance. Theodosius remained for some time in his palace in deep grief, and at last, in preparation for the Christmas Communion, divested himself of his Imperial robes, prostrated himself on the pavement of the church, spread out his arms in the form of the Cross, and like the humblest penitent repeated the Psalm, " My soul cleaveth unto the dust; quicken thou me, O Lord, according to Thy Word." The result of this was a wise enactment that no sentence of death or confiscation should be published for thirty days, when it was to be reconsidered and, if necessary, revised.

In 395 Theodosius died, and in 397 Ambrose followed him. To the end he was writing his Commentaries; the one on the 43rd Psalm was broken off before the last two verses. Paulinus, his Secretary, saw " a globe of flame playing on his forehead; then it floated on his lips; after which his face became as white as snow." He could do no more work, and on Good Friday he lay for five hours with his arms extended in the form of the Cross, and then died.

" The power of Ambrose lay not in his originality or profundity of teaching, but in his strong Christian personality, and his example of the practical form of Christianity." [1] The work that he did with his pen was, however, very important, because, being the last great Italian before the coming of the Goths, he presented a definite and practical Theology as a bulwark against their Arianism, and so prepared the way for the rule of the Church and the salvation of society. He was also the first great Italian, or may we say, Western preacher. Augustine declared that he " hung" on the sweetness of his words." [2] His influence therefore was threefold : (1) as Statesman, (2) as preacher, (3) as a concise and practical writer. Bishop Christopher Wordsworth, in his *Church History*,[3] gives a good account of his writings, and tells us that he did for Latin theology what Cicero did for Latin Philosophy. He enriched it from the stores of Greek Literature. Ambrose was a cultivated scholar as well as a poet;

[1] Barry's *St. Ambrose*, p. 390.
[2] *Confessions*, Book V.   [3] Vol. III. ch iii.

and in poetry he had a special reverence for Virgil.
It is appropriate, therefore, that in the Ambrosian
library at Milan, founded in 1606, there should be a
highly valuable edition of Virgil. "The poetical gifts
of Ambrose, his playful fancy, his fervid imagination,"
continues Wordsworth, "gave a rich warmth and
mellow glow, caught from Origen and Basil, to his
interpretations of the Old Testament, which rescued it
from the dryness and coldness that repelled many from
the exegetical writings of some of the Antiochene
school, and prepared the way for Augustine." The
alleged craving of Ambrose for the mystical, rather than
the literal meaning of Scripture, was the result probably
of his poetic sense. The allegory of Nature, which
first appeared in Clement of Rome, but is characteristic
of so many of the Fathers, is strong in Ambrose. He
also did much to elucidate the true perspective of the
Old and New Testaments in relation to one another.
"The shadow is in the Law; the Image is in the Gospel; the Truth is in Heaven." [1]   As an instance of his
debt to the Greeks, his *Hexameron* is entirely founded
on, and to a great extent a translation of Basil's work.
As an instance of his practical views, he strongly recom-
mends Virginity, not as an end *per se*, but for the sake
of detachment from worldly distractions, as Gregory
of Nyssa also viewed it. "The chains of matrimony
are good chains; still they are chains." [2] Similarly
he regarded fasting as useful as a discipline of the body,
but thought that no self-torture for its own sake is
pleasing to God.

Two works are attributed to Ambrose, *On the Mysteries* and *On the Sacraments*, both of which are, however, somewhat doubtful, and especially the latter. In
the former appears a celebrated argument on the
Eucharist. [3] "If Moses by a word could call down fire
from Heaven, will not the Word of Christ be sufficient

[1] Off. Min. I. 48.   [2] Virg. 32. 6.   [3] Myst. 52 to 58.

to change the species of the Elements? If Christ
could create things out of nothing, can He not trans-
form things which already exist? So this which we
make is the Body which is from the Virgin. Why do
you look for the ordinary course of Nature in regard to
Christ's Body, when the Lord Jesus Himself was born
of a Virgin contrary to the course of Nature (*Præter
naturam*)? It is the true flesh of Christ which was
crucified and buried. Therefore this is truly a Sacrament of that Flesh. . . . Before the benediction of the
heavenly words it is called another species, after the
consecration it is named [1] blood. . . . In this Sacrament
Christ is, because it is the Body of Christ. Yet it is
not a corporal but a spiritual feast. For the Body of
God is a spiritual body, the Body of Christ is the body
of the Divine Spirit."

The Old Testament expositions of Ambrose are on
the *Hexameron*, or Six Days of Creation, Paradise,
Cain and Abel, Noah and the Ark, Abraham, Isaac,
Jacob, Joseph, the benedictions of the patriarchs,
Elijah, Naboth, Tobias, Job and David, and many of
the Psalms; New Testament, St. Luke. The doctrinal works are on *Faith* (written for Gratian), on *The
Holy Spirit*, on *The Sacrament of the Lord's Incarnation*,
and on *The Mysteries and the Sacraments* (the last
being very doubtful). The practical works are on the
Duties of the Ministry, on *Virgins*, on *Widows*, on *Penitence*, on the *Advantage of Death*, and on *Flight from
the Age*. He has also left us ninety-one letters, but
their historical importance is not equal to those of
Basil or Jerome.

In the *Duties of the Ministry* we have a system of
moral philosophy (for the duties of Ministers are to a
great extent the duties of all Christians) founded on
the model of Cicero's *De Officiis*. Cicero began by
distinguishing between what is good and what is useful

---

[1] Nuncupatur.

(the *bonum* and the *utile*); Ambrose refuses to admit
the distinction, saying that everything good must be
useful, and the utility of a thing must depend entirely
on its usefulness for eternity, and not for this world
only. Moral obligation emanates from one principle
only, respect for the Divine Law. Ambrose then
applies this principle carefully to the details of life,
including such subjects as the military profession and
the discrimination of charity. Further he deals with
Cicero's treatment of what is " becoming "(*quod decet*),
and claims that it is not a secondary virtue. Nothing
is becoming, unless it is also good, and everything good
is becoming. What is becoming is the form, goodness
is the substance. Goodness is like what health is to
the body, while good manners are like its beauty.[1]

It is generally known that previous to the introduction
of Gregorian tones by Gregory the Great, some form of
Church Music prevailed in the West known as Ambrosian. In fact so thoroughly was St. Ambrose identified
with the Early Church music that at one time a Hymn
was often called an Ambrosian. But of the Ambrosian
tones very little is known, though a great many learned
conjectures have been offered. By some it is thought
that they were little more than musical speech, something perhaps like an " inflected " Gospel. In that
case one wonders that they could have moved Augustine to tears. " How did I weep, in thy hymns and
canticles, touched to the quick by the voices of thy
sweet-attuned. Church." [2] A great number of Hymns
are associated with the name of Ambrose, but only
twelve are given in the Benedictine edition as certainly
his. It is probable that a school of hymn-writers
grew up under his example. The *Te Deum* was at one
time ascribed to him, or to Ambrose and Augustine
jointly, but it is now made clear that it is not of earlier

[1] De Broglie, *St. Ambrose*, p. 412.
[2] *Confessions*, Book IX.

date than the fifth century. In *Hymns Ancient and Modern* three Ambrosian Hymns appear, and in the edition of 1909 four, besides four doubtful ones. They are as follows :—

	Usual edition.	1909 edition.
Splendor paternæ gloriæ .	No. 2	No. 2
Veni Redemptor gentium .	55	55
O lux beata Trinitas . .	14	36
Æterna Christi munera .	—	192

Doubtful Ones

Nunc sancta nobis Spiritus .	9	9
Creator potens verax Deus .	10	10
Rerum Deus, tenax vigor .	11	12
Jesu corona virginum . .	455	211

In the new edition they are much more closely translated than in the earlier ones. The characteristics of Ambrose's hymns have been given as "iambic verses, short clear sentences, sublime thoughts, masculine spirit, refined culture."[1] The iambic metre remained a general metre for Hymns to a much later date.

To what extent Ambrose realized the idea of the Papacy it is difficult to ascertain. During the whole of his Episcopate, he was as prominent a figure in the Church as Pope Damasus. He certainly said, "Where Peter is, there is the Church," but the sense in which he used this expression is not clear. In the work on the Sacraments (if that is his) he refers to a difference of custom between Milan and Rome in the rite of baptism. At Milan it was usual to wash the feet of the baptized, but not at Rome; and this passage occurs: "We wish always to follow the Roman Church; but still we as men have our own opinion;

[1] III. 5, 6.

and here it seems that Rome is not following the example of Peter." In Letter XI, to the Emperors he writes : " We beseech you not to allow the Roman Church, the head of the whole Roman world, and the sacred faith of the Apostles to be disturbed; for from thence (*inde enim*) flow all the rights of venerable communion to all persons." Does he mean that they flow from the Roman Church or from the faith of the Apostles?

But at this time an important step was taken in the development of Papal jurisdiction by an edict of Gratian. A Synod at Rome desired that if a condemned Bishop in Italy or Illyricum forcibly retained his See, or when summoned to a trial by his brethren, refused to attend, he should be arrested and sent to Rome; if he was in a distant part the metropolitan should act instead : or if a metropolitan were the offending party, he should be brought to Rome. An accused Bishop was also to have the right of appealing to Rome or to fifteen neighbouring Bishops. Gratian acceded to this, but added to Italy and Illyricum, Gaul, Africa and Spain. Thus by an act of the State Rome now practically acquired jurisdiction over the entire Western Church.

Note on the Relics.

Ambrose, writing to his sister, and quoting his own Sermon (Letter XXII), says, " You have seen, nay yourselves have heard many cleansed from evil spirits; many also, after touching the garments of the Saints, delivered from the infirmities under which they suffered : you have seen the miracles of old times renewed, when through the coming of the Lord a fuller grace descended on the earth. You see many healed by the shadow, as it were, of the holy bodies. How many napkins are passed to and fro ! How many garments placed on these holy relics, and endowed by the mere contact with the power of healing, are reclaimed by their owners." Further on he says, "They cannot deny the fact. The man is well-known; when in health he was employed in public trade, his name is Severus, a butcher by business. When his affliction befell him, he gave up his trade. He calls as witnesses those men by whose charity he was supported. He summons as witnesses of his present visitation the very men who bore testimony to his blindness. He declares that when he touched the border of the garment with which the martyrs' bodies were clothed, his sight was restored."

Augustine (*Confessions* IX.) says, " For when they (the relics) were discovered and dug up and with due honour translated to the Ambrosian Basilica, not only they who were vexed with unclean spirits (the devils confessing themselves) were cured; but a certain man, who had for many years been blind, a citizen, well known in the city, asking and hearing the reason of the people's confused joy, sprang forth, desiring his guide to lead him thither. Led thither, he begged to be allowed to touch with his handkerchief the bier of Thy Saints, whose death is precious in Thy Sight. Which when he had done and put it to his eyes, they were forthwith opened. Thence did the fame spread, thence Thy praises glowed and shone : thence the mind of that enemy (Justina) though not turned to the soundness of believing, was yet turned back from her fury of persecuting, thanks to Thee, O my God." It is impossible to suppose that men of the character of Ambrose and Augustine did not believe in the miracles, or were consciously encouraging a fraud.

CHAPTER XX

(Born 354.   Bishop of Hippo 395 to 430).

ST. AUGUSTINE is generally admitted, by Roman
Catholics, Anglicans, Protestants and Rationalists
alike, to have been the greatest of all the Church Fathers.
Endless quotations might be adduced to prove this
statement, but it is sufficient to refer on one side to the
Catholic Encyclopædia, and on the other to such
writers as Harnack and Rudolf Eucken. The last
mentioned alludes to him as " the one great philosopher
sprung from the soil of Christianity proper." To the
learned outside the Christian community he appears
not merely as a doctor of the Church, but as holding
a prominent position in the History of Philosophy, as
a deep and original thinker for all time. His writings,
however, covered the whole range of Christian ethics
and doctrine, and his teaching is consequently so
many-sided (to the extent even sometimes of appearing
contradictory), that he has influenced all succeeding
schools of Christian thought. This is the more striking,
when we remember that he was not a savant, or a
highly trained scholar like St. Jerome, and also that
he developed into a very strict Churchman, and was
distinctly limited by his position and environment.
Yet the first question of any one seeking light from the
Fathers on a disputed point will be, "What did Augustine
say about it ? " For he is sure to have said something,
so few things are there that he did not deal with; and
such weight does his view carry, that all schools try to

prove that their view was his, and to explain away any points in which he seems to differ from them.

" Augustine," says Martindale,[1] " shifts the theological centre of gravity from East to West. Handing on what religious inheritance the East bequeathed, rescuing the riches of old and newer Greece, he Romanized the double treasure. He translated speculation into life, and thereby set the current of genuine Catholic mysticism; he infused Christian activity with thought and thus inspired a true scholasticism. Indeed it is the power of his own life, where to know was to love, where search for truth was passionate, that alone explains his unequalled influx into the life of Christianity." Thus in Augustine we see three things : the speculation of the East, the practical theology of the West, and the combination of the two in the supreme doctrines of Grace and Love exhibited in the life and teaching of the man himself. Not only do the different lines of the past, both in East and West, converge in him, but his own thoughts show the converging of the various elements of his own education. An African by birth, he accustomed himself to the Roman point of view during his life at Milan and Rome; he imbibed the ideas of the Far East through his association with the Manichæans; the philosophy of Plato and the Neo-Platonists, which he studied, made him acquainted with Greek culture; and so his entire training fitted him to stand at the parting of the ways, and to point out to the world, when Rome was sacked by Alaric the Goth, and Genseric the Vandal was beating at the gates of his own city, that the old civilization of Rome was dead, and that for the future men must look to the Christian civilization, the " City of God."

The interest of Augustine's life lies almost entirely in the education of his mind and the development of his philosophical and theological position; since,

---

[1] C. C. Martindale, S.J., *St. Augustine.*

although he always kept in touch with the outer world, he never took any part in politics, beyond the occasional encouragement of the authorities to suppress a schism or heresy, or sometimes a plea for mercy. He was born in 354 at Thagaste in Numidia, and his parents were Patricius and Monica. Not much is known of his father, except that he was a man of somewhat low origin, who made a fair maintenance; and that he was a Pagan, who was late in life converted by his wife. But Monica was one of the most beautiful characters in Early Church History. Her whole soul seems to have been bound up in Augustine; his early dissipations and his wanderings after strange gods were a deep grief to her; and when at last he was baptised, the work of her life seemed ended. The relation of Augustine to his mother runs all through his *Confessions,* and is one of the most moving features of that great classic.

Till he was sixteen Augustine was educated at a Grammar School in his native town. Then he proceeded to Carthage. When nineteen his attention was turned, by reading Cicero's *Hortensius* (a lost work), to serious thoughts; but the religion that first satisfied him was that of the Manichæans, and he remained attached to that body for about ten years.

The religion of Manes the Persian was one of the many Oriental religions which exercised their influence over the dying Roman Empire, and like the Gnostic sects absorbed some of the Christian teaching and imitated Christian institutions, especially the two great sacraments. In place of good and evil the Manichæans imagined two great principles of light and darkness, occupying separate territories; the former was the territory of God, the latter of the Dæmon. Thus, and this is the only feature of much importance in their scheme, evil had a separate existence; so we find again the old dualism, which appeared in all the Gnostic sects and against which Christian philosophy

was always at war. The Matter of these two Kingdoms
having got mixed up in the struggle between light and
darkness, God commanded the Living Spirit to fashion
out of this confusion our world, in order that the good
and the evil might be gradually separated. It was
the mission of Christ and the Spirit to carry this out.
The Christ was in some mysterious way identified
with the sun, the Spirit with the air, and both were
opposed by the dæmons in the stars. Christ *seemed*
to men (the old Docetism again) to come in the body
in order to lead mankind to the true God, but promised
to send later the Paraclete; and the Paraclete was
Manes.

His followers were divided into the Elect and the
Hearers (a sort of Catechumens). To the latter class
was left a good deal of freedom from asceticism, for
the business of the world must be carried on and the
race continued; but the Elect, to whom Baptism and
the Eucharist were confined, were intensely ascetic,
having to abstain from all things of the flesh, even the
eating of meat. On the other hand, they had a curious
theory that Light was imprisoned in flowers and fruit
and vegetables, which caused their beauty; and that
when the Elect consumed these things, they freed
light, in fact good. Clearly the fruit of the vine would
come under this category, and the result to the Elect
was often the wildest self-indulgence.

The Manichæanism of Augustine reduced Monica to
despair, and there is a touching story of her entreating
a bishop to reason with him. But this wise bishop
declined the task as futile, and expressed a belief that
Augustine's own studies would in time bring him to
the light. "Farewell," he said, "and God be with
thee. It is impossible for the child of those tears to
be lost:" [1]

[1] *Confessions*, Book IV. Traces of Manichæanism appear in
the Albigenses who were persecuted in France in the thirteenth
century.

At twenty-one, after two years' reading at Carthage, Augustine set up a school at Thagaste; but owing to the death of an intimate friend removed it shortly afterwards to Carthage, where he remained for nine years, and in the course of time became altogether dissatisfied with the doctrines of Manes; especially when Faustus, a leader of that sect, visited Carthage and entirely failed to solve his difficulties.

At the age of thirty he went to Rome, where he remained for about a year; but curiously we know little about his stay there. The office of " Rhetoric Reader " at Milan became vacant, and he was appointed to the post. There he came under the influence of St. Ambrose, and the following year (386), being now thirty-two, he was converted, and after several months of preparation baptized. Soon after this event, Monica, her life work ended, passed away.

In the *Confessions* of St. Augustine we have one of the great books of all ages. It is one of the only works of the early Fathers which is read not only by students but by general readers, and it can be bought in the small Oxford edition for a shilling. But the purpose of it is often misunderstood. When Byron wrote in *Don Juan* of " his fine confessions which make the reader envy his transgressions," he was writing nonsense. They were not the diary of a self-conscious sinner, and there is nothing in them of a prurient character and no painting of vice in an alluring form. Augustine was not in his youth such a great sinner as is often supposed, or as his own subsequent penitence paints him. He seems to have lived the average life of a cultured young man of his age, and at the early age of twenty he began to take an interest in the most serious subjects; duty, God (of whose existence he never entertained a doubt) and the human soul. Besides, whatever he was in youth, the *Confessions* were written many years after his baptism, when he was already Bishop of Hippo;

and in his baptism Augustine believed that all his youthful sins had been washed away. He had therefore no further interest in them; but he lays before his Maker (to whom the *Confessions* are addressed) the whole history of his heart; not to seek pardon, which he had already found, but to offer gratitude for the grace which had by gradual steps brought him to the light. Doubtless also they were meant as a guide for others.

In the *Confessions* we can trace the whole education of Augustine's mind, and consequently his philosophical standpoint. When he first began to think at all, he was confronted with two great realities, the existence of God, and the existence of the human soul or mind. "The human mind is a thing apart in the universe, and the Divine mind embraces the whole in an all-seeing vision."[1] But between God and the Soul comes Evil. Why does Evil find a place in the scheme of an omnipotent and benevolent God? It was this primary difficulty that brought him to the Manichæans, who seemed to offer a rational solution of it: and at this period that passionate zeal for Truth appears, which is the special characteristic of Augustine. " O Truth, Truth, how inwardly did even then the marrow of my soul pant after Thee, when they often and diversely, and in many huge books, echoed of Thee to me, though it was but an echo!"[2]

But this earnest quest for Truth was only a part of the general thoroughness of Augustine's character. At every stage of his life, he aimed at the complete fulfilment of his being, "the unfolding and enjoyment of his own personality."[3] In his youth he was enthusiastic for the mere joy of living; when a Manichæan, he was full of zeal to make proselytes, most of whom he subsequently carried over to the Church: when he

[1] Maccabe, *St. Augustine and His Age*, p. 118.
[2] *Confessions*, Book III.
[3] Eucken, *Problem of Human Life* (section on Augustine).

read Plato, he was absorbed by Plato: when at last he finds " the blessed life," " religious longing is no longer meditative but active and full of vitality; he combines both the ideal and the practical." [1] Not only does he deliver to the West the teaching of the East in a practical, concise and popular form, but under Western influence he becomes such a zealot for the institutions and laws of the Catholic Church, that he is carried away into extreme views and intolerance; while finally, when confronted with the heresy of Pelagianism, which seemed to him to raise natural man too high in relation to God, in his zeal for the majesty of God he evolves an extreme theory of Election, which the Church was obliged to modify. It is his passionate quest for truth and certainty and his happy way of expressing his inward thoughts which make the fascination of the *Confessions*, and impress on us the individuality of the man.

The keynote of the book is, " Thou hast made us for Thyself, and our heart is restless, till it finds its rest in Thee." [2] George Herbert seems to have followed this thought in his little poem, " The Pulley," in which God gives man everything but rest; " that at least,

> If goodnesse leade him not, yet wearinesse
> May tosse him to my breast."

But it must be noted that in these early years, when Augustine was repelled by formal Christianity, he was always, as has been said of Anatole France, " haunted by the prepossession of Christ." When the study of Cicero " altered his affections and turned his purposes," and he says,[3] " How did I burn then, my God, how did I burn to re-mount from earthly things to Thee," yet " this alone checked me thus enkindled, that the name of Christ was not in it. For this name according to

---

[1] Eucken, *Problem of Human Life* (section on Augustine).
[2] *Confessions*, Book I.   [3] *Ibid.*, Book III.

Thy Mercy, O Lord, the name of Thy Saviour and Son, had my tender heart, even with my mother's milk, devoutly drunk in and deeply treasured; and whatsoever was without that name, though never so learned, polished and true, took not entire hold on me. I resolved then to bend my mind to the Holy Scriptures . . . but they seemed to me unworthy to be compared to the stateliness of Cicero." He never understood the spiritual intent of Scripture till he listened to Ambrose. But the Manichæan system attracted him quite as much by its use of the names of Christ and the Holy Ghost as by its explanation of Evil. However, the futility of Faustus, who frankly admitted he could not answer his questions, made it impossible for him to go farther with that sect, as we find in the Fifth Book. He leaves Carthage and goes to Rome and Milan. Faustus " could speak fluently and in better terms than the rest, but still the self-same things; and what availed the utmost neatness of the cup-bearer to my thirst for a more precious draft ? "

So at last we find him at Milan, received by Ambrose as a son; " loving him, not at first as a teacher of the truth (which I utterly despaired of in Thy Church), but as a person kind towards myself. And I listened diligently to him; I hung on his words attentively, but of the matter I was as a careless and scornful looker-on; . . . and yet was I drawing nearer by little and little unconsciously. And while I opened my heart to hear how eloquently he spoke, there also entered how truly he spoke." But still it was an open question. Ambrose was helping him by his spiritual interpretations of Scripture, and he became again a catechumen as in his childhood; but he failed to break down the Manichæan stronghold, because he could not yet conceive of God as a spiritual substance : there could be no personality, he thought, which was not material.

Then came the penultimate phase, the study of

Plato, while " Monica believed in Christ that before she departed this life, she should see me a Catholic." [1] The relation of Augustine to Plato is of extreme interest, because although later in life he modified his Platonism,[2] it had much to do with his conversion, and continued to influence materially the tenor of his earlier writings afterwards, while his later writings were hardly free from it.   The learning that he got from this source may be summed up by saying that from Plato he learned that the Word was God : from St. John he learned that the Word was made flesh and dwelt among us, which thought is expanded in the Seventh Book.   Along with this idea is another that " the invisible things of him are clearly understood from the things that were made, even his Eternal Power and Godhead; " [3] or as Plato would put it, " the things known (noumena) are taught us by the things that appear (phenomena) " :   and thirdly he overthrew the Manichæans at last by the Neo-Platonist doctrine that evil was not a substance but only a negation or defect.

The argument from the things seen to the things known, from the outward sense to the inner mind, is graphically illustrated in the Tenth Book. " I asked the earth, and it answered, ' I am not He '; and whatsoever are in it confessed the same.   I asked the sea and the deeps, and the living creeping things, and they answered, ' We are not thy God, seek above us.'   I asked the moving air :   and the whole air with its inhabitants answered, ' Anaximenes was deceived, I am not God.' I asked the heavens, sun, moon, stars, ' Nor (say these) are we the God whom thou seekest.'   And I replied to all the things which encompass the doors of my flesh, ' Ye have told me of my God, that you are not He; tell me something of Him '; and they cried out with a

---

[1] *Confessions*, Book VI.
[2] His mature thoughts on Plato are in *City of God*, VIII
[3] Rom. i. 20.

loud voice, ' He made us.'   My questioning them was
my thoughts on them; and their form of beauty gave
the answer.   And I turned to myself and said to myself,
' Who art thou ? '   And I answered, ' A man.'   And
behold, in me there present themselves to me soul and
body; one without, the other within.   By which of
these ought I to seek my God ?   I had sought Him in
the body from earth to Heaven, so far as I could send
messengers, the beams of my eyes.   But the better is
the inner, for in it, as presiding and judging, all the
bodily messengers reported the answers of Heaven and
earth, and all things therein, who said, ' We are not
God, but He made us.'   These things did my inner
man know by the ministry of the outer; I the inner
knew them; I the mind through the senses of my body.
I asked the whole frame of the world about my God;
and it answered me, ' I am not He, but He made me.' "

The process through which Augustine's mind passed
is thus described by Eucken.   First there is the radical
dissatisfaction with the condition of man and the natural
world; in fact with the existence of evil.   Yet man,
with all his ills, clings to existence.   Is it not conclusive
that man has something in his nature good and capable
of happiness?   There must then be something beyond
this world.   There must be somewhere Perfect Being;
and that is God.   All genuine life springs from Him,
and returns to Him.   The soul of man is equally real :
even if we doubt, we must possess a mind to doubt
with; the existence even of a physical world is less
obvious than the existence of Mind.   All this is Platonic,
but he breaks away later from Platonism, by gradually
putting more and more the Will in the place of Thought,
Volition in the place of Knowledge.   Both the Trinity
and the individual soul as well, which is a mirror of It,
consist of Being (power), Knowledge (wisdom), and
Will (love).[1]   In God is true Being, and the Highest

---

[1] Trin. 10. 14.

Good (perfect love); man, therefore, only attains to salvation and happiness by clinging to God. There are two ways of doing this : (1) Intuition and Love, (2) the purification and moral training of the individual life by fellowship with God, who has freely bridged over the abyss that lay between. Cunningham [1] says that Augustine differs from Plato by saying, not that Truth has its source in God, but that Truth *is* God : God is not above all Being and Reason, but *is* the highest Being and the completest Reason.

It is strange that, although Augustine owed so much to the Platonists, he seems to have only read their books in translations, knowing probably at the time very little Greek, which in his youth he detested. He always disclaimed much knowledge of it; even in the book on the Trinity,[2] written late in life, he hints that he hardly understands the Greek Fathers in the original. This is probably an exaggeration, as he freely handled the Greek of the New Testament; but of his youth it would be true. By what books he was influenced is uncertain, but he probably read the *Timæus, Phædo, Phædrus, The Republic, Gorgias* and the *Symposium,* and also the *Enneads* of Plotinus, to which last he owed much : probably the final conviction that somewhere there must be Spirit untouched by Matter.

Before leaving this subject, let us read one of the most exquisite passages in the *Confessions,* Ninth Book. A considerable part of this book records the last scenes with his mother, who did not long survive his baptism. Only a few days before her death, he discusses with her the life of the world to come. " If to any the tumult of the flesh were hushed, hushed the images of earth, and waters and air, hushed also the poles of heaven, yea, the very soul be hushed to herself, and by not thinking on self surmount self, hushed all dreams and imaginary revelations, every tongue and

---

[1] *Hulsean Lectures on St. Austin.*   [2] Trin., III. 1.

every sign, and whatsoever exists only in transition, since if any could hear, all these say, ' We made not ourselves, but He made us that abideth forever.' [1]— If, then, having uttered this, they too should be hushed, having roused only our ears to Him who made them, and He alone speaks, not by them but by Himself, that we may hear His Word, not through any tongue of flesh nor angel's voice nor sound of thunder, nor in the dark riddle of a similitude, but might hear Him whom in these things we love, might hear His Very Self without these—could this be continued on and other visions of kind far unlike be withdrawn, and this one ravish and absorb and wrap up its beholder amid these inward joys, so that life might be forever like that one moment of understanding, which now we sighed after; were not this, ' Enter into thy Master's joy? ' "

Augustine never soared higher than this; but compare it with the other two descriptions of the Beatific Vision already alluded to in this book. First there was the conception of Plato that the highest life would be to gaze forever on the ideal (abstract) Beauty, to hold communion therewith and so gain immortality.[1] Next we found St. Gregory of Nyssa following the same thought of the ideal Beauty, and so becoming detached from all worldly interest, till he arrives at his goal, the power of seeing God.[2] But this was less communion or fellowship than the striving for absorption into the Eternal Unity; it was metaphysical rather than ethical; it was speculative and Eastern. With St. Augustine the relation is quite different. " His strong sense of human personality prevents him from an aspiration towards absorption into God." [3] His Very Self is speaking to him as a separate entity. There is a beautiful passage in John Inglesant: " Amid the tumult of the Universe I should hear the faintest whisper of his voice." But here there is no tumult : all the Universe

---

[1] Ch. vii.   [2] Ch. xv.   [3] Cunningham, p. 38.

is hushed, his own soul is hushed; there is nothing but God—speaking to the human personality of Augustine.

The last stage of his conversion is told in the end of the Seventh and in the Eighth Book, and commences when he passes from Plato to St. Paul. Augustine became saturated with St. Paul, and the arguments in the *Confessions* continually fall into quotations from St. Paul. Bishop Wordsworth says that if transmigration of souls were a fact, St. Paul's soul would be found again in Augustine. For a long time his head was convinced, but his heart refused the great renunciation. "When Thou didst on all sides show me, that what Thou saidst was true, I, convicted by the truth, had nothing at all to answer, but only those dull and drowsy words, ' Anon, anon—presently, leave me for a little.' But my little while went on for a long while." At last he hears of the conversion of some simple folk, and cries to his friend Alypius, " What ails us? The unlearned start up and take Heaven by force, and we with our learning and without heart, lo, where we wallow is flesh and blood ! " Then comes the voice of the mysterious little child in the garden : " Take and read ";[1] he opens St. Paul at random and finds, " Not in chambering and wantonness . . . but put ye on the Lord Jesus Christ, and make no provision for the flesh." From that moment his mind is made up; he carries away Alypius, and the illegitimate child of his extreme youth, Adeodatus, into retirement, and after a few months of careful training by Ambrose, they are all baptized. `So came Augustine out of much tribulation and washed his robes.

With the Ninth Book end the *Confessions* proper, and the last words refer to his mother. At a later date he was asked to give an account of what he then was, and so wrote the Tenth, Eleventh, Twelfth and Thirteenth Books. The Tenth, in examining the

[1] " Tolle, lege."

relation of the mind to God, gives a wonderful analysis of memory; there is also some fine ethical writing on the three great temptations : " the lust of the flesh, the lust of the eyes, and the pride of life." But the last three books break away into a commentary on Genesis, giving incidentally a wonderful metaphysical treatise on Time.

The controversy with the Manichæans, which immediately followed his conversion, brought out the strength of Augustine as a commentator on Scripture. Ambrose taught him to see the spiritual interpretations, yet he followed closely on many occasions the letter, and even wrote one book on the literal interpretation of Genesis (De Genesi ad literam). But he always asked people to use their common sense; for instance, to guard against hazardous or unscientific interpretations, lest unbelievers should ridicule.[1] In dealing with the opening of Genesis, he combines the letter with a scientific point of view, by saying that all the principles of Nature were created in a week, but that they were afterwards gradually evolved. Again he held that Scripture is only a means to an end. Everything in the Bible is true and any thought is justified which can be proved from it; but Scripture is practical, and is a means towards faith, hope and love; " a man who depends on faith, hope and love, and holds by them invincibly, only needs Scripture to instruct others." [2] It is the substance of it that is important, yet " the authority of Scripture is paramount, being established from the time of Christ Himself by means of Apostolic ordinances and the succession of Bishops from those days to the present." [3] The Canon is therefore the testimony of Christ in the Catholic Church which is His Body. St. Augustine's view of the Apocrypha is not quite clear. He freely quoted from all the books, but seems to have

---

[1] De Genesi ad literam, I. 19 and 21.
[2] De Doctr. Christiana, I. 39.　　　[3] Faust 11. 6.

had a theory of different degrees of inspiration. A synod
at Hippo in 393, over which he probably presided,
included in the Canon, Esdras 1 and 2, Maccabees 1
and 2, Tobias, Judith, subject to consultation with the
Transmarine churches.

Bishop Christopher Wordsworth wrote a short book
on Augustine's sermon on the Sermon on the Mount,
which gives a critique of his general relation to Scripture.
He points out that, in Augustine's view, spiritual things
must be spiritually discerned; yet external helps are
valuable, such as natural science, history, logic, music,
philosophy. But after all the heart makes the theologian, and the right relation of reason to faith is not
" Know that you may believe," but " Believe that you
may understand." [1] He anticipated a principle of
modern interpretation, that a reading involving difficulty
was more likely to be correct, than one which made the
thought easy; yet obscurer passages must be interpreted by the clearer. The analogy of faith must be
followed, and an isolated text must not be taken to
counteract the general drift; thus metaphors and
symbols are used at different times in contradictory
meanings; for instance, Christ is a lion in Revelation,
Satan is a lion in 1 St. Peter: truth is leaven in St.
Matthew, malice and hypocrisy in 1 Corinthians. The
first foundations of doctrine must rest on plain and
literal passages: one half of truth must not be exaggerated, while the other half is obscured. He had
great skill in reconciling contradictions, as for instance
St. Paul's Judaizing and anti-Judaism in his correspondence with St. Jerome. Occasionally, but not as
a rule, Augustine allegorized to excess, as in his treatment of the 104th Psalm, where he gives a spiritual
meaning to the objects of Nature. Lastly, he thoroughly
recognized the progressive character of revelation;
and while he held such a strong view of Inspiration as

[1] Serm. 43.

that the Evangelists were the pen of the Holy Ghost, he also recognized the human element in their writings.

His sermons are remarkable for their tenderness, and the simplicity with which he unfolds all his wisdom to the humble congregation at Hippo. They present the closest analysis of scriptural passages, and gently lead his hearers to his conclusions. A good idea may be got of his style from reading the chapter in *Hypatia*, in which he converts a learned Jew by throwing new light on the Old Testament, in spite of manifest mistranslations of Hebrew words; for with Hebrew he was never acquainted.

After his baptism he spent about eighteen months in Rome, confuting the Manichæans; and then retired to Africa, where he lived quietly for some years in a confraternity of which he was the head, giving his possessions to the poor. On a visit to Hippo, he was induced to take Orders, built a hospital, and, following the custom at Milan, suppressed the last vestiges of the Agape. In 395 he became assistant Bishop of Hippo, and shortly afterwards Bishop. In that capacity he spent two hours every day in adjusting differences between members of his flock as an arbitrator; and this is supposed to have been the origin of ecclesiastical courts. The self-respect of Augustine required great cleanliness and neatness of person and dress. Although his diet was of the simplest, he did not abstain altogether from wine, and his spoons were of silver. On his table was fixed a little notice that at that board no one must speak ill of his neighbour. It is hardly correct to say that he was a monk; but he lived according to a monkish rule in a community consisting of his clergy, all of whom had to put their property into the common fund. Community of goods, chastity, labour; these were the three fundamental points of the Augustinian Rule. Not that he ever consciously founded an order, and the only definite rules that he issued are to be found in

Letter 211 and Sermons 355–6. But he encouraged everywhere the formation of communities like his own, and vigorously denounced in *De Opere Monachorum* idle monks. It was not till the time of Charlemagne that the name Augustinian was applied to any distinct class of monks; but from that time it was used by many different communities : and the various communities were brought together under one " General " in 1246. In his own community Augustine refused all donations and legacies which came from an impure source, such as defrauding children or rightful heirs; and to avoid scandal, he rendered a public account of all his expenditure.

The whole trend of thought in the *Confessions* is individual. They display the craving of the heart for God, to whom the soul appeals directly and without the apparent intervention of human ordinances or ministry; and for this reason they are dear to Protestants. The Church, it is true, is the ultimate authority on Doctrine, but personal piety and what is called experimental religion are prominent everywhere. Sin and misery are overcome by faith, humility and love. In faith the soul is at rest, yet it ever strives irrepressibly upward.[1] Faith, love, merits are the successive steps to salvation, although the merits themselves are gifts of God. " Give what Thou commandest, and command what Thou wilt." [2]

But when Augustine is confronted at Hippo with the Donatist schism, a quite different tone appears. The Church is seen as the exclusive medium through which grace is given; her Sacraments, as well as her teaching, are essential. The Sacraments are communicated through the minister, but are only redemptive where love is; that is, where unity is; that is, where the true and only Church is. Augustine, therefore, now becomes

[1] Harnack, *Outlines of Dogma,* p. 339.
[2] Da quod jubes, et jube quod vis (*Confessions,* Book X).

the highest exponent of Catholicism. Faith is exemplified in the individual by obedience to the Catholic Church, for the Church guarantees the truth of the Faith, where the individual fails to perceive it. The Church thinks for the uncertain : indeed Augustine himself says, " I should not believe the Gospel, did not the Catholic Church impel me to." [1]

, Donatism, which, as Canon Bright says, " wore out the great heart of Augustine," and at last led him to acquiesce in persecution, had its rise in Carthage in the beginning of the fourth century. The Bishop, Mensurius, being summoned to Rome, and believing rightly that he would never return, hid the sacred vessels, gave an inventory of them to an old woman, and told two men, Botrus and Celestius, where they were. These men, on Mensurius' death, opposed for ambitious reasons the consecration of Cecilian, setting up as an excuse that his consecrator was a " traditor." [2] By the help of some corrupt Numidian Bishops, Majorinus was set up as a rival Bishop, and in time succeeded by Donatus : hence the name of the schism.

The first act of Constantine, after his conversion, was to summon the Council of Arles, which condemned the schism ; but nevertheless it grew and by this time possibly a majority of the African Christians were Donatists. Although there were good men among them, they were on the whole a bad and mischievous sect. Their origin was bad, and their subsequent story one of hatred, intolerance and violence. Since the Catholic succession of Carthage came, they said, through a traditor (though it actually did not), they repudiated Catholic orders and sacraments, even Baptism. When they seized a Catholic Church, they scraped the walls, burnt the altar, and threw the Eucharist to the dogs : and, further, they maintained a sort of militia of ruffians,

---

[1] Contr. Ep. Manich, 5. [2] See ch. viii.

Y

known as the Circumcellions, who with a battle cry of
" Praise the Lord," fell upon Catholics, and murdered
and mutilated them. If Augustine became their
persecutor, he was sorely tried, and it was not till after
holding councils and many attempts at friendly discussion, that he agreed to call in the aid of Honorius
to suppress them.   Even then for a time he deprecated
extreme punishment; but we can only regret that such a
man as Augustine should be found using such expressions
as " The worst death of the soul is freedom to err,"
and " Better that a man's body should be destroyed
(i. e., by his fellow men) than his soul."   We all know
what that doctrine led to.   The result anyhow was that
Donatism was stamped out.   It is worth noting that
Augustine's great argument against it, that what the
bulk of Christianity believes must be the truth,[1] had
a remarkable effect on Newman, and seemed to him to
pulverize his earlier doctrine of the *Via Media*.   It
was this that made him first see " the shadow of the
hand upon the wall ! " [2]

But it was the struggle with the Donatists which
brought out Augustine's dogmatic statements about
the Church.   " Whoever is separated from the Catholic
Church, however laudably he thinks he is living, yet
for that crime alone, that he is severed from Christ's
unity, he shall not have life, but the wrath of God
abideth in him." [3]   " The question between us and the
Donatists is, ' Where is the Church?   With us or with
them? '   That Church assuredly is one, which our
ancestors called the Catholic, that they might show by
the very name, that it is through the whole.   For this
Church is the Body of Christ, as the Apostle says, ' His
Body, which is the Church.'   Whence surely it is manifest that he who is not in the members of Christ cannot
have Christian salvation." [4]   Eucken says about this:

[1] " Securus judicat orbis terrarum."
[2] *Apologia.*   [3] Ep. 141.   [4] *Unity of Church, 2.*

" At one time the individual is summoned to the boldest activity, and confident of victory feels himself superior to all existence. At another, overcome by distressing doubts as to his own capacities, and passionately longing for some secure support, he obediently submits himself to external authority "; and he somewhat maliciously adds that Augustine deeply needed the Church, to save him from his own contradictions.

The principle reasserted and finally established in the African Council dealing with the Donatists, was that holiness resides in the Church, which contains both the wheat and the tares, not in her ministers. The unworthiness of the Minister (the consecrator for instance of Cæcilian) does not affect the validity of his ministerial functions. However harsh and intolerant Augustine seems in dealing with the Donatists, we have always to thank him for the saying which is attributed to him : " In essentials unity, in non-essentials liberty, in all things charity."

Whether the Church, in Augustine's view, was entirely bound up with, and subservient to the See of Peter, is of course a different question. The feeling of the African Church at this time was strong against Roman interference. The Church is traced by its succession of bishops, and on various occasions Augustine quotes the Roman succession as an example. Irenæus also did this, on the ground that there was no time to quote all the successions. Augustine says, " For if the succession of Bishops is to be considered, how much more securely and beneficially do we reckon from Peter himself, to whom, as personating the Church, the Lord said, 'Thou art the Rock,' etc." [1] He then traces the Roman succession. Again, and this is rather more obscure, " Shall we hesitate to fling ourselves into the bosom of that Church, which even by the confession of mankind has from the Apostolic See, through the

[1] Ep. 53.

Y 2

successions of Bishops, obtained the loftiest pinnacle of authority." [1]   Augustine argues that while Donatism is a mere African community, the Catholicism of Africa is in communion with the Churches beyond the seas and takes the Roman Church as an example. It is difficult to contend for more than this in view of the strong assertion of independence of Rome made by the African Church during Augustine's life, at Councils at which Augustine was present. On the other hand it is not clear that he took such a prominent part in them, as his pre-eminent importance in that Church would lead us to expect; and it is quite possible that his great reverence for the Apostolic See may have caused him to shrink from active defiance of it. Space does not allow us here to relate the whole story in connection with the canons of Sardica, which ended in a general Council of the African Churches, protesting to Pope Celestine against Rome harbouring refugee priests, in spite of the rule that all such should be tried by their own bishops, and bishops by their own metropolitans.

The authority of Augustine is claimed by both Catholics and Protestants in defence of their Eucharistic views. He occasionally gives a symbolical view of the elements. "He commended and delivered to His disciples the *figure* of His own Body." [2]   "The Lord hesitated not to say, ' This is My Body,' when He gave them a *sign* of His Body." [3]   He also says, "In the Holy Sacrifice and communion of the Body of Christ, Christians celebrate the memory of the Sacrifice He accomplished." [4]   On several occasions he explicitly describes the Eucharistic Sacrifice as the offering up of the Church, which is Christ's Body. [5]   Yet over and over again he expresses the strongest belief in a Real Presence. " The bread which you see on the Altar,

---

[1] Util. cred., XVII.   [2] Ps. iii. 1.   [3] Adimant Man. 12.
[4] Faust, XX. 13.   [5] *City of God*, X. 6 and 20 and elsewhere.

after being sanctified by the Word of God, is the Body of Christ. So with the wine. By means of these things it was the will of Christ to bestow on us His own Body and Blood." [1] "When He said, 'This is my Body,' He carried that Body in His own Hands." [2] "He walked here in the very flesh, and that very flesh He gave us to eat unto Salvation." [3] The spiritual character of the mystery he explains thus : "What ye see then is bread and a cup, but what your faith needs to be taught is that the bread is the Body, and the cup contains the Blood. If it is asked, how these things can be, these things are called Sacraments, because in them one thing is seen, another thing understood. What is seen has a bodily species; what is understood has a spiritual fruit." [4]

On Masses for the dead, Augustine says : " It is not to be denied that the souls of the departed are relieved by the piety of their living friends, when the sacrifice of the Mediator is offered for them, or alms are performed in the Church. But these things benefit those who merited when living that these things should be able to benefit them afterwards. . . . Let no man hope that after death he can merit before God what he has neglected here." [5] St. Augustine's view of the after life by no means coincides with that of Origen, that all would at last be saved, though he tolerated those who held that view, calling them "*misericordes nostri*"; but he had clear views of punishment. First it was not so much intended to be corrective, as a vindication of right. Secondly, it was loss. " It is the most just punishment for sin, that every one should lose what he would not use well, when he might have done so so easily, had he wished; that is, that he who knows what is right, and does not do it, should lose the knowledge of it, the power of doing it. Ignorance and incapacity are two penalties

---

[1] Serm. 127. [2] Ps. xxxiii. [3] Ps. xcviii.
[4] Serm. 272. [5] De octo Dulcit. quæst, II.

for the sinner." [1] " Future punishment will in some cases be only temporal and partly material." [2]

St. Augustine was essentially the Doctor of Grace. Throughout the *Confessions* the leading thought is the wonderful way in which he had been led by grace, in spite of all his wanderings, into the light. His whole theology is based on the relation of God to the human soul; in other words the working of grace, of which the mainspring is the historic manifestation of God to humanity in the Incarnation. He emphasizes the fact that grace is not exhausted by the retrospective for-giveness of baptism. Harnack holds that the earlier Church had uncertain views on this matter, which would account for the deferring of baptism. As regards what happened afterwards they hoped all would be well, but they were not sure. Hope remained, but also fear. But with Augustine hope became conviction. The work of grace was continuous, and instead of hope and fear, he taught rest, faith and love.

Now about 405 a Briton or Breton (probably ·the latter), who was known as Morgan or Pelagius, began teaching a series of propositions of a quite contrary character. There was, he said, no such thing as original sin. Sin did not create death. Adam would have died just as much, whether he sinned or not. God made us men, but it rests entirely with ourselves whether we are good or not, for man's will is absolutely free and self-sufficient. There were three ways of salvation: the law of Nature, the law of Moses, the law of Christ. The works of heathens were acceptable independently of the grace of God. Perfection was attainable here by man unaided; either actual, so that believers do not sin, or at any rate possible, that they might live without sin.

Teaching such as this struck at the root of Christianity, for it denied the necessity of the Atonement, and

---

[1] *Free Will*, 3. 52.   [2] *City of God*, XXI. 13.

Augustine's whole soul was on fire. In 412 he entered the lists. The Augustinian reply, stated simply is this: Man, owing to the fall, has lost sanctifying grace, is subject to death and suffering, and feels an impelling inclination to evil. Hence his free will is changed in nature, it is now corrupt, and can do no good thing without grace. And this grace is an entirely free gift of God, which we have not merited, could never merit, and without which merit is impossible.[1] Augustinianism then, to start with, is simply an expression of the thought that nothing good can be done without grace, and that grace is freely offered. Original sin is universal, yet man is not, as Calvin taught, utterly rotten and defiled. Man's nature is a good thing corrupted. " Sin is the defect of a good nature, which contains elements of good even in its most diseased and corrupted state." [2] How did sin come? All things are good, because God created them, who is good. But they are changeable (God only is without change), and every falling away or privation of good is evil. Following the first change evil crept in, even against man's will, with ignorance and concupiscence, which brought in their train error and suffering.[3]

But in the course of the controversy, Augustine was carried on to further positions. God, being omniscient, must have known that man's free will would err. He foresaw those who would believe, and gave them the grace of well-doing, withholding it from those who would not. Yet in a later stage, instead of merely saying with St. Paul, " those whom He foreknew, them did He also predestinate," he develops predestination into election, so that grace is now a free gift offered to some and not to others, according to an arbitrary choice. Hooker tells us that his view developed in this way in

---

[1] This statement of the two positions is taken from Hook's *Church Dictionary*.
[2] *Free Will*, 3. 35.   [3] Enchir, 12, 23-4.

the Pelagian controversy, though Augustine in his
Retractations (a work written towards the close of his
life, and the title meaning rather revising or re-editing
than retracting his earlier opinions), denies that his
views changed. It would seem that in the earlier
treatise on Free Will he distinctly states that the will is
free. This is explained, however, by saying that he
was then speaking of the human will before the Fall;
since then it had been crippled. The ultimate
position then is, " Since the fall human nature is a
corrupt mass liable to God's wrath and punishment,
and while in His mercy He chooses some by an eternal
decree of Predestination to eternal life, He leaves others
to eternal damnation." [1] To those who are predestined the gift of perseverance follows. How all
this can be consistent with Divine love and justice,
Augustine would say, is a mystery into which we cannot
look: we can only wait for the Beyond, where all
enigmas will be solved.

All this is what is known as the gloomy side of
Augustine's theology, and it certainly led to extreme
Calvinism, although he never explicitly said that God
predestined any to damnation. Still that Augustine
should, in the heat of his controversy with Pelagius,
have made the statements that he did, is strange when
the doctrine of love runs so clearly through all his
work. The Abbé Martin finds a reconciliation of Free
Will with Predestination in the City of God.[2] " Your
memory imposes no necessity on the past: so God's
prescience imposes no necessity on the future." Certain
it is that Augustine never reduced his theory to practice.
When he preached to his flock at Hippo (and they must
have been a rough lot), they were all his " beloved,"
and he assumed that they were all destined to salvation.
In a sermon on John vi. 44, he says: " Mighty en-
hancement of grace! No man cometh unless drawn.

---

[1] Enchir, 98.   [2] V. 9–10

Whom He. draweth, and whom He draweth not,, why He draweth one, and draweth not another, wish not to judge, if thou wilt not err. Once for all take and understand; art thou not drawn? *Pray that thou mightest be drawn.*" This of course seems to beg the whole question.

In 529 the Council of Orange modified the Augustinian teaching by a series of general statements. Original sin is universal : Free Grace is offered to all : Justification is by that grace, and not by our own merit, but proceeding through Christ's death; Man's love to God is a gift of God : No one is predestined by God to evil.

The Council of Trent reaffirmed original sin and the necessity of grace; but proclaimed the freedom of man and both his power of resisting grace (as opposed to the doctrine of irresistible grace for the elect), and of choosing between good and evil.

The Church of England, in Article 17, while admitting that, Predestination to. Life is " full of sweet, pleasant and unspeakable comfort to godly persons," declares that " to have continually before the eyes the sentence of. God's predestination is a most dangerous downfall, whereby the Devil doth thrust them either into desperation or into wretchlessness of most unclean living, no less perilous than desperation."

In contrast with the theology of the East, Western theologians always made practical use of metaphysics. They are not so much concerned with the nature of God as with His relation to man : they seek less an objective knowledge of Him than the subjective knowledge of His image in man defaced and restored. God no longer reveals, but communicates Himself; Christ is more thought of as the Redeemer than the God Man : the moral aspect of theology is therefore of more importance than the metaphysical.[1] This aspect is

[1] See Wordsworth's book on the homily on the " Sermon on the Mount."

nowhere more clearly shown than in Augustine's
Enchiridion and his work on the Trinity.

The *Enchiridion*, or little book to hold in the hand,
or handbook, is a summary of the Christian faith,
dealing concisely with all the articles of the Creed
and the various doctrines which can be deduced
from them; for instance, the explanation of Evil,
questions of grace and predestination, and even the
future life, which, for the lost, he says, will consist in
alienation from the life of God. But what is especially
noticeable here is that the subject matter of the book
is concerning Faith, Hope and Charity; so that
Christian dogmas are really considered, not merely
speculatively, but in their relation to these three great
Christian virtues.

The *De Trinitate* is a work of fifteen books, which
shared with other books many years of Augustine's
life—at least sixteen; it was apparently the work that
he reserved for his times of peace and leisure. But of
these fifteen books, while the first eight deal with the
correct dogma as to the nature of God, the remaining
seven deal with His relation to man, and His reflection
in man, since man is the image. The human image
displays the Trinity in the memory, the intelligence
and the will; and again in mind, knowledge and love.
In this life the Trinity is only seen through a glass darkly,
and man will only be a perfect image when the vision
is made perfect. But God is Love, and no gift of God
is greater than Love. " The whole Christian conception
of God is brought out with tremendous fullness when
Augustine sums up the doctrine of the Trinity in the
revelation of Love." [1]

When Rome was destroyed by the Goths, a great
outcry was raised that it was because Rome had for-
saken her ancient gods and turned to Christianity.
Augustine therefore wrote his great work on the *City*

[1] Headlam, *History, Authority, Theology*, p. 75.

of God; first to prove (in the first five books) the falsity of the charge; secondly, to make a final denunciation of Paganism and especially its futility as a preparation for an after life, which he does in Books Six to Ten; and thirdly in twelve further books to compare and contrast the city of this world with the City of God, showing the legitimate claims upon mankind of each of them. The work was begun in 413 and not completed till 426, and the germ of it is to be found in Letter 138, a reply to some one who had asked how the Christian precept of turning the other cheek was compatible with the principle of Roman rule. Augustine declares that the Gospel is not opposed to righteous war, and that Christian principles are a strength, not a weakness, to the State. Rome was destroyed by her venality, corruption and immorality, and the Cross was now her only hope.

In the *City of God*, after denouncing Paganism and showing how even Pagan philosophers derided it, and proving also the insufficiency of natural religion, he traces the growth of a sounder philosophy up to Plato, whom he acknowledges as having reached a point much nearer to the Christian; but he breaks with the Platonists because they taught the impossibility of direct approach by man to God, and interposed dæmons as intermediaries. This naturally brings him to the mediation of Christ, and so to an exposition of the doctrines of the Trinity and Incarnation. From this he proceeds to the account of the Creation; explains the origin of evil and the Fall, which latter was the cause of death; and writes at some length on the whole question of death. Then follows an enquiry into the two states of man, life after the flesh and life after the spirit; and he then devotes four books to the biblical authority for his previous statements. In the last of these books comes incidentally an interesting note on the Septuagint, which Augustine treated to all intents and purposes as inspired. Lastly, after explaining the limits of the two cities, of God and of the world, he asks what have been the various ideals and aims of philosophy, and teaches that the ultimate aim of the Christian is eternal peace. This brings him to a description of the life to come, which includes some very curious reasoning about material punishment, almost mediæval in character. To the Christian who attains to Heaven will come the capacity of seeing God everywhere and in everything, and a complete restoration of the freedom of the will.

It is of great importance, in studying St. Augustine, to know at what period his various books were written : indeed it has often been said of him, that to understand him, the mind must grow with his. His works were so numerous, that only some of the most characteristic are here given.

Among the earliest works after his conversion are *Against the Academics, On the Blessed Life, On Order,* the *Soliloquies, On the Immortality of the Soul* (the last two are strongly Platonic) and *On Music.*

The second stage of his work (still previous to his ordination) includes the *Books against the Manichœans,* and part of the treatise *On Free Will;* and after he reaches Africa, *On True Religion,* the *Commentary on Genesis,* which he developed later into *On the Literal Interpretation of Genesis,* and *The Master.* The last was a sort of In Memoriam of his son, Adeodatus, and gives one of their last discussions before his son's death.

The third stage follows his ordination (391), and here we have *On the Utility of Believing* (against the Manichæans), the conclusion of *On Free Will,* the homily *On the Sermon on the Mount,* and part of the Donatist controversy.

After his consecration in 395 come : *On Christian Doctrine* (Books 1 to 3 in 397; the Fourth Book not till

420) and immediately after the turn of the century most of the controversy with the Donatists, such as *Against the Letter of Pœtilian, On Baptism,* and many others. The book *On the Work of the Monks,* came in 400; in 401, *On Holy Virginity* and *On Conjugal Love.* With the *Literal Interpretation of Genesis* he was occupied from 401 to 414, and with *On the Trinity* from 400 to 416. The *Confessions,* at least the first nine books, were one of his earliest works as a bishop (397), the remaining four books were written later. In 412 he took up arms against Pelagius, and in the next two or three years followed *On Nature and Grace, On Corruption and Grace, On the Perfection of Human Justice, On Grace and Original Sin, On Predestination, On Perseverance* and the other anti-Pelagian books; contemporaneously he was at work on the *City of God,* which he began in 413 and finished in 427, within three years of his death. The *Retractations,* in which he reviewed and revised the whole of his own literary work, was published in 426. In 430 at the ripe age of 76, he died.

There has been hardly any phase of subsequent Christian thought which does not refer for its sanction to St. Augustine. Catholics claim that he was not only the Doctor of Grace but the Doctor of the Church, on account of his strong support of Church authority and his devotion to the Sacraments. The Scholastic Theologians inherited his acuteness, his subtlety of intellect, his dialectical skill. Protestants love him for his reverence of the Bible, his careful distinction between the law and the gospel, and for the doctrine that faith and man's good will are gifts of God. The modern spirit admires his gift of individualizing and self-observation. Mystics have caught much inspiration from his Neo-Platonism and his doctrine of Predestination.

The great Jansenist movement in France and Holland

consciously and avowedly referred to Augustine as its great authority. Jansenius, who was Bishop of Ypres in the middle of the seventeenth century, having read the whole of St. Augustine's works ten times, wrote a book called *The Augustinus*, which nearly rent the French Church in two, and probably would have done so but for the activity of the Jesuits and the intervention of the State. In the Catholic Church of Holland it produced a lasting schism. The main tenets of this book, which were denounced by a series of Papal Bulls, were—that it is not possible for all men to do good, even if they will, for grace has not been offered them; that grace, when given, is irresistible; that moral actions, though free from external restraint, are not free from interior necessity; and that Christ did not die to save all men, but only the elect. However dangerous these doctrines may be, they influenced such excellent Christians as Pascal and Fénelon; and the School of Port Royal, though it was stamped out in France by the middle of the following century, exhibited one of the purest phases of religious life, which were ever seen in the history of the French Church.

Shortly before Augustine's death, the province of Africa was overrun by the Vandals under Genseric, who had been foolishly called in by Count Boniface, himself a well-meaning Catholic, to help him in his revolt against Rome; and with their coming commenced the downfall of the great African Church. At Augustine's death she had 500 Bishops; twenty years later only eighteen. While Augustine was dying, all Africa was in the hands of the enemy except Carthage, Hippo and Cirta. But he died at his post, and continued his correspondence to the end; giving his views to the neighbouring bishops as to the duty of awaiting martyrdom. The city of Hippo held out for two years after his death, and then was entirely destroyed, nothing being spared but his church library. Little more, indeed, is heard of the African Church till it was eventually overwhelmed by Mahomedanism.

It is not well to dwell too much on the gloomy theology into which Augustine was led through being " very jealous for the Lord God of Hosts "; nor on his tendency to persecution, which came only when he was sorely tried. Like many others who have taught a grim theology, he belied it by the sweetness and grace of his character. Let us think rather of his untiring devotion to duty; his absorption in the quest for the Divine and in the revelation of It to others; his brave death at his post, when all the work of his life seemed falling to pieces; and listen to his tender words of consolation: " Pray that you may be drawn." " Lift up your hearts, and your tears shall be dried."

INDEX

PRINTED IN GREAT BRITAIN BY RICHARD CLAY & SONS, LIMITED,
BRUNSWICK ST., STAMFORD ST., S.E. 1, AND BUNGAY, SUFFOLK.

9 780259 509387